Who Runs Edinburgh?

Who Runs Edinburgh?

David McCrone

EDINBURGH
University Press

Edinburgh University Press is one of the leading university presses in the UK. We publish academic books and journals in our selected subject areas across the humanities and social sciences, combining cutting-edge scholarship with high editorial and production values to produce academic works of lasting importance. For more information visit our website: edinburghuniversitypress.com

Edinburgh University Press Ltd

The Tun – Holyrood Road
12 (2f) Jackson's Entry
Edinburgh EH8 8PJ

Typeset in 10.5/12pt Sabon by
Manila Typesetting Company, and
printed and bound in Great Britain

A CIP record for this book is available from the British Library

ISBN 978 1 4744 9830 2 (hardback)
ISBN 978 1 4744 9831 9 (paperback)
ISBN 978 1 4744 9832 6 (webready PDF)
ISBN 978 1 4744 9833 3 (epub)

Contents

List of Figures and Tables   vii
Preface   ix

1. Who Runs Edinburgh?   1
2. Politics in Edinburgh   24
3. Winners and Losers: The Political Economy of
    Edinburgh   51
4. Treading Angels: Edinburgh and its Festivals   81
5. Are You One of Us? Status in the City   112
6. What School did You Go To? Education and
    Status in Edinburgh   140
7. Enlightened City: Cultural Power and University Life   168
8. Developing Edinburgh: Pies in the Sky, Holes in
    the Ground   195
9. Lost in Leith: Accounting for Edinburgh's Trams   224
10. Does Anyone Really Run Edinburgh?   248

Bibliography   279
Index   288

Figures and Tables

FIGURES

1.1 Discerning power in the haar   13
2.1 Seats on Edinburgh Town Council, 1946–73   36
3.1 Broken biscuits: McVitie's at Fountainbridge   54
3.2 Changing employment patterns, SOC 2010, 1–3   58
3.3 Changing employment patterns, SOC 2010, 8 and 9   58
3.4 Gross weekly pay for FT workers   60
3.5 Industry in the city: Bertrams of Sciennes on the Southside   62
5.1 Talking Edinburgh   113
6.1 Climbing the ladder   141
8.1 City of Edinburgh Council Local Development Plan – Spatial Strategy   198

TABLES

2.1 District elections in Edinburgh, 1974–92   38
2.2 City of Edinburgh council elections, 1995–2017   39
2.3 Percentage of councillors who were property owners   43
3.1 Industrial structure of resident workforce   55
3.2 Occupational structure (NS-Sec), 2001 and 2011   56
3.3 Employment by occupation (2020)   57
3.4 Percent employed in largest single occupational category, 1861–1951   64

Preface

Another book on Edinburgh: why one of those? There is, indeed, no shortage of books on the city, but they are mainly about buildings and history and heritage; nothing wrong with that, but arguably it gives a distorted impression of Edinburgh. When I came to Edinburgh in the 1960s as a student, Sandy Youngson's book *The Making of Classical Edinburgh* was about to be published. Edinburgh University Press was nervous about sales, and drummed up subscribers whose names appeared at the back of the first edition. They need not have worried, as Youngson's book became a classic in its own right, especially in its sumptuous first edition. To a young impecunious student (who could not afford to subscribe) it was a lesson in writing lucidly and laterally, for Youngson was an economist, or rather, an economic historian, and was able to tell the story of the building of the New Town across economics, politics and culture. It was, though, about classical Edinburgh, of the eighteenth and early nineteenth centuries, and to a student of sociology the puzzle was who ran (and runs) this city today.

In the 1970s, with my friend and colleague Brian Elliott, I began a study of landlordism in Edinburgh, and in 1989 we published it with the title *Property and Power in a City: The Sociological Significance of Landlordism*. Truth to tell, the book was far more about landlordism than it was about property and power in Edinburgh, but it sowed seeds which lay in the ground a long time and took a while to come to fruition. We got side-tracked by writing another book, *The City: Patterns of Domination and Conflict* (1982). The allusion to Max Weber's classic *The City* was deliberate, because we thought that much of urban studies in those days underplayed the role of politics and power for our liking. Although we thought of ourselves as urban sociologists, other activities intervened. Brian went to Canada, to Vancouver, and had much to say about property and power in that city. I got heavily involved in the sociology and politics of Scotland, culminating in *The New Sociology of Scotland*, published in 2016.

The question, Who Runs Edinburgh?, never went away. Coming to a city you do not know because you were not born and brought up there can be disconcerting, and a source of puzzlement, because you cannot take many things for granted. They become problematic.

I recall my fellow sociologist at Aberdeen, Ian Carter, writing a fine book called *Farm Life in North-East Scotland, 1840–1914*, published in 1979. Ian, who came originally from Luton, told the story of social gatherings in Aberdeen where in conversation, people spoke about coming from 'the country', the Aberdeenshire hinterland, and their 'auntie in Echt'. This reiteration of rural roots by lawyers, doctors and professions generally, puzzled Carter, that somehow they 'belonged' somewhere else. Ian went on to write his book which arguably came about because he was an outsider, someone from Luton, possibly as unlike Aberdeen as one could get.

Who Runs Edinburgh? falls into a similar frame. Being asked 'what school did you go to?', and discovering that this was really about 'placing' you in an Edinburgh system of castes, and hence irrelevant because you were an outsider, set me thinking. Robert Park, another urban sociologist, had written in the 1920s of the 'marginal man', someone who could not take things for granted, but had to work at puzzles which insiders took for granted.

In one sense, this book has taken forty years to write, but in another sense, six years. I am grateful to Michael Rosie as editor of *Scottish Affairs* for allowing me to publish, as early articles, some of my work, notably Chapter 4 (on festivals), Chapter 6 (on Edinburgh schools), and Chapter 9 (on the trams). I am also grateful to Bob Morris and *The Book of the Old Edinburgh Club* for publishing an earlier version of Chapter 2 (politics in Edinburgh).

So what kind of book is this? It is written by a sociologist, and is thus sociological (like the belief that, to the cobbler, there is nothing quite like leather). It is, however, framed by other social sciences, by history, geography, politics and economics, if those disciplines will accept the social science framing. It goes without saying that no discipline has a monopoly of wisdom, and that trying to understand a place requires all the weapons that one is competent to muster.

Social science is in essence a collaborative activity, and I am grateful to many people for their insights, comments and help, even when they are unaware of doing so. In alphabetical order: to Alan Alexander, Keith Anderson, Mike Anderson, Steve Bruce, Matthew Bond, Tony Cohen, Sam Friedman, John Hall, Jon Hearn, Andy Inch, Jim Johnson, Hamish Kallin, Michael Keating, Bob Morris, Lindsay Paterson, Gianfranco Poggi, Aaron Reeves, Richard Rodger and Michael Rosie.

I am grateful to the Blomfield family for permission to use three photographs (Figures 1.1, 5.1 and 6.1), and to do so free of charge. I am also grateful to the National Railway Museum at York for permission to use Figure 3.1 (Fountainbridge), and to Historic Environment Scotland (HES) for Figure 3.5 (Sciennes).

Living with a social scientist means that you learn a lot of social science along life's way, and my greatest debt is to my partner, Jan Webb. Her daughters, Islay and Catherine, are able to say with authority which school they went to. I am grateful to all three for enriching my life, as well as my work.

St Andrew's Day 2021

1

Who Runs Edinburgh?

Why study any city or 'place' these days? The conventional argument is that power has moved away from localities, first, to reside at the level of the state, and then at the global level. There seems little point in focusing on localities, even ones as putatively interesting as Edinburgh, a historic capital city, historic in both senses: once the capital of an independent state, as well as a city full of old buildings, and one with an international reputation for culture reflected, above all, in its festival(s).

There is another intriguing reason for studying Edinburgh. It is a capital city, albeit one which is 'historic' (formally ending in 1707). That may seem obvious, but it introduces another level of tension: between the local and the national. Simply put, to what extent is the city operating to serve its citizens and hinterland, and to what extent fulfilling its role as a national capital? This matters, because while not the capital of an independent state, there are civil institutions to be housed and serviced: of law, courts, professions, social and political order and civil regulation. The fact that there is a parliament in Edinburgh since 1999 makes the point: that is both a national as well as a local institution. Furthermore, Edinburgh is a small city, of half a million people, small in proportional terms – less than 10 per cent of Scotland's population – compared with the likes of London, Paris or even Dublin, which has about a quarter of Ireland's. Accommodating national agencies is, arguably, a challenge for a small city; think of Bonn in West Germany before reunification, or Ottawa in Canada, dwarfed alongside Toronto and Montreal. While Edinburgh receives national financial support for its duties as a capital city, there are tensions, most notably over tourist footfall. Such tensions, like points of conflict, are analytically interesting because they help to make *explicit* various systems of power and influence. The more contested they are, the easier it is to see power in action.

STUDYING POWER

We might well ask: who does power studies these days? That tradition of studying local elites, notably in the US in the 1950s and 1960s (associated with Robert Dahl, Nelson Polsby, Floyd Hunter), ended long ago. Why that happened is interesting. The conventional wisdom is that cities have been hollowed out by global economic forces, that they are nowadays interesting because of that process; after all, the purpose of studying Detroit is to show the devastation of global capitalism (see, as a good example, Mark Binelli's book *The Last Days of Detroit: Motor Cars, Motown and the Collapse of an Industrial Giant*, 2013); how production has moved away to other places and other countries, obviously China. Studying the void would seem the new attraction for studying cities; that, plus bootstrapping into a new urban economy: the bottom line being, this place is miles better than it once was.

This business of studying urban collapse has little relevance here, and in any case, throwing babies out with bathwater has a long and misguided pedigree in the social sciences. In order to justify what we do, it is often thought necessary to present it as 'new', to argue that old orthodoxies are dead, that we have fresh sets of problems, or at least new ways of getting at old ones. The conventional wisdom is: if cities were once places of considerable power, they are no longer. Yet all is not what it seems. We might assert, however, that studies of local power matter, otherwise cities would all be, and indeed look, the same; and patently they are not, and do not. Then there is people's attachment to places, that they feel they belong to somewhere. (*I Belong to Glasgow*, is not simply a song made famous by Will Fyffe;[1] it confers identity on its inhabitants. How else would it have become iconic?)

In any case, we can show from survey work that people identify above all with the local: their street, district, town or city, far more than with the state, or even the nation. When Frank Bechhofer and I did our identity surveys in the early years of this century, we found that place identification is highly local. More than a quarter of people in England, and almost a third of Scots, identified most strongly with their town or city. Furthermore, roughly one-third of the English as well as Scots identified strongly with their local area or district within their town or city (McCrone and Bechhofer 2015: 51). Think about that for a moment: four out of five people in both England and Scotland identified most strongly with their locality, whether defined as street, district, town or city. So local places matter a lot: they are where people feel they belong. These figures far outweigh identification with nation or state. Only 7 per cent of people in England, and 17 per cent of Scots (that's still only 1 in 6) invested most pride in 'country'. Even in Scotland where there is a strong identification with the nation, people opt, above all, for the 'local'. Are people simply misguided? Don't they know that local places do not matter anymore? Are we back in the realms of false consciousness? I think not: place, in whatever form, continues to matter to people.

This book focuses on Edinburgh but we could be studying anywhere in the sense that all places matter and have meaning, even, perhaps especially, in these 'global' times. Follow the money. Why does tourism matter so much; why do visitors traipse the streets of cities, seek out local 'visitor attractions'; and spend so much money in so doing? Bootstrapping cities has become the means of economic and social regeneration, sometimes spectacularly: witness Glasgow, Edinburgh's near-neighbour forty miles away, famously 'miles better', and subtly ambiguous – better than what/where, one wants to know. Post-industrial cities have reinvented themselves (Glasgow, Manchester, Bilbao, Lille and many more), and even where they did not think of themselves as ever primarily 'industrial', they see the value, and the profit, in encouraging tourism. Post-industrialism sells. But it is not simply about tourist footfall; cities are hubs of the digital economy, offices, cultural promotions; and they continue to be centres of industrial production, such as it is. It has not all decamped to China.

From City to State and Beyond

Taking the longer view, there is an orthodoxy in social science that cities ceased to matter a long time ago. Their role was taken over by the state. Max Weber's famous essay *The City*, published posthumously in 1921, argued that the legal and political foundations of the modern state derived from the autonomy of the medieval city-state. Weber's essay is, however, largely misunderstood. Part of the problem lies in the English translation of the essay's title *Die Stadt* as 'the state', which quite misses the point. Weber's *Die Stadt/The City* got buried in his larger corpus of work, *Economy and Society*, and was taken merely to be Weber's attempt at an urban sociology. Except that it wasn't.

The City was about how in the West the medieval city-space provided the legal and cultural means for developing capitalism free from the constraints of national and regional feudal rulership. It was, par excellence, the place where *stadtluft mach frei* (conventionally translated as 'city air makes free'). The city was the place to escape the strictures and constraints of the national and regional ruling classes, frequently aristocratic and rural. After all, the notion of the 'citizen', which we nowadays associate with membership of the state (marked most obviously by having a passport) derived from membership of *civis*, the place, the town, the city. Citizens were locals, not nationals. Furthermore, the burgher class, the bourgeoisie, were in essence citizens of the city (the burgh/burg/bourg/borough, in its various linguistic forms). The point is that the city in Western Europe gave rise to the modern state in bestowing and guaranteeing the necessary freedoms upon which it was built. In the early 1980s, Brian Elliott and I wrote a book using Weber's essay as a tribute-title, calling it *The City: Patterns of Domination and Conflict*, in which we set out a Weberian perspective on the city. What we appreciated about Weber's approach was that it gave proper attention to the 'political' (as opposed to the narrowly 'economic'), as well as a willingness to study cities from the bottom up rather than the top down.

All this might seem to be ancient history; but it matters. It lies in the mindset that places, especially towns and cities, no longer are important; that we have become citizens of the world. Except that we are manifestly not. The survey data do not lie. Furthermore, we live in a world where 'nation' and 'state' are not the same thing; that the concept of nation-state, where culture and politics are equivalent, is the exception not the rule. Nor do localities no longer matter. If, on the other hand, they

do, who runs them? How are decisions made? Is there a ruling
elite which makes decisions, and to what extent are these transparent or opaque?

THE ECOLOGY OF GAMES

To help us answer these questions, here is an old idea which
deserves reviving. In the 1950s, the political scientist Norton
E. Long published an article entitled 'The local community as
an ecology of games' (Long 1958: 251–61). He began his paper
by saying: 'it is psychologically tempting to envision the local
territorial system as a group with a governing *"they"'* (252).
Hence, the dominant question in studies of community elites:
who runs this place? Long observed: 'it is comforting to think
that the "executive committee of the bourgeoisie" is exploiting
the community' (256), and he goes on: 'most newspapermen and
other professional "inside dopesters" hold that there is a "they"'
but that they themselves are merely the court chroniclers of the
doings of the 'they'. 'Public and reporters alike are relieved to
believe both that there is a "they" to make life explicable and
also to be held responsible for what occurs', and 'the community
needs to believe that there are spiritual fathers, good or bad,
who can deal with the dark' (256).

If nothing else, magic has to be performed. The Hopi Indians
did a rain dance to overcome drought; medieval Europeans
said a High Mass to ward off plague; but, says Long, our own
practices can be thought of as equally magical. 'Top leadership' is largely confined to carrying out ritual and ceremonial
roles, and 'doing a terrific job' turns out to be 'a few telephone
calls and possibly three luncheons a month' (Long 1958: 257).
'*They*', said Long, are often people holding private rather than
public office. Newspapers report the activities of these 'lords
of creation', for top community leaders provide the sense that
they are 'gods in the heavens' as well as a convenient set of
demons to blame when things go wrong, as they usually do
eventually.

Long gave the nice example of one mayor of a large (unspeci-
fied) American eastern city who toured Rome, Dublin, Tel Aviv,
Paris and Le Havre, who was confronted by the press on his
return asking what he had learned from his travels. He couldn't
admit to having been on a junket at the taxpayers' expense, and

in some desperation he recalled an anti-noise campaign in Paris. That was it; it took off in the press as his anti-noise campaign, which suited the press as it had something to report, and, with luck, sell some newspapers. For the politician, his 'success' was to be measured in column-inches devoted to the story which had been fabricated out of thin air on the spur of the moment. That was then (the 1950s) and this is now (2020s), but if anything, things have got worse (or better, depending on your point of view). Publicity becomes the accomplishment. PR is all. Announcing what is *going* to happen is the name of the game, rather than recounting what has been achieved. In short, branding is everything.

The point of Long's title – the ecology of games – is that 'place' is the arena for a series of distinct games: politics, banking, contracting, the media, churches, schools and colleges, civic groups and so on, each with its own focus and set of rules and goals in which the participants 'know how to behave, and they know the score' (Long 1958: 253). Much of cooperation in the local territorial system, said Long, is unconscious and unnoticed. Games go on within the territory, occasionally extending beyond it, though in practice central to it. Few treat the territory as their proper object. The common interest is realised through institutional interactions rather than deliberate and self-conscious rationality. In that way, coordination is largely 'ecological', rather than the result of conscious, rational contriving (255). What happens is akin to Adam Smith's 'hidden hand', not because it is defined narrowly as 'market behaviour' (which, in any case, is a misreading of Smith's famous *Wealth of Nations*) but as the outcome, almost the by-product, of sundry games played out according to different rules. Each set of rules produces outcomes, in which the whole is greater than the sum of the parts.

It suits those who report on these games, notably the media (who manifestly have their own games to play), to be able to identify the winners and losers, and to translate the game for the spectators accordingly. It is handy for them to construe an identifiable 'they' because it makes life, and explanation of outcomes, that much simpler. Long points out that to do so is 'psychologically tempting', but misleading. The ecology of separate games produces outcomes, often unintended and unexpected. Things happen. It is, furthermore, a systemic thing.

Who Governs this Place?

Long, a professor of 'urban politics', was writing in the late 1950s when it was fashionable to do community studies of elites, and there was a considerable literature on 'community power', with debates about methods, ways of getting at power: how to identify and measure the 'them'; whether one could depend on who citizens thought were powerful (known as the 'reputational method'); or whether it was necessary to measure outcomes by analysing decisions: *cui bono?* who benefits? It also threw up a broader literature on measuring power, famously, the work of Steven Lukes who argued for power having three faces (Lukes 1974). One face is the decisional, focusing on who makes overt decisions about place, and has a strong association with what has come to be called a 'pluralist' view of power; the short answer to 'who governs?' in this framework is: no one, for power is decentred and dispersed. This view was built around the studies by Robert Dahl in his book, *Who Governs?* (1961), and by his student Nelson Polsby (*Community Power and Political Theory*, 1963). The second 'face' of power, according to Lukes, is *non*-decision-making, whereby the trick is to avoid making adverse decisions by setting the agenda in advance. In short, certain issues (and interests) are excluded from debate such that the status quo is taken for granted. It was, in fact, Peter Bachrach and Morton Baratz who identified this second face in their 1962 seminal article 'Two faces of power'.

Steven Lukes added the third face, that of ideological power, even more subtle than the other two in that people were deemed to 'want' certain things even if, objectively, these things were not in their material interests. In other words, they became willing dupes. There are many examples of that in the contemporary world. Why did so many working class people in England vote Tory in the 2019 general election which brought Boris Johnson to power?[2] It is hard to argue that they thought they would be better off financially. Why, indeed, did Donald Trump manage to retain the support of a significant proportion of white working class America until his downfall in 2020? We see here the power of ideas. In his seminal, and short, book (a mere 150 pages of text, first published in 1974), Lukes argued for the organisational mobilisation of bias in which people's wishes and preferences were so influenced that overt conflict usually did not arise.

Critics latched on to the argument that there was a clear distinction between 'interests' and 'preferences', and particularly how to work out what people's real interests might be. Arguably, exploration of their 'preferences' is the more intriguing puzzle. In essence, Lukes's was a theoretical, a conceptual, discourse on power. However, its bedrock was a suite of local studies in the 1950s and 1960s on power in US cities, given the general title of 'community power studies', associated with Robert Dahl, Nelson Polsby and Floyd Hunter.

There is, of course, a prior argument: why bother with the question: who has power? Does it matter? What Lukes's seminal book showed us is that it does, and often in ways we hardly discern. That is the point. Indeed, the apparent non-operation of power is the most powerful of all forms. It is in there somewhere, even if it is hard to identify, and apparently benign. Outcomes do not simply happen; they reflect inbuilt biases and tendencies. Even assuming that it is an 'it' is instructive, and misleading. Furthermore, local power systems are usually even more opaque and mysterious, and there is the convention that place-power is so hollowed out that it hardly matters any more. But the community power analysts were on to something.

Getting at Who Governs

It is instructive to give a brief overview of the classical studies of community power here because they raise many of the issues about studying local power and rulership, and one in which the method of research is closely tied to what one comes up with as findings. There are many more than these studies, and they were the *fons et origo* on which most subsequent studies were based. The fact that most of them were studies of American cities, rather than European ones, reflected the relative autonomy of such cities in the wider governmental context. Arguably, they help to identify the key dimensions of local power which may operate in a city like Edinburgh.

Robert Dahl's *Who Governs? Democracy and Power in an American City* (1961) was the path-breaker. The city was New Haven in Connecticut, dominated by Yale University, much as Cambridge, England, is dominated by its university today.[3] Dahl was arguing against Floyd Hunter's 1953 study of Atlanta, Georgia, which showed that a handful of business leaders

dominated that city. Dahl compared 'social notables' (231 families) and 'economic notables' (238) and found that there was little
overlap between them (only twenty-four belonged to both networks). Furthermore, he argued that Yale University was on the
periphery of local politics, while the best the business community
could do was to veto downtown developments, but seldom took
an innovating role. Power lay in the hands of the (Democratic)
mayor and his aides. Thus, claimed Dahl, power in New Haven
was fractured, decentralised and uncoordinated. Based on interviews with members of these two elites, and focused primarily on
decision-making, Dahl's study was confirmed by his former student Nelson Polsby in his book *Community Power and Political
Theory* (1963). Polsby was critical of what he termed 'sociological studies' which asserted that power was concentrated, at either
the local or national levels. Different disciplines produced different kinds of studies. The Dahl/Polsby versus Hunter approaches
became reified as 'pluralism' based on decision analysis, vis-à-vis
'elitism' based on reputational analysis.

Then came Bill Domhoff's much more radical approach
in 2005, updated in 2014, and helpfully documented online
(http://whorulesamerica.net/local/new_haven.html). Domhoff
took Dahl/Polsby to task for their argument about 'dispersed
inequalities' and a lack of concentrated power. He restudied New
Haven with the data which Dahl himself had used, along with
Dahl's interview material, kindly provided by the author himself.
Domhoff's analysis of the key social clubs in New Haven – the
Lawn Club, the Country Club and the Graduate Club – showed
that social notables in New Haven in the late 1950s when Dahl
studied them, were a close network of overlapping social circles
consisting roughly of 1350 families (less than 1 per cent of New
Haven's population). Furthermore, there were tightly-knit inter-
locks among businesses in the town, especially law firms and the
banks, which represented a 'well-knit downtown business community', with First New Haven National Bank at the centre of the
business network. Of twenty-five members of the bank, twenty-
four were in at least one of the three social clubs, and thirteen
(over half) were members of two of the three social clubs.

Rather than being peripheral, Yale University was well connected to the business network through corporate law firms.
Alumni 'Yalies' were in places which mattered. Domhoff criticised Dahl for his poorly constructed list of economic notables

such that the 'whole enterprise is stacked against any appreciable overlap'. He noted that Dahl had a priori excluded by default people of Jewish and Italian heritage, and that his focus was on WASPs (white Anglo-Saxon protestants) who were exclusionary and anti-Semitic. Domhoff was grateful to Dahl for giving him access to his material, but judged that Dahl had not actually *read* Domhoff's manuscript draft which he had previously sent him for comment. Polsby, he noted, was Dahl's former student and 'hatchet man'. In short, Domhoff judged Dahl's study as having a very narrow definition of the upper class; an arbitrary definition of economic notables; a list of social notables, containing a large number of Yalies, which by Dahl's definition could not be included in the list of economic notables; and as a result of exclusionary practices by WASPs, could not include Jews or Italians in the list of social notables. The result was 'an inadequate and invalid sociological mishmash'.

Dahl's study began in 1957 when the programme of urban renewal, which involved federal funding for slum clearance, was well-nigh settled, and in the hands of Mayor Lee and his aides who played a clever game of keeping Yalies and their allies onside. Then there was the role of Prescott Bush, who was to become Republican Senator for Connecticut. Familiar name? Yes, because his son, George Bush (senior) became US President, as did Prescott's grandson, George W. Bush ('Dubya'). Here was a key conduit of power from federal to local, passing through New Haven. Dahl, according to Domhoff, had bought into Mayor Lee's account in the late 1950s (verified by his interview transcripts), and Lee, a non-Yalie, while a Democrat, steered cleverly between different interests, careful not to upset traditional power, having constructed a narrative which Dahl was only too happy to accept. In retrospect, Dahl had begun his study in 1957 when the old controversies about urban renewal had been settled, and before the 1960s when the previous settlement began to unravel. When Domhoff looked into the archival evidence in the 1990s, he found clear evidence of cahoots between holders of power – and Dahl. Domhoff is clear about where Dahl went wrong: Dahl argued that:

- social and economic notables did not overlap, and they did;
- business leaders were not interested in urban renewal, and they were;

- business leaders did not have any impact on the town, and they did;
- Yale University was uninterested and powerless, which was not so;
- there was no downtown power structure, and the opposite was the case.

Dahl's reliance on the 'decisional method', Domhoff concluded, was flawed because it was an interview-based study, and hence he swallowed what his informants told him. Doing careful analysis of archival material provided Domhoff with a quite different tale. What is interesting is that it involved a reconstruction of events and processes, and re-analysis of Dahl's interview material which Domhoff was grateful for. Does it matter? It does, because subsequent local power studies were powerfully framed by Dahl's, and Polsby's, assumptions, even when Hunter, who had been criticised by Dahl and Polsby, redid his study of Atlanta in 1980 which confirmed the findings of his previous 1953 study. By then, too late: the Dahl/Polsby account had become conventional wisdom both in terms of methodology and findings.

And then such studies came to an end; not because we knew all the answers, but because, arguably, 'communities' were no longer thought of as primary sites of power. Who cared anymore? The debate had moved on. With hindsight, social science is just as susceptible to fashion and moving on as most other activities in life. Studies of elites either shifted their focus on to the national or global level, or became more nuanced in terms of processes rather than people. Studying what the sociologist Meg Stacey (1969) called 'local social systems' (she thought the term 'community' too emotionally overloaded) went out of fashion. The classic review of British community studies by Colin Bell and Howard Newby was published in 1971 (and re-issued by the publisher in 2022, suggesting that there is life, or at least interest, in this sociological genre). In reflecting on the American studies above, Bell and Newby commented: 'For comparable material on Britain we must await the current work being done in Birmingham, Sheffield, Aberdeen, Colchester and elsewhere' (1971: 220). We waited in vain. Academics stopped doing community studies, described in any case by Stacey as a 'myth'. Long's ecology of games went on to the shelf, where it gathered dust. Yet Long and others had been on to something. The complexity of games, with diverse and frequently implicit rules, is a good metaphor for studying power in localities. Now is the time to take it off the shelf.

EDINBURGH GAMES

How does Edinburgh fit in? What 'games', and their key players, can we identify? And do they matter anyway? That is for the reader to decide, but here is my justification. There is no shortage of written material on Edinburgh, but most of it is represented by 'coffee table' books; not surprising, given that it is such a photogenic city, and as a consequence is much written about, and photographed, if somewhat hagiographically. Even a cursory look at those Edinburgh books reveals that they are about buildings, rather than people. The city appears empty, apart from tourists. Covid-19 in the early months of 2020 put a sudden stop to that, and the place took on a new look, but in many ways a familiar one. In an article in *The Guardian* (https://www. theguardian.com/travel/2020/jul/12/edinburgh-empty-novelist-ian-rankin-locals-see-city-through-tourists-eyes), journalist Peter Ross observed: 'Edinburgh is uncanny. Streets that should be busy with tourists, phones and voices raised, are deserted.' He went on: 'No one would have wished for a health crisis to crash the money machine, but this is an opportunity to see the place clearly in a way that hasn't been possible for years. It is a chance for Edinburgh and Edinburghers to renew their vows.'

But to what, exactly? To the city that it had become, replete with tourists, or as it had once been, or at least remembered? What *is* this place which so many claim as their own? Which, and, above all, whose, Edinburgh are we talking about? In Scotland, we tend not to ask: 'where do you come from?',[4] but where do you belong? Think about that. It is a double-edged question, passive and active. In the first place, it assumes that you are attached to a place whether you like it or not. Secondly, you affiliate yourself with a place that matters to you. '*I belong to Glasgow . . .*' is iconic for that reason.

Edinburgh, or for that matter any city, is, above all, a place in which many processes, conflicts and 'games' are played out. It is typified as a 'city of castes', a description attributed to the nineteenth-century journalist, John Heiton, who started his

Figure 1.1 Discerning power in the haar; courtesy of the Robert Blomfield collection

book strikingly: '"Look you, sir. Your city is a very fine city, but it swarms with castes". The American was right: Our beautiful Modern Athens is in a swarm of castes, worse than ever was old Egypt or is modern Hindostan,' (1859: 1). A city of castes. Change the metaphor: think of cities as palimpsests; stories, as well as buildings, are layered one upon the other.[5] They are repositories of what has gone before. Their features are blurred by what layering does, transforming accounts of what the place means. Previous histories poke through the surface to shape and influence the present.

A Tale of Two Cities

So there is a history to be tackled; less about its architecture, which though fine, is arguably much too written about. Buildings, after all, reflect who built them, lived in them, demolished them, preserved them, often in aspic. Edinburgh is a city of aspirations and aspersions: 'east-windy, west-endy', as the saying goes; or demotically, 'fur coat and no knickers'; where pretensions matter most: tight with money, 'you'll have had your tea'. Classically, how people spoke seemed to matter.

The strangulated vowels of Morningside speech became a music-hall joke: sex was something the coal was delivered in.[6] Go to the local pantomime at the King's Theatre during the Christmas season to encounter joking riffs which only make sense if you live in and around Edinburgh, and you are able to pick up the cues.

The city, however, has an 'other', an alter ego, Glasgow, in the west, against which it is compared, and usually to its detriment. If Glasgow is friendly and frowsy, Edinburgh is uptight and up itself. Robert Crawford, poet and academic, even wrote a book about the pair (a 'famously scratchy relationship', it says on the book's dust cover), though more about the city in the west whence he came. His book begins:

> Like good and evil, Glasgow and Edinburgh are often mentioned in the same breath but regarded as utterly distinct. The rivalry between these cities, which is so longstanding that it has become proverbial, set them alongside other urban centres – Los Angeles and San Francisco, Moscow and St Petersburg, Rio de Janeiro and Sao Paulo – which like to jockey for supremacy within their nations. (Crawford 2013: 1)

Nice idea; Crawford's book is interesting. He has manifestly a much better 'feel' for Glasgow. Born in Bellshill (Lanarkshire), brought up in Cambuslang on the eastern fringes, educated at Hutchesons' Grammar School ('Hutchie's'), first degree at Glasgow University, he treats Edinburgh fairly, but there is a lack of knowingness about his account; it is a place to visit, to pass through, but not in which to live. Getting under its skin is difficult for those who have never lived in the city. Crawford observes: 'Only people from Edinburgh could dwell in a universe without Glaswegians; only Glaswegians could live on an Edinburgh-less planet. Everyone else may enjoy this pair of stubborn cities; no-one can understand Scotland without paying attention to both' (2013: 40). His key point is central: 'self' and 'other' are in intimate relationship. You cannot understand one without the other. Crawford did elsewhere capture one essence of Edinburgh in his poem *Camera Obscura* (*London Review of Books*, 8 January 2015: 15).

Nae knickers, all fur coat
Slurped Valvona and Crolla,

Tweed-lapelled, elbow-patched, tartan-skirted,
Kilted, Higgs-bosuned, tramless, trammelled and trammed,
Awash with drowned witches, prematurely damned,
Prim as skimmed milk, cheesily floodlit, breezily,
Galefully, Baltically cold with royal
Lashings of tat and Hey-Jimmy wigs, high on swigs
Of spinsterish, unmarried malt . . .

Nowhere in poem or title is 'Edinburgh' mentioned, but we get the multiple points, a bit like pantomime allusions, we're in on the joke. And Crawford was not the first poet to write about the city. Here is Hugh MacDiarmid's *Midnight*, 1978, usefully drawing comparison with its city peers.

Glasgow is null,
Its suburbs, shadows,
And the Clyde a cloud.
Dundee is dust
And Aberdeen a shell.
But Edinburgh is a mad god's dream,
Fitful and dark,
Unseizable in Leith
And wildered by the Forth,
But irresistibly at last
Cleaving to sombre heights
Of passionate imagining
Till stonily,
From soaring battlements, Earth eyes Eternity

Moreover, for a city proverbially tight and self-contained, even if it is a mad god's dream, Edinburgh has the distinction of having a large number of inhabitants who were not born in the place; people like the author of this book who came, liked it and stayed: what I call the Edinburgh syndrome. Nor is it necessary only to belong to one place. Here is Norman MacCaig, with such strong associations with Edinburgh, describing the condition of being-between ('two places I belong to as though born in both of them'):

From the corner of Scotland I know so well
I see Edinburgh sprawling like seven cats
On its seven hills beside the Firth of Forth.
And when I'm in Edinburgh I walk
Amongst the mountains and lochs of that corner

That looks across the Minch to the Hebrides.
Two places I belong to as though I was born
In both of them.
They make every day a birthday,
Giving me gifts wrapped in ribbons of memory.
I store them away, greedy as a miser.
                                    (*The Poems of Norman MacCaig*,
                        edited by Ewen MacCaig, Polygon, 2005: 505)

Edinburgh is a city of only half-a-million people, where living
within a few miles of the city centre is unusually common, a
city with many layers, like peeling an onion, best done slowly,
and possibly at arm's length. Those of us 'outsiders' long felt
that there was something intriguing and unknown about our
adopted city; we know that we don't quite 'belong'. We are frequently asked: what school we went to, and when we might reply
(apocryphally) 'Auchtermuchty High', the native's eyes glazed
over. Irrelevant answer. What they usually wanted to know was
which Edinburgh *caste* we belonged to; which of the private
schools we had attended. If we hadn't, and worse still, came
from outwith the city, it was of little concern to them, and in
the city of John Knox (who didn't come from Edinburgh either;
he hailed from Haddington in East Lothian, about twenty miles
away), and the 1843 Disruption between auld and new kirks,
religion hardly mattered very much. We did not quite fit in, we
could not be 'placed', as the saying goes. But being an 'outsider'
has its benefits: we took less for granted, we had to learn the
ropes for ourselves, even if we don't get 'the rules of the game'.
Recall the value of Long's metaphor of games.

TACKLING THE QUESTION

So how to tackle the question: who runs Edinburgh? Manifestly,
there is formal party politics. Who runs this city? What sorts
of people govern the place? How are economic interests represented on the council? How has that changed over time, if at all?
How did we come to be governed as we are? What sort of city, in
political terms, is Edinburgh? That is the subject of Chapter 2. It
is, however, only the start, something of a desk-clearing exercise,
because the formal political process may be masking an altogether complex and implicit system of power. In other words,

there may be a hidden game lying behind the formal political one, a shifting sand of political–economic fortunes. We cannot avoid giving an account of money and economy, how material interests are translated into political ones, indeed, whether this is the case at all. If Edinburgh is 'a city of castes', how do these operate today, and particularly affect the spatial distribution of power? Where do rich and poor people live, and does it matter anyway?

And then we have to face its current reputation. We cannot assume that because Edinburgh is a city of culture and festivals, it has always been so. We find that, especially post-1945, decisions were taken to excise much of small-scale industrial production from the city, to banish it to the suburbs or beyond, as unfitting of a 'festival city' (Rodger and Machin 2013[7]). But be careful what you wish for. Edinburgh was deliberately re-invented as a quintessential *non*-industrial city, aided and abetted by central governments of the day, on the grounds that the city was too 'well-off' to be awarded economic development status, and hence not eligible for government grants.

So its myriad small-scale industrial and proto-industrial capacity withered, or decamped elsewhere. Take a walk around the city and you will find warehouses, small workshops – my favourite is the anchor-maker/blacksmiths next to the up-market bistro on Leith's Shore. Except, in late 2020, it announced it was decamping to the western suburbs,[8] and the site would be sold to a developer for (yet more) housing. Little, however, remains of small, local production. Other examples of shifting out of the city abound: eponymous 'Edinburgh Crystal' went to Penicuik; Ethicon health products and Uniroyal Tyres to Newbridge in Midlothian where development grants were available, and parking/deliveries were possible when they were lacking in Fountainbridge. Breweries, which bestowed on Edinburgh the unique smell of malted barley if the wind was in the right direction, emanating from the North British distillery at Haymarket among others, moved away. The fruit market had been in Market Street close by Waverley station, where in the 1960s you would literally slip on a banana skin as you dodged the delivery pick-up vans. The fruit market became The Fruitmarket, an Arts and Culture Centre, which says it all, or most of it: real fruit having decanted to the western outskirts.

This political economy of Edinburgh is described in Chapter 3. We will explore the contention that Edinburgh is a socially segregated city, with distinct neighbourhoods with special cachets, a notion that derives from things which are hidden (from the French verb, *cacher*, to hide). Like many cities, Edinburgh comprises diverse districts, with historical rivalries, most obviously Leith (quintessentially not-Edinburgh). It is also a city where more than half of its population lives within a couple of miles of the city centre.[9] Think of this chapter as an 'economic history' of Edinburgh, with a focus particularly on the decline of manufacturing industry and its social and political implications; the rise and fall of the Edinburgh banks, and the investment industry; and the relative ease with which Edinburgh was 'invented' as a city of culture to the extent that the conventional wisdom was that the city had never been a place of manufacture whatsoever.

Then there are festivals, the subjects of Chapter 4. The most famous is EIF, Edinburgh International Festival, which began in the dog days of the late 1940s, and has blossomed or morphed, depending on one's point of view, into all sorts of other festivals, grown like Topsy, the Fringe, but now also encompassing the winter solstice period. This chapter explains how this came to be, and how Edinburgh reinvented itself in such a way that it takes considerable mental agility to think of the city as not being about festivals. Like 'The University', there is the accusation that 'The Festival' (in truth, many festivals) is in the city, but not of it, at least insofar as the accusation has generated counter-movements.

The following two chapters focus on the status groups of Edinburgh, that world of social castes: first, in Chapter 5, we identify the elites, who inhabit the shady social worlds, based indubitably on wealth, but discretely manifest, underplayed and often unspoken. This is the world of clubs, associations which you don't join without an invitation. If you have to ask, then you're not their sort of person. The Merchant Company is one such, which has direct connections into certain schools and professions, and which still has its exclusive golf course at Muirfield out near Gullane (pronounced Gillane if you're posh; another of the in-jokes) in East Lothian. Women members had to wait until 2019 before being admitted, not that there was a stampede to get in the door. Just as well, as only twelve were formally invited to join. Ask who runs Edinburgh in conversation, and it is likely you will be told about the New Club on Princes Street, hard to find – and next to a shop selling women's lingerie – but key to many accounts of power in Edinburgh. We will see what we can find.

This raises the complexity of gender relations around issues of power, for historically at least Edinburgh's was a firmly patriarchal society; women had ancillary, walk-on, parts. One such is the Company of Archers (all men too, it seems) who retain premises at the Boroughloch end of the Meadows on the Southside, and who are observed, when the weather is right, practising their defence of the monarch during her stay at Holyroodhouse. No foot soldiers therein: everyone is either a General or a Captain: pure Lewis Carroll, all shall have prizes. The current Captain-General (you get to be both at the top) is the Duke of Buccleuch.

Ostensibly feeding this elite, as well as the professions of law, accountancy and medicine among others, is the schools system which is analysed in Chapter 6. This is the sphere of 'cultural' power, although that is a matter of emphasis and not distinct from matters of economics. It is captured by the seemingly innocent question which does the social rounds in the city: 'what school did you go to?' Unlike the west of Scotland where it is a device for ascertaining religion, in Edinburgh the question is which social caste you belong to; which of the private schools you had attended: are you a Herioter, Watsonian, Academical, and so on. Things, of course, ought to have changed since John P. Mackintosh, professor of politics and himself a local politician (MP for East Lothian),[10] wrote in 1966 in the Edinburgh volume of the Third Statistical Account of Scotland:

> Social attitudes in Edinburgh are carefully compartmented and of long standing, and it is expected that political opinions will fall into place. If one Edinburgh man [*sic*] wishes to place another, he picks up the accent, and once he knows school, address and occupation, all the rest can be assumed. (Keir 1966: 319)

There is, of course, more to schooling than the private sector. We will examine the implications of being educated in the state sector for Edinburgh's bourgeoisie in the context of private schooling. How women fit into this complexity of educational institutions will also figure in this chapter, for, almost seamlessly, schools, public and private became co-educational, for reasons of economy rather than equality.

In Chapter 7, we examine cultural power and university life. 'The University', which means the one founded in 1582 as the Tounis College, is *primus inter pares*, compared to Heriot Watt, Queen Margaret, and Napier, universities which are peripheral, both socially and geographically, in relation to the elder one. Despite its foundation as the toun's college, 'Edinburgh' is often accused of being *in* the city, but not much *of* it (shades of Yale in New Haven). This is usually the cue to raise its 'destruction' of George Square, and its blighting of much of the Southside in the 1970s, which many have not forgiven, and certainly not forgotten. As far as we can tell (a common refrain in relation to Edinburgh, because a lot of its dealings were, and are, conducted behind the hand), the university was not in the forefront of opposition to inner city road building (for which, by the way, see Glasgow's ruinous destruction of its inner city), though many academics lent their expertise to the stop-the-roads campaign. The university's own planning department under Percy Johnson-Marshall[11] was too *parti pris* to be outright opposed. Large parts of the inner Southside, however, lay blighted for decades by red-lining before an alternative set of university academics got together and formed Edinvar[12] housing association to provide much-needed accommodation in the inner city.

Cultural power, defined broadly, is not simply about 'The University', but ramifies into the knowledge industry more generally. Edinburgh is a city of medicine and science, at least as important as law and finance, and historically deeply rooted. Its workforce is highly skilled, with almost two-thirds educated to degree level, reflecting the demands of hi-tech and service industries.[13]

Edinburgh, then, is indubitably a city constantly on the make. In Chapter 8, we examine planning controversies which the city has never been short of. Developers come and go; skylines are altered, and holes appear which weren't there yesterday. This is the place to discuss Place, for the social ecology of the city is an interesting one. Two notable features matter: the fact that the city has a disproportion of its population living within three miles of the city centre, thus sustaining many local services, making it a liveable city; second, it is also highly socially segregated, at last by conventional measurements. Decanting historic slums in the city centre to the periphery created significant areas of social deprivation (SIMDs, in the official parlance) in a city with above-average levels of affluence and occupational skills.

Studying power can usefully be done by controversies, whereby what is usually opaque becomes transparent. Suddenly we find that 'who runs this place' becomes more explicit; that the rules of the game become easier to decipher. Such was ('is' would be the more appropriate tense) the controversy about 'The Trams'[14] which we analyse in Chapter 9. There are citizens of Edinburgh today who refuse to travel on the trams on principle, that it cost the city a lot of money, and more importantly, made their city into a laughing-stock, in Edinburgh never a laughing matter. Here we deal with the controversy and its continuing aftermath, as the trams continue to make their slow journey to the sea, at Newhaven.

Re-casting Edinburgh

The book concludes by bringing this material to bear on our question: so who runs Edinburgh? (Chapter 10). Can we identify a social–political caste who hold power, or is it nowadays a function of technocratic structures and financial sleights of hand? Could it be that no one actually runs the city, but that a series of complex games with their inner logics, political, economic, cultural, keeps the show on the road? We live in a world of 'new public management', its hegemony reflected in its acronym, NPM, rife in governments, cities, institutions; to its critics, the cost of everything and the value of nothing (it comes as a shock that the phrase, so redolent of our twenty-first-century times, was invented by Oscar Wilde).

Perhaps, rather than looking for the 'guilty men' (and they conventionally are men), we ought to consider cities as systems, not in the nineteenth-century sense of civic provision and municipal enterprise, but, in Irving Lapsley's phrase 'calculable' (Lapsley et al. 2010):

> Cities have come to mimic large corporations, as they engage in various kinds of exercises aimed at projecting and visualizing the city as it should become, and how it should transform itself to get there. The targeted audience of visions and strategies can be developers, businesses or residents. The reputation of a city, its image, is perhaps the most visible sign of these visualizing efforts.

This segues into a discussion of who gets airbrushed out of the city's history: women, the working class, and in-migrants. Edinburgh is rarely thought of as a city of 'immigrants', although it happens to be, in terms of having a high proportion of residents born outwith the city. Its largest 'ethnic group' of incomers proportionally are people from England, classically 'minus-one ethnics'.[15] We will set that in the context of historical migration patterns: Irish, Jews, Italians, people from the Indian subcontinent, and latterly East Europeans.

CONCLUSION

And so to Edinburgh. This is a book about social, economic and political realities, set in the context of how these have evolved. It does not conform to conventional wisdoms. It is a book written by a sociologist who has lived in the city most of his life; who came to study and never left, an insider-outsider. It is for the reader to judge the evidence and the argument therein.

NOTES

1. Will Fyffe was a star of Music Hall in the 1920s and made the song his theme tune. It became a party piece for many. According to Albert Mackie's *The Scotch Comedians* (1973), Fyffe got the inspiration for the song from a drunk he met at Glasgow Central Station. The drunk was 'genial and demonstrative' and 'laying off about Karl Marx and John Barleycorn with equal enthusiasm'. Fyffe asked him: 'Do you belong to Glasgow?' and the man replied: 'At the moment, at the moment, Glasgow belongs to me.' Thus are iconic songs made. Note, in passing, that there is no Edinburgh equivalent.

2. According to the British Election Study 2019, a majority – 56 per cent – of those in 'routine' (largely unskilled manual) occupations voted Tory, and only 31 per cent Labour. The figures for 'semi-routine' manual occupations were, respectively, 48 per cent and 33 per cent.

3. That is an interesting comparison to make because today the two towns are virtually identical in size: New Haven has a population of 130,000 (2012 figures), and Cambridge England, 124,000 (2011 figures), each dominated by their universities.

4. Not strictly true. 'I come fae Pumphie' (Pumpherston, a former shale mining village in West Lothian) has a pleasing alliteration to it, and made it as a car bumper sticker in the 1990s.

5. Palimpsests were originally manuscripts which were superimposed on previous ones because paper was so expensive, the previous texts faintly showing through. As a metaphor, it has been used to make sense of towns and cities where buildings are not tabula rasa but impinge on the new.

6. Glasgow, too, had its version in Kelvinside, conveniently forgotten, in which extending the final vowel sound 'i' to 'a' (-side to 'said') was taken as a mocking sound of refinement.

7. Machin and Rodger (2013), 'Inspiring Capital? Deconstructing myths and reconstructing urban environments, Edinburgh, 1860–2010', *Urban History*, 40(3), 507–29.

8. '"Dark Satanic mill" blacksmiths find new home' – BBC News, 15 October 2020.

9. 55 per cent of the city's population in 2011 lived within 4 km (2.49 miles) of the centre of Edinburgh, compared with 48 per cent in 1981. See: <https://www.edinburgh.gov.uk/downloads/file/24263/population-distribution-and-density>.

10. Mackintosh, though born in Simla, India, was brought up and educated in Edinburgh, and attended Melville College in the city, later merged with Daniel Stewart's. Mackintosh, hence, could be 'placed'.

11. Percy was a fan of development, and cut his teeth working for the post-war London County Council. For those with time and patience, there are three metres of his papers on the Southside development lodged in the University Library archive: <https://archiveshub.jisc.ac.uk/search/archives/19596a3c-5096-3380-bb67-4b71ac0e6db9?component=1fce83a0-9a9e-3773-8aba-8728c2072614>.

12. Edinvar became part of Castle Rock Housing Association, a much bigger and more professional housing association working across nine Scottish local authorities.

13. <https://www.edinburgh.gov.uk/downloads/file/25200/edinburgh-by-numbers-2019>.

14. It is interesting that certain institutions and events/processes become so significant in public discourse that they are simply referred to by the definite article: *The* University, *The* Festival, *The* Trams. We know whereof they speak.

15. I am indebted to the late Michael Banton for that term, which refers to a group who do not consider themselves 'ethnic' at all.

2

Politics in Edinburgh

Let us begin our exploration of the question 'who runs Edinburgh' by focusing on formal political power.[1] The point is not that this will provide an easy answer our question, but that it is the obvious place to begin. It is, as it were, necessary in finding an answer, but not sufficient. After all, power may be veiled; formal politics may (or may not) be a front for other, and deeper, interests. It is, however, one of the key games to explore in Norton Long's ecology of games.

We have three ways of assessing formal political power in Edinburgh: who runs the council (our main focus here); who gets elected as MSPs for city seats in the Scottish parliament; and who gets elected as MPs for Edinburgh constituencies at Westminster. At council level, which uses the single transferable vote system (STV), the Scottish National Party shares power with Labour in coalition, and is the senior partner with nineteen council seats following the 2017 election, to Labour's twelve. This is just short of an overall majority in a council of sixty-three members. In fact, the SNP took 27.1 per cent of the popular vote, about half a per cent behind the Conservatives, but the SNP were in a much better position to form a coalition, having been the junior partner with Labour in the previous 2012–17 administration (with eighteen seats to Labour's twenty). The Tories are less attractive coalition partners for any other party with the possible exception of the Liberal Democrats with whom they shared power back in the early 1980s in Edinburgh District.[2]

What of 'national' politics? There are two levels to consider: Scottish and British. In terms of the Scottish parliament, elected by another system of proportional representation, the additional member system (AMS),[3] the Nationalists are dominant, holding four of the six Edinburgh constituency seats in 2021, three in 2017, and five of the six in 2012. As far as Westminster seats are concerned, elected by traditional first-past-the-post, there are five Edinburgh seats[4]; in the 2019 UK general election, three were held by the SNP, Edinburgh East, Edinburgh North and Leith, and Edinburgh South-West, all with five-figure majorities, one by Labour (Edinburgh South, also with a five-figure majority), and one by the Liberal Democrats, Edinburgh West, with a 3000 plus majority. In the latter two, non-SNP, seats, the Nationalists are the main challengers.

It would appear, then, that in the second decade of the twenty-first century, the Nationalists are the dominant political force in Edinburgh; after all, they are the majority party in running the council, and have a majority of Edinburgh seats at both Scottish and British parliamentary levels. Furthermore, we might expect that, given Edinburgh's position as national capital in a Nationalist-dominated polity. That is somewhat misleading, because the rise of the SNP to city dominance is relatively new, and only emerged in the last decade or so. It is further misleading because it tells us very little about how the city was shaped by its politics in the longer duration. The task of this chapter is to tell that important tale.

THE RISE AND FALL OF POLITICAL PAROCHIALISM

Focusing merely on the current state of Edinburgh's politics tells us little or nothing about the dominant mode of the last century: the hegemony of 'political parochialism', the view that local politics is for local people, and highly resistant to 'national' intrusion, even to keeping political parties out of politics. In this respect, Edinburgh was not unique; many other towns and cities had similar formations (see Peter Hennock's *Fit and Proper Persons: Ideal and Reality in Nineteenth Century Urban Local Government* (1973); and Avner Offer's *Property and Politics, 1870–1914* (1981)), but what marks out Edinburgh is that this ideology far outlasted other places. It was not until the mid-1970s that politics in Edinburgh were 'nationalised', ending what George Bernard Shaw, in another context, called 'rule by shopkeepers'. The manifestation of this was the denial that 'politics' had anything much to do with running the town. In W. H. Marwick's words, the cry was for 'economy', to limit spending unless absolutely necessary, and sometimes not even then. Its most obvious manifestation was the absence of party labels, especially on the political Right. It was not until 1973, for instance, that the Conservative party, at least in its modern form, fought local elections in Edinburgh. Hitherto, right-wing interests – although they would deny such a thing – were managed by the Progressive Association (a description it preferred to 'party'). In the first half of the twentieth century it was more common to find such interests calling themselves 'Moderates', as they did in the other Scottish cities: Glasgow, Aberdeen and Dundee. Why not in Edinburgh? Such interests were mobilised by what, or who, they were opposed to – Labour – and so were defined by what they were not. In the inter-war period, there were 'Moderates' in Edinburgh, but at the behest of the Liberals, and Lord Provost Andrew Murray, the term 'Progressive' replaced it, because, it sounded more, well, 'progressive' and up-to-date.

Ostensibly, it was the emergence of Labour in the 1920s which had the effect of mobilising the Right, and in 1928 the Edinburgh Good Government League (EGGL) was formed with one (negative) platform: 'opposition to Socialism'. The catalyst was the election of 1926 – the year of the General Strike – when 'Labour' candidates doubled its number of councillors to fourteen, and took more than 50 per cent of the vote in electoral contests. Still, such a number was dwarfed by non-Labour councillors in a council of seventy-one members. *The Scotsman* newspaper gave EGGL, and the Moderates, formed in 1929, a fair wind.

The Scotsman had skin in the game,[5] to use an American expression. The newspaper, like many institutions in Edinburgh, was both local and national in focus, serving local clientele and calling itself 'Scotland's national newspaper'. Founded in 1817, *The Scotsman* was a supporter of reform from about 1820 until the mid-1840s (Marwick 1969). From the third quarter of the century, under the editorship of Alexander Russel, it tended to support conservative Whiggism in opposition to what it described as 'the disorderly elements of radicalism as voiced by Duncan McLaren' and his radical Liberals.[6] McLaren's 'advanced' or 'independent' Liberals were criticised by *The Scotsman* as 'disorderly' and 'extremist', and there was a personal feud between the paper's editor, Russel, and McLaren, which at some point involved a libel action. Marwick observed: 'in 1886, *The Scotsman* became Unionist, and inclined towards Conservatism, though professing support for non-intrusion of party politics in local government' (Marwick 1969: 31), a refrain repeated down through the twentieth century in support of the 'non-political' right, and its defining enemy 'municipal socialism'.

We might conclude from this that party politics had little or no part to play in municipal affairs in Edinburgh, and only emerged in mid-twentieth century, but this was not so. Indeed, we can find 'Liberal' and 'Conservative' party labels employed by councillors in the nineteenth century; in 1875, for example, twenty-four out of forty-one councillors were Liberals, eight were Tories, and nine had no party affiliation. By 1905, fourteen out of fifty were Liberals, three were Tories, and most, thirty-one, had no formal party affiliation. The remaining two councillors were Labour. Much depended on who was entitled to vote. In 1855, there were only 4230 electors, all male, who had premises worth £10 or more.

The 1867 Act extended the franchise to urban workers who stood for election as Trades Council candidates without success. 'Lib-Lab' candidates were more common until the turn of the century, with attempts to form working class representation by means of the Scottish Labour Party which merged with the Independent Labour Party (ILP) in 1893. The Edinburgh Trades Council did not affiliate, and supported instead the 'Scottish Trades Council Labour Party' which did not survive beyond 1892. In 1889, Andrew Telfer, a 'so-called working man', according to *The Scotsman* whose dislike of candidates could always be ascertained by the use of the descriptor *soi-disant*, won in St Cuthbert's ward, and two years later, John Cubie was also elected in the Canongate. The Trades Council recognised such candidates as 'Labour representatives'. The plethora of labels on the Left encompassed the Irish republican James Connolly as an Independent Socialist in St Giles in 1894, ILP, and SDF (Social Democratic Federation) candidates. In 1899, there was a Workers' Municipal Committee, supported by the Trades Council, one of whom got elected to the council. *The Scotsman* took to branding such leftist groups as 'Socialists', although it more commonly treated it as a synonym for Labour.

As long as there were few electoral contests, apathy ruled, and few council seats were contested: in 1849, only two, and in 1889, none at all. Over a ten-year period in the 1880s, there were on average three elections per year, but *eleven* in 1889, attributed to the granting of freedom of the city to the Irish home ruler Charles Stewart Parnell, as well as to a rise in the city rates, the touchstone of right-wing politics. Apathy, however, was a useful device, and, as Marwick observes, '(t)he cry of "economy" was so frequently raised as to incur the jibe that Edinburgh residents, unlike the Apostle Paul, could not claim to be "citizens of no mean city"'.[7] The intrusion of the 'Irish vote', notably in the Canongate in the 1870s, was resented by *The Scotsman*, and in 1889 the award of the freedom of the city to Parnell provoked violent opposition.

From 1882, women householders were entitled to vote in Edinburgh municipal elections (but not parliamentary ones), and numbered around 20 per cent of the electorate. The electorate was fewer than 30,000 in 1880, and only around 60,000 in 1900, as results of inclusion of women, and of Portobello. In short, between 1880 and 1900, there were small electorates and few contests (only four or five per year on roughly 50 per cent turnouts).

Religion was an issue, notably after the Disruption of 1843. Until 1874, the council held the patronage of city churches, and the growth of 'Dissent' sought to cut the number of established church clergy and their stipends which the council had to support. An Annuity Tax dated from the seventeenth century to cover clergy stipends, and selective exemptions (including advocates, for no obvious reason) simply heightened the grievances. Matters of religious dissent were never far away from politics in the nineteenth century, and in 1856 among councillors, seventeen were Free Church, fourteen were dissenters, seven belonged to the established church, and there was a solitary Episcopalian. Matters of education (control of the university, the tounis college, was vested in the council until 1858) also played a part, with appointments to university chairs a matter of politics rather than expertise. 'Christopher North' (the Tory journalist John Wilson), for example, was appointed to the chair of Moral Philosophy, although he openly professed ignorance of the subject.

Matters of municipalisation were not particularly contentious. Marwick observed that it was regarded 'in Edinburgh as elsewhere, merely as an expedient for the administration of recognised public utilities, and most of its champions would have been horrified to be regarded as Socialists' (Marwick 1969: 36). The water supply to the city *was* contentious. Outbreaks of cholera (1831–2) and typhus (1848–9) in the city made the case for a pure water supply, and reservoirs in the Moorfoot hills (1879) and at Talla (1895) were established to serve the city with clean water (a St Mary's Loch scheme was rejected). A city gas company was formed in 1817, but only in 1888 was gas municipalised; municipal electricity came seven years later. The Tramways Act of 1870 legalised municipal ownership of horse-drawn trams, with municipal ownership largely achieved by 1893 with the introduction of cable traction. Not until after the First World War did the city run the trams directly rather than lease them to a private company.

So who were councillors in early nineteenth-century Edinburgh? Marwick (1969: 37) observed:

> There seems some warrant for the view that citizens more prominent in other respects, in business or professions, took a larger part in public life than has been the case later; a probable explanation is that municipal duties then demanded less time than now, particularly at attendance at committees . . .
>
> Bernard Shaw once said that the system of local government led to rule by shopkeepers. Certainly, many such, though usually bearing the more honorific designation of merchants, became councillors. Among Lord Provosts, besides those already mentioned, were Sir William Johnston, printer, Charles Lawson, seed merchant, William Law, coffee merchant, James Cowan, paper manufacturer, Sir James Falshaw, Chairman of North British Railway, Sir Thomas Boyd and Sir Thomas Clark, publishers, Sir Andrew Macdonald, clothier, Sir Mitchell Thomson, timber merchant, Sir George Harrison, woollen merchant, and Sir James Steel, builder. Four may be classified as professional – Sir James Forrest and Francis Brown Douglas, advocates; Sir John Melville WS; and Sir James Russell, physician, though latterly company director.

In truth, shopkeepers as such seem thin on the ground, and rule by the substantial merchant class seems more obvious.

By end of the nineteenth century, Labour was putting up around twelve candidates in council seats, with a couple being elected (a Labour candidate contested the parliamentary seat of Central Edinburgh in 1892). In 1900, the number of wards increased to sixteen, with fifteen contested. However, this fell back to average of six, until the Great War, with around 60 per cent turnout. Henderson[8] comments: 'One interesting feature is the regularity with which a small group of Labour candidates contested, and with five members, formed a little group in the Council by 1914.'

Early Twentieth-century Municipal Politics

The century started with *The Scotsman* making plain where its politics lay. Using the occasion of the extension of the city boundaries to absorb the suburb of Portobello, the editorial took exception to the fact that the Liberals had put forward candidates:

> they are put forward by a party political body. This is in strict keeping with the doings, or rather the misdoings, of the Radicals in the Town Council in the past. Though they burned their fingers over the Parnell freedom they do not seem to have taken the lesson to heart, and they are as ready as ever to make politics the test of fitness for the Council.[9]

Issues of temperance exercised the editor, who probably wrote or instigated the comments, but his attack went wider:

> In other directions attempts are being made to force what are already Imperial politics into the discussion of municipal matters. The electors ought to see that this course is not successful. The Municipal Council has its own business to do. It has not to interfere with the duties of the Imperial Parliament.[10]

What these municipal matters were is unclear, but certainly they should not interfere with the workings of local markets. Thus, on the pressing matter of housing in Edinburgh, *The Scotsman* offered its own version of 'let them eat cake':

> the man who tells us that the proper way to deal with the housing of the poor is for the city to build houses talks pernicious nonsense. The way in which overcrowding in the city can be disposed of best is to make facilities for travelling to the outskirts easy and cheap. There, land can be got upon which houses can be built at less price than they can be built in the town.[11]

Whether the newspaper would support subsidised fares is moot; it was much exercised by the business of the city being 'conducted efficiently without the intrusion of party politics'. Issues such as temperance, or women's suffrage ('"The British women" are the tools of Radical wire-pullers', it asserted[12]), or wider social reform, are deemed pretexts in the pursuit of power. It is sufficient to be 'non-political' in the pursuit of the city's business. *The Scotsman* opposed 'so-called Labour candidates'[13] ('so-called' again), and all the more so when 'Socialists' come to challenge this curious form of non-party politics. It is sufficient that politics have not been talked about at the ward meetings, even though 'pro-Boerism has attempted to raise its head'.[14]

The Edinburgh Workers Municipal Committee had the temerity to put forward a Labour candidate in St Leonard's ward in the 1902 election, focusing on issues of housing and overcrowding, while *The Scotsman* was more exercised by 'the evils of betting' and other nefarious Sunday activities,[15] although the newspaper was quite taken with Sunday music in the parks. It reported at some length the annual dinner of the Merchant Company of Edinburgh,[16] and extolled the comments of Sir James Steel, Lord Provost, that 'there is a good deal of similarity between the Town Council and the Merchant Company, not only because of their antiquity, but because of their connection with various public trusts'. Moreover, said the provost, he 'was only sorry that there were so few of the large merchants of the city who came forward to give their services in the Town Council'.[17] Somewhat elliptically, the newspaper thought, 'party politics are undesirable in municipal life; sex prejudices and preferences would assuredly be worse'.[18] For example, it certainly did not approve of the provost's widow Lady Steel (her husband having died in 1904) who was nominated, and defeated, for a council seat. *The Scotsman* judged it to be 'the wayward promptings of an 'ill-regulated temperament'.[19] Municipal politics was a man's game, and required men of substance at that.

Non-political politics were the order of the day, at least as *The Scotsman* could manoeuvre matters, reporting that the 1909 election resulted in 'uneventful campaigns' – 'the election contests have been largely "gas and water" affairs'.[20] It was happy for there to be 'fewer contests than usual', but resented Labour's intrusion such as that of William Smith in the Canongate who 'appeared as an advocate of the Socialistic propaganda'. The city establishment, reflected in the newspaper's views, walked a fine line between stirring up apathy, and getting out the (right-wing) vote in order to counter the perceived evils of 'Socialism'. Issues of municipal services such as electricity, the municipalisation of the tramways (vis-à-vis buses) were framed by the city treasurer by the principle which can be taken as the leitmotif of early twentieth-century municipal politics, that 'it behoved [councillors] to be extremely careful before they embarked on any expenditure which could be at all avoided'.[21] Extending city boundaries into Leith was an issue, and amalgamating the western suburbs was justified on the economistic grounds that 'getting these Edinburgh people outside the city bounds who were enjoying its privileges' to pay for them. Municipal parsimony ruled. 'Socialist' candidates pressed for elections in the inner-city wards, Calton, Canongate, Gorgie, Dalry and St Leonards, extending to contests in Broughton, Liberton and George Square.

In 1914, the last election before the Great War, *The Scotsman* was pleased to report 'the rout of the Socialist candidates',[22] and the newspaper regretted that 'Socialists had forced contests', considering that 'Socialists' were 'one of the extreme bodies of the kind in the city'. 'Socialist' was manifestly a useful, if imprecise, term of political abuse; at times *The Scotsman* used it to describe ILP and leftist parties, and Labour was so described in later years. The newspaper was staunchly right-wing, hostile to public spending and anything which smacked of 'Socialism', seeking to equate low rates with 'efficiency'.

Inter-war Municipal Politics

While it suited *The Scotsman* to inveigh against 'Socialists', Labour councillors in the inter-war period only numbered a handful, even after the amalgamation into the city in the early 1920s of Leith, Colinton, Corstorphine and Cramond. Labour doubled its representation – from three to six – between 1919 and 1925, but the council numbered seventy-one members. Labour's breakthrough came in 1926, the year of the General Strike, when it more than doubled its number of councillors to fourteen, and took more than 50 per cent of the vote in electoral contests that year, which, as we have seen, alarmed *The Scotsman* and the Edinburgh Good Government League (described by the newspaper as 'an Edinburgh movement'). Despite adding a further seat in 1928, Labour 'failed to repeat its success of two years ago [1926] when they gained no fewer than 8 seats'.

EGGL 'has arisen through increasing support for "Labour" candidates [note the quotation marks, more *soi-disant*], and there were now 14 Socialist members'.[23]

EGGL described itself as 'non-Socialist'; it was defined merely by what it opposed. Thereafter, EGGL, the Moderates, and *The Scotsman* (all singing in unison from the same song-sheet) set about encouraging people to vote, to counter 'apathy' which would simply encourage the 'Socialists'. 'If electoral indifference continues', pronounced *The Scotsman* in 1930, 'Edinburgh's reputation for sound management may be impaired by the rise to power of the Socialists'.[24] By 1931, The 'Moderates' (soon to be relabelled as 'Progressives') took 63 per cent of the municipal vote, to Labour's 35 per cent. The newly-moulded Progressives had fifty-two councillors to Labour's sixteen. This, however, did not reflect the fact that Labour took 42 per cent of the vote in wards contested. While we may wonder why the Right made the fuss it did, given Labour's small number of councillors, it was manifestly 'The Socialists' share of the vote which especially startled them.

Nineteen thirty-five was also the year when Protestant Action took three council seats. *The Scotsman* deplored the 'emergence of sectarianism in local politics',[25] but could not quite decide whether this was to the detriment of 'the Socialists' or its own favoured candidates on the Right. In 1936, Protestant Action won six seats, mainly at the expense of Progressives, which suggested the latter explanation, and in post-war years, Progressives stood aside to allow PA to challenge Labour, almost exclusively in the Leith wards. By the final council elections (1938) before the Second World War, *The Scotsman* commented: 'If Edinburgh may be regarded as a Progressive stronghold, the Socialists consider their own position in Glasgow impregnable' (ibid.). Glasgow stood as a reminder to Edinburgh's electorate of the dangers of 'Municipal Socialism'. By the outbreak of war, Progressives had forty-five councillors to Labour's eighteen (even though Labour took 41 per cent of the vote, once more alarming the Right), and Protestant Action's six.

Post-war Politics

In 1945, Labour had made seven gains, mainly from the Progressives 'who still hold an emphatic majority', said *The*

Scotsman; by 1946, Labour had twenty-seven council seats to
the Progressives' thirty-eight, and the writing looked to be on
the wall. Gradually, Protestant Action receded, largely defeated
by Labour, holding on to a single seat (South Leith) held by
its founder John Cormack until 1961.[26] *The Scotsman* took
comfort, in 1949, in 'Labour's Severe Setback', 'setting it back
20 years'. Elsewhere, in Glasgow and Dundee, the Right had
control at municipal level (in Glasgow, there were forty-seven
'Moderates' to Labour's thirty-seven; and in Dundee, nineteen
and sixteen respectively); results attributed to the nationalisation of gas and electricity, and the loss of local autonomy, as well
as rising prices. In 1951, Labour in Edinburgh was reduced to
fifteen councillors (on a third of the vote), to the Progressives'
fifty-two. Other Scottish cities were also controlled at the time
by the Right: even Glasgow, fifty-nine to Labour's fifty-three;
Aberdeen twenty to seventeen; Dundee twenty-two to fourteen.

   By the mid-1950s, the tide had turned. By 1954, in Edinburgh
Labour had twenty-four councillors (on 44 per cent of the vote),
with Progressives on forty-two councillors (and 53 per cent of
vote). In Glasgow and Dundee, Labour were back in power on
the councils. Successive council elections in Edinburgh showed
a narrowing of the gap between Progressives and Labour in
Edinburgh, with the Liberals re-emerging from the late 1950s
(one seat in 1959, two in 1961, and five in 1962). Commented
The Scotsman, presumably through gritted teeth: 'Liberals and
Labour jubilant as Progressives wane'.[27]

   By 1962, the Progressives had lost overall control of
Edinburgh council for the first time in their history, with thirty-
three councillors to Labour's thirty-one, and Liberals on five. In
Glasgow, Aberdeen and Dundee, meantime, Labour was comfortably in power. By the mid-1960s Progressives and Labour
in Edinburgh were virtually neck and neck (respectively, thirty-
three and thirty-two councillors), and there was an expectation
that Labour would make the breakthrough to power sooner
or later. Nevertheless, the Progressives managed to hold on to
council control (in 1967, they went into the municipal election
with thirty-six councillors to Labour's thirty-two, the Liberals
having fallen away), but right-wing representation was being
challenged.

   The chairman of the local Conservative Association pronounced that 'the entry of Conservative candidates in local

government elections is a recognition of the inevitable'[28] and while in 1966 two candidates stood in wards where there was no Progressive standing, in 1967 a Tory won a seat which also ran a Progressive candidate. Plainly, the Conservatives were becoming alarmed at the failure of the parochial Right to hold on to municipal power; they also realised that building a local political base was essential to getting constituency Tory MPs elected.

Nevertheless, contrary to expectations, the Right did not lose council power. In 1968, the SNP won seven seats, all at Labour's expense, with thirty-four Progressives, twenty-one Labour and three Tories, with Liberals holding a single seat. The Right was managing to hold its own.

Post-1967, the demise of two-party council politics is shown in Figure 2.1. Plainly, first-past-the-post elections did not properly reflect seismic shifts in vote shares. In the 1968 municipal elections, these were as follows: SNP 36 per cent, Progressives 28 per cent, Labour 20 per cent, Conservatives 10 per cent, and Liberals 7 per cent; a startling victory by the Nationalists. This was largely repeated the following year when the SNP won 29 per cent of the vote, but first-past-the-post awarded them only ten council seats. Plainly, the voting system was producing considerable distortions in a multi-party system. Thus, the Progressives had twenty-nine seats (on 27 per cent of the vote), Labour seventeen (on 21 per cent), and the Tories seven seats (on 15 per cent). However, the Tories warned what was to come: 'the Edinburgh City Conservative Committee . . . wishes it to be known that a Conservative candidate will contest such seats in the city as are most suited to the interests of the citizens of Edinburgh, regardless of confrontation with the Progressives'.[29]

The 'War on the Right' as *The Scotsman* put it in a headline on 6 June 1969, drew attention away from Labour's failure to win a majority on the council (in 1970, Labour had twenty-one seats to Progressives' thirty-one). While they won twenty-eight to Progressives' twenty-seven seats in 1971, an uneasy, right-wing alliance between Tories and Progressives kept the Right in power. By 1972, in the final years of 'old politics' before council reorganisation, Labour managed thirty-three seats to the Progressives' twenty-one, and Conservatives' nine. By this time, the SNP vote had collapsed, and the Liberals were on five.

Labour may have won the plurality of seats (thirty-three out of seventy-one), but insufficient to give it a majority. That proved to be the running theme of post-war Edinburgh politics; so near, and yet so far, and this arguably helps to account for the enthusiasm with which local Labour councillors embraced proportional representation at the end of the twentieth century. First, however, the reorganisation of local government into two tiers lay ahead, following the Wheatley Commission of 1969, introduced by the Local Government (Scotland) Act of 1973.

The battle on the Right had its own epitaphs: said the leader of the Progressives, Mrs Catherine Filsell, later to defect, unusually, to Labour, 'The Progressive Party believe that Edinburgh must be governed by local people who will always put Edinburgh first.' Replied the leader of the Tories, Brian Meek: 'I am afraid the Progressive Party is a bit of a dead duck.'[30] And so it proved in 1972, with a council line-up of eighteen Conservatives, ten Progressives, thirty-four Labour, five Liberals and two Independents. As Figure 2.1 shows, political parochialism, at least in that form, had come to an end. By the final old-council elections of 1973, Labour held thirty-four seats, the Conservatives twenty-one, there were seven Liberals, and five others, including Progressives almost all of whom eventually joined the Tories. Half a century of 'non-party' politics to the Edinburgh Corporation, manifestly right-wing, had ended.

Why focus on the 'history' of the city's politics, and in particular, the hegemony of right-wing and ostensibly non-political 'economy'? Because it laid down some of the most fundamental parameters of the city's political economy, in particular

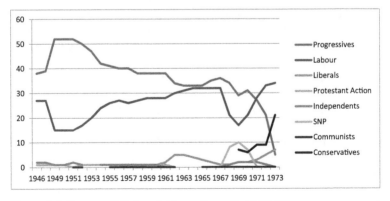

Figure 2.1 Seats on Edinburgh Town Council, 1946–73.

how the city developed and stratified its population, which we will examine later in this chapter. The key is that politics were closely aligned with property interests. Beliefs about 'economy' and parsimony had an important part to play in shaping how the city developed, notably who got what and who lived where. Before exploring that further and systematically, let us complete the political story of Edinburgh, and in so doing, set the parameters of what the city became in the following fifty years.

Reorganised Politics, Post-1973

In 1969, the Labour government had set up the Wheatley Commission into local government, which proposed the two-tier system, to get around the problem that many people lived outwith the main towns and cities, yet used their services. The Commission argued that it made for more efficient use of planning and resources. Regions had control over police, fire services, consumer protection, education and transport. Districts had responsibility for local planning, housing, libraries and licensing. Labour held an overall advantage in Lothian Regional Council elections because they took in the 'landward' areas of East Lothian, West Lothian and Midlothian, as well as the City of Edinburgh. Labour's strength in the landward areas offset its relative electoral weakness in Edinburgh. In the six regional council elections between 1974 and 1992 (see Table 2.1) Labour had a majority on Lothian Region in all but one,[31] in 1982, when there was a narrow Conservative/Lib-SDP[32] majority (twenty-two Tories and three Lib-SDP councillors out of forty-nine).

In terms of understanding the politics of Edinburgh, it is more meaningful to focus on district elections. In the city we find a much more competitive form of politics than in the region. Labour were more likely to run the council over the twenty-year period, but only in 1984 and 1988 do they have a clear majority, with minority status in 1974, and again in 1992. Across the period, the Conservatives, by now no longer competing with Progressives, take a higher share of the vote than Labour, but fewer council seats. Notice too that Edinburgh's municipal politics are shaping into a four-party race, with two major (Labour and Tories) and two minor parties (Liberal/Dems and SNP), which is formalised and given expression after the further reform of the electoral system in 2007 when the single

Table 2.1 District elections in Edinburgh, 1974–92

District elections	1974	1977	1980	1984	1988	1992
	Seats votes	Seats votes	Seats votes	Seats votes	Seats votes	Seats votes
Labour	29 (36.2%)	23 (26.6%)	25 (36.8%)	34 (38.8%)	33 (36.8%)	30 (29.2%)
Cons	30 (41.4)	34 (44.8)	31 (40.0)	22 (33.0)	23 (36.4)	23 (40.2)
Lib	3 (13.5)	1 (7.9)	2 (11.4)	4 (21.6)	4 (11.9)	7 (15.4)
SNP	1 (6.7)	5 (19.3)	3 (9.3)	2 (4.6)	2 (14.2)	2 (14.4)
Indep.	1	1	1	1		
Outcome	Lab minority	Conservative	Tory/ LibDem	Labour	Labour	Labour minority
Seats	64	64	62	62	62	62

Source: District election results, 1974–1992.

transferable vote (STV) system is introduced. Compare, for example, municipal elections pre- and post- the introduction of STV in 2007 (Table 2.2).

Labour, which had been winning overall council control on a minority of the vote (most obviously in 2003 when it won just over a quarter of the vote but took more than half of the seats) found itself either out of power, or forced into coalition. Compare, for example, in Table 2.3, its tally of seats and votes in 2003 and 2012. Its marginally greater share of the vote in 2012 gave it ten seats fewer under STV, a tally three or four seats more generous than proportional.

Let us take stock of Edinburgh's municipal politics. There had been a vibrant party politics between Liberals and Conservatives at the end of the nineteenth century, but this gradually faded into an ostensible 'non-party politics' with the rise of 'economy' and the view that keeping the rates as low as possible was the key to electoral success. 'Politics' could then be blamed on 'the Socialists' whose challenge at elections was usually magnified (raising the rates) to scare the middle-class electorate into line. The Moderates, later 'Progressives', held on to power much longer in Edinburgh than elsewhere, and not until the mid-1970s

Table 2.2 City of Edinburgh council elections, 1995–2017

City of Edinburgh Council	1995	1999	2003	2007*	2012*	2017*
	Seats votes	Seats votes	Seats votes	Seats votes	Seats votes	Seats votes
Labour	34 (40.7%)	31 (32.5%)	30 (27.4%)	15 (22.9%)	20 (28.1%)	12 (18.4%)
Cons	14 (23.3)	13 (22.5)	13 (24.7)	11 (22.1)	11 (19.7)	18 (27.7)
Lib	10 (18.1)	13 (24.4)	15 (26.9)	17 (22.0)	3 (9.3)	6 (13.6)
SNP	0 (17.3)	1 (20.5)	0 (15.6)	12 (20.3)	18 (26.9)	19 (27.1)
Green				3 (8.3)	6 (11.4)	8 (12.4)
Outcome	Labour	Labour	Labour	NOC LD/SNP	NOC Lab/SNP	NOC SNP/Lab
Seats	58	58	58	58	58	63

*Under single transferrable vote system (STV).
Source: City of Edinburgh Council election results, 1995–2017.

was its hegemony challenged, by the Conservative party who thought itself much better suited to fending off 'the Socialists', and in any case, municipal politics provided a useful training ground to educate the electorate for 'national' elections.

Once the Progressives were ditched in favour of Conservatives, party politics ostensibly were an integral part of municipal affairs. Labour, which had threatened to take power from the Right in Edinburgh from the 1960s onwards, did not in fact do so until the introduction of two-tier local government in 1974, albeit as a minority administration. It was not until 1984 that it took a majority of seats on the (district) council. By the end of the twentieth century, Labour in 1999 had a firm grip on local power, but its majority of seats (53 per cent) was achieved on only one-third of the popular vote. The main losers were the SNP whose fifth share of the vote produced a single seat, reflecting the fact that its vote share was spread uniformly across the city. Coming a good second in first-past-the-post elections does not win seats.

Two thousand and seven saw the first election following the introduction of PR (the single transferable vote (STV)) for local government, part of the deal struck by the Liberal Democrats in alliance with Labour following the 2003 Scottish parliament elections. Almost uniquely in Scotland, by 2007 four parties in Edinburgh were getting around one-fifth of the vote each, roughly reflected in numbers of councillors.

By the end of the twentieth century, Edinburgh's municipal politics had been transformed. Dominated for most of the century by 'non-party' politics in the shape of the Progressive Association which had kept out all-comers, from Labour, Protestant Action, even Tories, it succumbed in the final quarter of the century. The questions remain: why should Edinburgh be unusual, and to what extent did its politics have an impact on how the city developed? Did it actually matter that 'political parochialism' dominated municipal politics in Edinburgh for so long, and if so, with what effect?

THE POLITICAL ECONOMY OF EDINBURGH

Recall John Heiton's characterisation of Edinburgh in mid-nineteenth century as 'a city of castes'. He started his book, published in 1859, with this observation: '"Look you, sir. Your city is a very fine city, but it swarms with castes". The American was right: Our beautiful Modern Athens is in a swarm of castes, worse than ever was old Egypt or is modern Hindostan.' The point Heiton was making was that a simple division between capital and labour has never been Edinburgh's way. Rather, there are longstanding and complex nuances of status, class and power.

Lying behind Edinburgh's politics is the issue of its economy, or rather, economies. Edinburgh was not a heavily 'industrial' city, although it was far more devoted to manufacture than is commonly conceived. Rebecca Madgin and Richard Rodger (2013: 510) make the point that

> Professional employment accounted for one worker in six in Victorian Edinburgh – more than twice the national average – and provided a steady demand for furniture and fine art, prints and pianos, and generally underpinned the consumption-based industries in the city. In turn, this supported highly skilled, craft-based firms and sustained a substantial labour aristocracy. Edinburgh in the late nineteenth century was described as 'the greatest retail shop-keeping centre out of London' and so 'small-scale crafts, catering for a "luxury" market, constituted an important component of this employment'.

At root is political economy. In Liverpool or Manchester, commented Heiton, "twas cotton that did it'; in Sheffield, "twas steel that did it . . .'; in Dundee, "twas tow [rope, that is, flax/jute] that did it'; in Glasgow, "twas pig-iron that did it'; in Leith, "twas Dantzic wheat that did it'.[33] And Edinburgh? For lawyers, "twas quarrels that did it', but the lawyerly caste did not rule the city directly. Rather, it was the merchant class

> often worth a plum, and what is more, they are generally highly educated, and carry the manners of gentlemen. They can boast, moreover, of their corporate representative, the Chamber of Commerce – an institution of national celebrity and importance, whereby they contrive to draw within their cognisance, logic, and discretion, most of the great questions of the day . . . Edina forms mostly from out of them her Provosts, Bailies and Councillors, her Police Board and Paving Board.[34]

Thus, Heiton concluded, 'we suspect, indeed, that if the motto were to be of any form of that kind, it should be, "'Twas the Merchant Burghers who did it".' To be sure, merchants were a class differentiated from shopkeepers, who in turn were divided into 'Big Panes' and 'Little Panes' according to size of 'establishment' (never anything as common as simply a 'shop'). 'Shopocracy has its castes, its emulation, its envy. There is something about a shop altogether peculiar. It is a sign; it is an advertisement.'[35] Labour, in mirror image, was also made up of castes, largely comprising small masters and tradesmen, rather than gathered up in major manufactories.

Here is the basis of Heiton's 'city of castes'. Not only was there no unified industrial bourgeoisie, but the city's elites did not, by and large, come into common contact with industrialised labour, who nevertheless comprised half of the male workforce in the century up to 1951 (Madgin and Rodger 2013). In his study of the labour aristocracy in Victorian Edinburgh, Robbie Gray (1976: 21) commented:

> The most prominent middle-class groups were not directly involved in relations of production with the manual working-class, but were engaged in the professions, wholesale and retail distribution, commerce and finance. The industrial structure was itself heterogeneous, with a considerable amount of smaller-scale labour-intensive industry and a consequent diffusion of ownership.

On both sides of the capital–labour divide there was considerable diversity, a feature of the local bourgeois consumer
market, and reflected in the numbers employed in domestic service.[36] Even in a situation where most men were in industrial
employment, Edinburgh's heavy industry (engineering, brewing,
rubber) was composed largely of single firms, and thus differs
from those in large cities such as Glasgow and Birmingham
(Gray 1976: 24). While industrial structure does not determine
'politics', it undoubtedly shapes how electoral conflict is manifest. The first part of our answer, then, to the question: why did
'political parochialism' have such a long and successful run in
Edinburgh is that its industrial, and hence, occupational, structure was diverse.

People of Property

The second part of our answer is that in Edinburgh the connection between politics and 'property' was continuously close.
When municipal rates raised locally were a much higher proportion of city revenues than they are nowadays, those on
whom the burden fell, notably people of property, were far
more likely to engage in local politics simply to 'keep the rates
down'; they had a material interest in so doing. In the absence
of local taxes on income, trade or sales, the burden of taxation
fell on those who held property, not persons of great wealth but
owners of tenemented houses, small businesses, or parcels of
land.

In our study of landlordism in Edinburgh (McCrone and
Elliott 1989), we explored the intimate connections between
property and political power in Edinburgh between 1875 and
1975. In the first phase, between 1875 and 1918, party politics were replaced by ostensibly non-party labels. The Master
of the Merchant Company of Edinburgh's statement in 1873
that he was 'thankful that the Town Council had nothing to
do with politics' became the motif for the next century. As
many as 80 per cent of councillors in 1875 were landlords, and
even by the 1930s the figure was around half. Property interests were disproportionately represented on committees dealing
with building works, public housing and city extensions. There
was deep resistance to the 'nationalisation' of politics especially over public housing which was seen as a direct threat to

private interests (recall *The Scotsman*'s suggestion that working men take to the outer fringes of the city in search of affordable housing).

We might think of the links between property and power in Edinburgh as having three phases: the first, from around 1875 until 1918, covers a period in which the city was largely responsible for solving its own problems. This was the period of greatest autonomy, when local matters could be solved with minimal reference to central government. In these years, material interest in property, and especially the landlord interest, was shared by almost all councillors (see Table 2.3), and a sizeable number had direct involvement in the building industry. To reinforce the point, several of the council committees directly concerned with regulating property and its development were dominated by 'building interests' such as builders, landlords or house factors.[37] These included Plans and Works, Streets and Buildings, Cleaning and Lighting, Planning, Transport; as well as senior committees such as Lord Provost's, and Treasurer's committees. We observed: 'it is hard to resist the suggestion that careers in the "property game" as builders or factors might well be advanced through involvement in those committees involved in real estate' (McCrone and Elliott 1989: 79).

The second, inter-war, phase saw the expansion of local government activity, stimulated by central government's determination to tackle problems of housing and planning, and the beginnings of social welfare. The *Edinburgh Evening News*, companion of *The Scotsman*, and sharing its political line, reported on 3 November 1930 that in the council: 'Housing has been the main topic; the effects of rent subsidies on tenants . . . and the need to have sound businessmen on the Town Council.' Louis Gumley, house factor and soon to be lord provost, recorded his approval of the fact that in the four years up the election of 1935, a record number of houses (11,000) had been built, and with disarming frankness, advised his election audience that

Table 2.3 Percentage of councillors who were property owners

	1875	1905	1925	1935	1955	1965	1975
%	80	72	57	45	32	14	20

Source: McCrone and Elliott 1989: 77.

'in the advertisement pages, there are pages of houses for sale' (*The Scotsman* 1935).

The final, post-war, period sees the demise of political parochialism in Edinburgh. It is the period of major growth in state power, and the extension of local government responsibilities, creating large bureaucratic agencies to meet new obligations. With so much central decision-making, and concomitant funding, coming from central government it was difficult to maintain non-partisan and localist ideologies. There emerged a new cadre of politicians who wished to make local government more 'professional', and, on the Right, a new breed of Conservative councillor, especially lawyers, who came to dominate right-of-centre politics. While some councillors simply changed their party affiliation, from Progressive to Tory, they were more likely to be professionals than their small business counterparts. We concluded:

> Reform of municipal government in the nineteenth century, the transfer of responsibilities for education and housing in the inter-war years in the twentieth century, and the greatly extended tasks allotted to local authorities in the period since 1945 had all, by the 1970s, transformed the local arenas into important polities. (McCrone and Elliott 1989: 98)

The twilight creed of the Progressive Association, made in their manifesto in 1973 – that 'Progressives stand for local government by local people, whose duty is to the ratepayers of Edinburgh alone and not to any national political party. We see the good government of the city as an end in itself' – could have been issued at any time during the previous century. By the late twentieth century, it had become its swansong.

Segregation in Edinburgh

And the legacy? It shaped the patterns of social and spatial segregation in Edinburgh. The Third Statistical Account for Scotland, published in 1966, commented in its Edinburgh volume: 'Segregation began in the 19th century, but not until the 1920s did open development allow the creation of coherent areas of development, not only housing one social stratum of the city's community but separated by open space' (Keir 1966: 59). In the 1970s, geographers were arguing that there was in Edinburgh 'extreme spatial segregation of social classes' (Richardson et al.

1975) using measures such as indices of dissimilarity in the context of other cities. Truth to tell, a limited number of cities were
studied, and mainly in North America, so systematic comparisons were impossible to make, but it made an important point,
and seemed to reinforce the general perception of a socially segregated Edinburgh as highly plausible. If it were so, how had it
come about? What were the mechanisms which mattered?

This period of municipal history was over, but it had one
major legacy. It shaped who got what, in terms of land, in the
city. Particularly in the inter-war period, Edinburgh Corporation
used low-interest loans and subsidies to encourage private builders. Miles Glendinning (2005: 150) has made the key point that
in Edinburgh:

> Of the private sector housing constructed between 1918 and 1932,
> 7 per cent was built with Corporation assistance, the vast majority
> for owner occupation. The corporation also provided low-interest
> loans for building and purchasing houses. Its officials came to
> believe that it should not, through large-scale council building, raise
> the price of building materials and labour and thus damage the pri-
> vate enterprise market.

Having successfully 'farmed' state subsidies set up by John
Wheatley's Housing Act of 1924, Edinburgh Corporation
helped building firms erect low-cost houses for rent. They did
this by releasing land on favourable feuing terms, and even provided builders with cheap loans up to 75 per cent of the value
of the houses. One-quarter of all new private-sector housing
in the city after 1933 was built for renting under post-subsidy
schemes (Glendinning 2005: 151). The point is clear. It is not
simply a matter of having councillors whose ideological bent
is to 'keep the rates down', but to provide material assistance
to local builders, who, as we have seen, were well represented
among councillors themselves.

The doyen of this system was James Miller who, between 1927
and 1934, built almost 2000 subsidised houses, over twice as
many as the next ten largest firms put together. By 1932, Miller
had built 64 per cent of all subsidised houses in Edinburgh, and,
as if to make the point about the connection between property
and politics, became Lord Provost of the city from 1951 to 1954,
and Lord Mayor of London in 1964. By 1939, Miller's company
had amassed a land bank of 489 acres on seventy-two different

sites in Edinburgh. Miller Homes[38] was but the tip of a large iceberg of private builders who were indebted to the policies and practices of the Progressives, not merely to defend their interests but to promote actively new building opportunities.

If Edinburgh had a reputation for defending its patch against large-scale state and outside private developments such as 'system-building', it was at the behest of local business and political interests. Whereas two-thirds of houses built between the wars had been privately built, from 1946 to 1963 two-thirds were council houses. By 1962, Edinburgh Corporation lent more than £6m for house-building, and, in Glendinning's words, 'the Corporation doggedly revived its policy of subsiding the private sector' (Glendinning 2005: 158).

Politicians worked across parties. The Labour councillor Pat Rogan was made convener of the housing committee by a Progressive council in the early 1960s, and Glendinning observes that 'because the Progressive's parsimony had left the financial resources to support the sudden boost to the housing drive, and the large, low-density schemes of prefabs had bequeathed him a tempting land bank to raid' (Glendinning 2005: 160), Rogan in 'Tory' Edinburgh was in a much better position than his counterpart in Glasgow. When the Progressive councillor George (born Adolf) Theurer[39] took over the housing convenership in 1965, he worked closely with Pat Rogan,[40] culminating in the last major public housing scheme in Edinburgh, Wester Hailes, built between 1967 and 1975. Said Theurer (quoted in Glendinning 2005: 163):

> My intention, just like Pat, was to build houses for the people! Some of my fellow-Progressives grumbled bitterly: they didn't want council houses because the low rents would be exploited by the Labour Party; they didn't want to add to national Labour 'successes'. But I didn't care one bit!

In truth, a large-scale plan such as for Wester Hailes was the exception not the rule. A 'conservative' housing strategy was reinforced by the policies and practices of successive burgh engineers whose remit included building houses. A. Horsburgh Campbell was burgh engineer from 1910 until 1926, and appointed as director of housing in 1920 by the Housing and Town Planning Committee, and strongly advocated the continuing use of tenements in slum clearance. Campbell pursued a policy of 'Geddesian small-scale redevelopments' making use of small in-fill schemes, and low-rise suburban estates (such as those in Niddrie Mains – not to be confused with Craigmillar – and Prestonfield). His successor, Ebenezer MacRae, became city architect and was in post until 1951. MacRae reinforced the philosophy of piecemeal redevelopment and suburban over-spill schemes. Stephen Robb (2017: 72), who has done much to revive the reputation of MacRae, observed:

> MacRae's inter-war housing is now at least seventy-five years old, a timescale that should allow a proper assessment of his legacy. As part of a sustainable approach to Edinburgh's housing stock in a growing city, and with a likely intensification of future upgrading for fuel poverty, it is to be hoped that MacRae's best work might now be regarded as an asset to Edinburgh, part of its wider built heritage. Hopefully, in the future it will benefit from sensitive and sympathetic revitalisation, redecoration and upgrading.

MacRae's legacy is to be found literally all over Edinburgh, and includes 'numerous public toilets, pavilions, stores, bandstands, sheds and around a hundred electricity substations. Bespoke street furniture for Edinburgh included boundary signs and light columns, and the building type for which MacRae is most widely celebrated, the Edinburgh Police Box' (Robb 2017: 43). MacRae's policy of Geddesian small-scale developments and in-fill across the city could be accommodated within a 'conserva-tive' strategy of house-building, while in no way derivative of its political implications. MacRae also contributed the 'Historical Review' introductory chapter to the grandiose Abercrombie Plan of 1949, and took care to distance himself from radical propos-als by Abercrombie such as running a triplex roads system along Princes Street. He warned pre-emptively: 'this chapter has been written independently and its inclusion does not necessarily indicate the writer's agreement with the conclusions or recom-mendations of the main report' (MacRae 1949).

MacRae (1949: 9) had a good feel for the social fabric of the city, commenting on its early modern form in the Old Town:

> Gradations of society were made vertically, all classes entering by one door and passing each other on the turnpike stair, the lowest and the uppermost storeys of each tenement housing the poorer families. This had at least the advantage that each class was familiar with the mode of life of all the others.

There was little that MacRae could do to turn the clock back, but in his slum clearance programmes and developing new housing schemes across the city, he avoided the strategy of corralling the poor in peripheral estates. There was nothing comparable to the policy pursued in Glasgow by the legendary housing convener David Gibson, of driving round the city with the city engineer and planting tower blocks on available sites as he found them, without any social facilities to speak of.[41]

CONCLUSION

So this is Edinburgh and its politics. It is a city which had a long hegemony of parsimonious politics, dominated by a curious political formation which denied that 'politics' had much to do with running the city. And yet its 'conservative' strategy meant that Edinburgh had far less physical disruption brought about by pursuing 'development' at all costs. We will see in a later chapter that Abercrombie and Plumstead's famous 1949 *Plan for Edinburgh* produced very little on the ground, and that resistance to fashionable designs for roads in the sky on stilts to accommodate the car did not happen in the city, unlike in Glasgow in the west. Edinburgh is by no means bereft of planning mistakes, but carving up the city as proposed in the post-war period, and again under the 1965 Development Plan Review, did not happen, with its threat/promise: 'A primary objective of the Plan is to provide for road traffic by improving the network of principal roads. Additions to the existing principal road network include an inner ring road, to new radial roads and a bypass road.'

In fending off such developments, the city remains one in which a high proportion of its population live within a few miles of the city centre, making it feel a 'liveable' city. Throughout this chapter, issues of political economy have intruded because so much of the city's politics both have an effect and are dependent on how the city's economy (better still, economies, for they are various) has developed, and it is to that topic that we now turn in Chapter 3.

NOTES

1. An earlier version of this chapter appeared in *The Book of the Old Edinburgh Club* (McCrone 2017b).

2. Between 1974 and 1994, local government in Scotland had two tiers, District and Region, the former covering Edinburgh, and the latter, Lothian which comprised East-, West- and Mid-Lothian plus Edinburgh.

3. The AMS system for the Scottish parliament is a mix of constituency seats (seventy-three) and list seats (fifty-six), the latter being a means of balancing out the disproportional effects of the former. There are six constituency seats in Edinburgh, and seven list seats in Lothian, which covers the city plus adjacent local authorities. The focus here is on constituencies to give a measure of party strengths in the city.

4. In 2005, the Scottish constituencies were redrawn, and the number reduced from seventy-two to fifty-nine.

5. The term derives from US horse racing, and relates to having betting interests in the race; it was made popular by institutional investor Warren Buffett.

6. Duncan McLaren was Lord Provost of Edinburgh in 1851, and became a city MP in 1865.

7. Marwick, 'Municipal Politics in Victorian Edinburgh', p. 34.

8. J. Henderson, 'Seventy-Year Survey of Edinburgh Voting', *Edinburgh Evening News*, 20 April 1953.

9. *The Scotsman*, 3 November 1900.

10. *The Scotsman*, 27 October 1900.

11. *The Scotsman*, 27 October 1900.

12. *The Scotsman*, 7 November 1900. 'The British Women' was a temperance group. It later changed its name to the White Ribbon Association.

13. *The Scotsman*, 10 November 1900.

14. *The Scotsman*, 6 November 1901.

15. *The Scotsman*, 1 November 1902.

16. For histories of the Merchant Company of Edinburgh, see Alexander Heron's *The Rise and Progress of the Company of Merchants of the City of Edinburgh, 1681–1902* (Edinburgh: T. and T. Clark, 1903); covering the period from 1681 to 1902, and, subsequently, Rosalind Marshall's *The Edinburgh Merchant Company, 1901–2014* (Edinburgh: John Donald, 2015).

17. *The Scotsman*, 6 November 1902.

18. *The Scotsman*, 6 November 1907.

19. *The Scotsman*, 17 October 1907.

20. *The Scotsman*, 2 November 1909.

21. *The Scotsman*, 29 October 1912.

22. *The Scotsman*, 4 November 1914.

23. *The Scotsman*, 7 November 1928.

24. *The Scotsman*, 1 November 1930.

25. *The Scotsman*, 29 October 1938.
26. Cormack won (and lost) the North Leith ward early in his career, and transferred to South Leith which he held for a number of years.
27. *The Scotsman*, 2 May 1962.
28. *The Scotsman*, 6 April 1967.
29. *The Scotsman*, 5 June 1969.
30. *The Scotsman*, 3 May 1972.
31. In the first regional elections in 1974, Labour won twenty-four of the forty-nine seats, and technically were a minority.
32. In 1982, the Liberal party and the recently formed Social Democratic party (1981) had not yet amalgamated to form the Liberal Democrats, first as the Social and Liberal Democratic party in 1988, and adopting its present name a year later.
33. Heiton, *The Castes of Edinburgh*, 1859, p. 282.
34. Heiton, *The Castes of Edinburgh*, 1859, pp. 282–3.
35. Heiton, *The Castes of Edinburgh*, 1859 p. 295.
36. Gray puts the proportion of people employed in domestic service in 1881 at 20.5 per cent (1976: 26).
37. House factors in Scottish cities often managed properties for landlords, collecting rents, instructing repairs and vetting tenants. They often owned large swathes of property in their own right, and latterly became estate agents, buying and selling property (McCrone and Elliott 1989).
38. Miller Homes was sold for £655m in 2017 to the private equity group Bridgepoint, whose holding also included Pret a Manger, the sandwich chain.
39. Theurer, wig-maker to trade, died in 1997. See his obituary in *The Herald*: <http://www.heraldscotland.com/news/12323425.George_A_Theurer/>.
40. Rogan's influence in Edinburgh can be gauged by his obituary in *The Scotsman* in 2011. It is a far cry from *The Scotsman* 100 years before.
41. For the definitive account of Glasgow's council-house building, see Sean Damer's *Scheming: A Social History of Glasgow Council Housing, 1919–1956* (Edinburgh: Edinburgh University Press, 2020).

3

Winners and Losers:
The Political Economy of Edinburgh

Lying behind the changing fortunes in politics in Edinburgh is its changing economy. It is, however, not a question of reading one off the other, assuming that 'politics' is simply the expression of the 'economy'. Furthermore, we have grown so used to defining Edinburgh as a city of professions, money and culture that we tend to assume that this has always been so. Our examination of the city's politics indicates otherwise. Small, local, capital had expression in its 'non-political' politics for such a long time, occupying most of the twentieth century, and thus shaping what came after it.

In 1914, the Merchant Company of Edinburgh proclaimed its local patriotism:

> The Company is not merely a company of merchants. It is the Company of Merchants of the City of Edinburgh and nothing that concerns Edinburgh or the district included in the definition should be a matter of indifference to it. In everything that concerns the welfare of this district as a whole the Company has a direct responsibility.[1]

This begged many questions which the Merchant Company was aware of. It was no longer

> a compact association of members with identical and limited interests, but includes merchants, bankers, traders, principals or agents engaged in any department of commerce, trade, manufacture or handicraft, architects, engineers or surveyors, managing directors, managers and principal officers of banks, insurances or other companies.[2]

The Company, in other words, now represented 'many various and sometimes antagonistic interests'.

EDINBURGH CASTES

It had tended to be ever thus. John Heiton's *Castes of Edinburgh*, fifty years previously, had made that plain:

> The Merchants – not great with us – stand between the Professionals and the Shopkeepers; these are getting up; the Big Panes despise the Little Panes. The latter expel the Tradesmen, who erect a *nez troussé* against the Labourers. And these lord it over the Irish Fish-dealers, who will cut an Applewoman of a Sunday. (Heiton 1861: 6–7)

Robbie Gray's study of the labour aristocracy in Victorian Edinburgh showed how status differences – caste distinctions – ran all the way down Edinburgh's class system, but that 'the city's notorious snobbery seems to have derived from social and political rivalries encouraged by this heterogeneity of the wealthier classes' (Gray 1976: 20). It is not difficult to characterise Edinburgh as a city of class distinctions – 'snobbery' – but these social distinctions were not bi-modal, but subtle and multi-varied. Gray (1976: 12) argued that the working class in the city was formed in the context of no unified industrial bourgeois elite:

> The most prominent middle class groups were not directly involved in relations of production with the manual working class, but were engaged in the professions, wholesale and retail distribution, commerce and finance. The industrial structure was itself heterogeneous, with a considerable amount of smaller-scale labour-intensive industry and a consequent diffusion of ownership.

Edinburgh's bourgeoisie and proletariat, then, did not stare fixedly across a uniform class divide; indeed, they had little opportunity and reason to do so, because the city's economies (plural) were diverse and variegated.

> The industrial working-class in 19th century Edinburgh was thus marked by considerable occupational diversity. A range of old-established crafts catered for the large middle-class consumer market, while newer, more capital-intensive enterprise were geared to national and world markets. One feature common to many

local industries was their high proportion of skilled labour. (Gray 1976: 26)

In the final quarter of the nineteenth century, the stratum of 'superior artisans' espoused values of 'respectability', 'independence', and 'thrift'. This 'upper stratum created relatively autonomous class institutions and had a distinctive cultural life, articulating a sense of class identity' (Gray 1976: 184). The labour aristocracy also provided leadership of any working-class movement.

> The result was transmutation of socialism into labourism, programme of gradualist reforms; a negotiated response to capitalist society; strong sense of class pride and an ethic of class solidarity. This class identity was transmitted in the later nineteenth century to a wider class movement and culture – it is not the least of the legacies of the Victorian labour aristocracy. (Gray 1976: 190)

The heterogeneous character of Edinburgh's economy, notably the importance of consumer crafts as well as domestic service (especially for women) was also reinforced by the character of its heavy industries. Ian MacDougall, editing the minutes of the Edinburgh Trades Council for the period 1859 to 1873, noted that Edinburgh's heavy industry is composed largely of single firms of outstanding reputation in each sector. Thus it differs from the concentration of similar firms in large conurbations such as Clydeside or Birmingham (MacDougall 1968). It was not that Edinburgh lacked heavy industries, notably in engineering, brewing and rubber, and the number of workers in these industries grew fast in the second half of the nineteenth century. Even the 'consumer' industry was on a large scale, as this image of McVitie's biscuit factory at Fountainbridge shows.[3] (Figure 3.1).

And so the Edinburgh economy by the turn of the century saw growth in three sectors: old-established handicrafts catering for local 'luxury' market; larger-scale industry and transport which, if anything, grew more rapidly; and the building industry characterised by cyclical fluctuation in numbers employed.

EDINBURGH TODAY

Leap forward a century, and what do we find? The city has been transformed. Industry, large and small, has been airbrushed from

Figure 3.1 Broken biscuits: McVitie's at Fountainbridge

its story. Indeed, one would hardly know that 'industry' had existed, because it is no longer part of the city's narrative. As the 2011 Census[4] observed: 'The historical decline in manufacturing is particularly striking.' In 1961, one-quarter of Edinburgh residents were employed in manufacturing; by 2011, less than 4 per cent, a mere one in twenty-five. The Census comments: 'Edinburgh now has one of the smallest manufacturing and construction sectors of any major city in the UK' (para. 79). On the other hand, nine out of ten are employed in 'services', up from 64 per cent in 1961 (Table 3.1).

We can bring these data further up to date using Nomis,[5] and furthermore, view them comparatively. By 2019, a mere 2.3 per cent of jobs in Edinburgh were in manufacturing, compared with 6.8 per cent in Scotland as a whole, and 8 per cent in Britain. On the other hand, the finance and insurance industries in the city employed one in ten, almost three times the proportion employed in Scotland, and in Britain generally. Twice as many

Table 3.1 Industrial structure of resident workforce

	1961	2011	Percentage point difference
Manufacturing	25.3	3.5	-22
Distribution, catering	20.7	19.9	-1
Transport and communications	9.5	7.8	-1.5
Other services	33.4	62.4	+29

Source: Census (Scotland) 2011.

were in information and communication (6.4 per cent), and dis-proportionately more (around 20 per cent more) in professional, scientific and technical employment than in Scotland as a whole. There are also proportionately more employed in education in Edinburgh (around 10 per cent) than in Scotland – and in Britain. Even the fallout from the banking crash in the early 2010s had only a marginal effect on the proportion employed in finance and insurance (from 10.9 per cent in 2015, to 9.6 per cent in 2019). The proportions in Edinburgh employed in finance and insurance, information and communications, professional, scientific and technical, as well as education taken together, represent about one-third of the city's labour force, compared with just over one-fifth of Scotland's, and one-quarter of Britain's. These data make the point that Edinburgh nowadays is a city of money, transactions, information and knowledge-processing.

These data, of course, relate to the industries in which people are employed (what is known as the city's 'industrial structure'). A related, but different, matter concerns the kinds of jobs which people do within those industries, the 'occupational structure'. Let us begin with the Census data for 2001 and 2011 (Table 3.2).

While the reclassification of occupations in 2000 means that we cannot make straightforward comparisons with what had gone before, we can gauge significant changes in Edinburgh's occupational structure as follows. In 1961, over half (54 per cent) of employees in the city worked in manual occupations (whether skilled, semi-skilled or unskilled), and by 1991, this had fallen by more than half, to 23 per cent. In many respects, what came after 1991 did not change a great deal: 19 per cent were in routine or semi-routine jobs in 2001, as well as in 2011. In other words, the major fall in manual employment in Edinburgh had occurred between 1961 and 1981 (when it fell from 54 per cent to 30 per cent), so these two decades were

Table 3.2 Occupational structure (NS-Sec), 2001 and 2011

	2001	2011
Large employers, higher managerial	4.1	2.0
Higher professionals	10.6	12.6
Lower managers and professionals	24.4	22.3
Intermediate	12.9	12.4
Small employers	5.5	6.1
Lower supervisory and technical	5.7	5.5
Semi-routine workers	11.1	11.0
Routine workers	7.7	8.3
Never worked	2.8	2.8
Long-term unemployed	1.0	1.5

Source: Census (Scotland) 2001 and 2011.
Note: NS Sec (National Statistics Socio-economic classification) was introduced in 2000, and superseded previous classification systems such as SEC (socio-economic categories), making direct comparisons over time inappropriate. See https://www.ons.gov.uk/methodology/classificationsand standards/otherclassifications/thenationalstatisticssocioeconomicclassification nssecrebasedonsoc2010

crucial in the transformation of the city's economy. Meanwhile, the proportion of intermediate and junior non-manual workers had increased from 21 per cent to 38 per cent (and to 41 per cent in 1991), virtually doubling. The numbers of employers, managers and professionals had grown far less proportionately, from 15 per cent in 1961, to 16 per cent in 1981, and to 23 per cent in 1991, suggesting that the 'professionalisation' of Edinburgh in employment terms came at the turn of the century or later. By 2011, 13 per cent were higher professionals, and 22 per cent lower managers/professionals, broadly speaking, one-third of employees in the city.

What has happened since 2011? Bringing these data up to date, we find a reinforcement of Edinburgh's non-manual, but especially its professional and managerial status. Note that the city has consistently and proportionately more managerial and professional workers than either Scotland or Britain (see Table 3.3).

We can draw the following points from the table:

• While Edinburgh has a disproportionate number of people employed as senior managers, professionals and officials, its

Table 3.3 Employment by occupation (2020)

	Edinburgh	Scotland	GB
Soc 2010 Major Group 1–3	**62.6%**	**47.5%**	**50.2%**
Managers, directors and senior officials (1)	10.4	8.9	11.5
Professional occupations (2)	34.1	23.5	22.8
Associate professionals and technical (3)	18.1	14.9	15.8
Soc 2010 Major Group 4–5	**14.0**	**19.1**	**19.3**
Administrative and secretarial (4)	9.1	9.6	10.0
Skilled trades (5)	5.0	9.4	9.2
Soc 2010 Major Group 6–7	**13.8**	**17.7**	**15.7**
Caring, leisure and other services (6)	8.3	9.6	8.8
Sales and customer services (7)	5.5	8.1	6.9
Soc 2010 Major Group 8–9	**9.6**	**15.8**	**14.8**
Process, plant and machine operatives (8)	3.6	5.9	5.5
Elementary occupations (9)	6.0	9.8	9.2

Source: https://www.nomisweb.co.uk/reports/lmp/la/1946157416/report.
aspx?town=Edinburgh#tabempocc

particular advantage lies in the proportion of professional occupations.

- While it has fewer workers in the remaining categories, Edinburgh has significantly fewer employed in skilled trades, sales and customer services, and as process plant and machine operatives.

We can see from the graphs in Figure 3.2 that Edinburgh's superfluity of managers, professionals and senior officials has been the case for at least a decade and a half; and likewise its deficit of machine operatives and those in elementary[6] occupations.

Concomitantly, Edinburgh has fewer workers in manual trades (categories 5, 8 and 9 in the table) than either Scotland or Britain[7] (see Figure 3.3). This reinforces the point that far fewer are employed in manufacturing and allied trades than at the respective national levels, Scottish or British.

We can look at this another way. Taking again the period between 2004 and 2020, but this time calculating change in

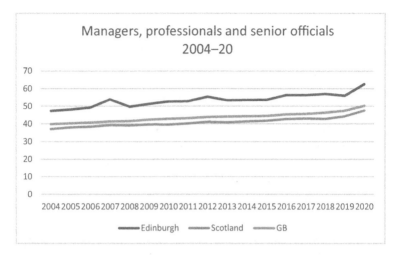

Figure 3.2 Changing employment patterns, SOC 2010, 1–3
Source: Nomis: ONS National Population Surveys: https://www.
nomisweb.co.uk/reports/lmp/la/1946157416/report.aspx?town=
Edinburgh#tabempocc

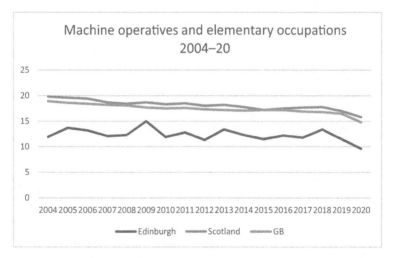

Figure 3.3 Changing employment patterns, SOC 2010, 8 and 9
Source: see Figure 3.2.

terms of the number jobs in the respective sectors, we find the following:

- In Edinburgh there has been a 60 per cent increase in the number of jobs in category 1–3 (that is, among managers, professionals and senior officials); which compares with a 38 per cent increase in Scotland as a whole, and 45 per cent in Britain.
- Furthermore, Edinburgh's disproportionate increase is in *professional* occupations (plus 60 per cent) and especially in 'associate professional and technical' jobs[8] (plus 77 per cent), and less so for managers, directors and senior officials (plus 38 per cent).
- There has been a disproportionate loss of jobs in categories 4 and 5 (administrative, secretarial and skilled trades) of the order of minus 27 per cent in Edinburgh,[9] compared with a fall of 18 per cent in Scotland, and minus 12 per cent in GB.
- There has been a modest decline in caring, leisure, sales and customer services – categories 6–7 – of the order of minus 5 per cent, comparable to Scotland as a whole (minus 6 per cent), in contrast to a plus 10 per cent increase in such employment in GB over the period. This decline masks an *increase* in Edinburgh in caring, leisure and related services (plus 27 per cent), but a *decline* among sales and customer services (minus 32 per cent).
- Finally, and somewhat unpredictably, Edinburgh is *least* likely to have lost jobs (a decline of 3 per cent) among process plant and machine operatives (group 8) and in elementary occupations (group 9), compared with a fall of 14 per cent in Scotland as a whole, and of 10 per cent in GB. This, however, reflects the fact that the de-industrialisation of Edinburgh had already happened by 2004, the beginning of the period in question. Nevertheless, the loss of employment in process plant and machine work was of the order of minus 23 per cent in the city, continuing that process of de-industrialisation, rather than in the loss of elementary occupations.

Our next task is to explore why these changes have taken place in Edinburgh, and put simply, whether they are the result of 'secular' changes which affect all similar labour markets,

and/or whether there are specific shifts in policies, locally or
nationally, which have had a differential effect on employment
in the city. Before we do that, we might reinforce the point that
Edinburgh is a city of above-average income levels, and of educational skills. Taking the latter point first, the percentage of
the city's population with degree qualifications or above (technically, NVQ4 and above, according to Nomis), virtually two-
thirds (66 per cent) reach this level, compared with 49 per cent
in Scotland, and 43 per cent in GB. This is also reflected in
earnings in the city, where the median income for FT workers is
higher than both Scotland and GB (Figure 3.4):

The Transformation of Edinburgh

Historians are divided as to why Edinburgh was econom-
ically transformed. Broadly speaking, there are two views: in
Bob Morris's words: 'Edinburgh de-industrialised with relatively good grace' (Morris 2010: 20); and the view expressed
by Richard Rodger that de-industrialisation took place, contra
Morris, 'as a conscious series of decommissioning decisions by

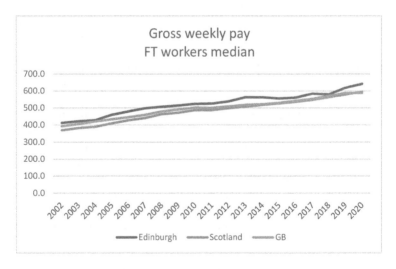

Figure 3.4 Gross weekly pay for FT workers
Source: see Figure 3.2.

planners' (Rodger and Machin 2013: 527). We will explore this transformation as these historians account for it, and examine key moments and reports, notably Abercrombie and Plumstead's comprehensive survey of 1949.

The first point to be made is that juxtaposing 'production' and 'consumption', as if these were separate economic spheres is misleading. In Edinburgh's case, for example, much 'production' was precisely *for* 'consumption' – recall McVitie's biscuits. Rebecca Madgin and Richard Rodger make the point:

> Professional employment accounted for one worker in six in Victorian Edinburgh – more than twice the national average – and provided a steady demand for furniture and fine art, prints and pianos, and generally underpinned the consumption-based industries in the city. In turn, this supported highly skilled, craft-based firms and sustained a substantial labour aristocracy. (Madgin and Rodger 2013: 501)

And in any case, as Bob Morris points out, in 1911, Edinburgh was 'a place for shopping, for hotels and eating places' (2010: 15). Still, he observes:

> The dominant feature was the substantial portion of the Edinburgh economy involved in manufacturing. In terms of absolute numbers employed, Edinburgh was the second manufacturing city in Scotland. Manufacturing has a reluctant place in the history of the city, but it dominated the life of much of the population. (Morris 2010: 15)

Morris points out that in 1911, the major male occupations included printers (3502), second only to commercial clerks (3839). There were bread, biscuit and cake makers (McVitie's again) (1402), India rubber, gutta percha workers (1251),[10] and the ubiquitous brewers (1013) who gave the city its distinctive odour. Printing and publishing employed 6090 men and 3856 women in firms like Nelson, Chambers and Bartholomew in and around Newington. Iron manufacturers which employed 4520 made a diversity of products, and included Bertram of Sciennes which employed 2954 making machinery for the printing industry in nearby Newington. The factory in Sciennes, a residential district on the Southside (Figure 3.5), did not close down until 1985, and the site was developed for housing.[11]

Figure 3.5 Industry in the city: Bertrams of Sciennes on the Southside

Despite its ubiquity in Edinburgh, displaying

all the features of an industrial economy, division of labour, use of technology and a world market . . . manufacturing tended to be ignored in Edinburgh's self-image, in part because of the greater social prestige of the lawyering and banking, but also because of the enormous variety of outputs which were involved. (Morris 2010: 15–16)

In the 1930s, it could be claimed that 'Edinburgh is to printing and stationery what Manchester is to cotton and Birmingham is to hardware' (Morris 2010: 16); in Heiton's terms, ''twas printing and publishing that made it'.

Richard Rodger's disagreement with his fellow historian seems to rest on Morris's view that 'in the last thirty or forty years of the [twentieth] century, Edinburgh had de-industrialised but had done this with little fuss or debate' (Morris 2010: 17). That, of course, is a judgement call, and derived from alternative forms of economic activity: 'income and employment offered by tourism, by finance and business services and by the banking and finance sector', making the Edinburgh experience 'more like Leeds and New York than Bradford or Detroit' (Morris 2010: 17). What Edinburgh also had in its ostensible favour was a high degree of cultural capital, that, in Morris's words, 'Edinburgh lay at the centre of a symbol system that meant Scotland – not just for Scots but on a world scale' (Morris 2010: 20). As we shall see in later chapters, such a degree of cultural capital threatened to overwhelm the city not only in terms of cultural meaning but, quite literally, feet on the ground as tourism became the name of the game.

The question is to what extent Edinburgh's shift in political economy was the result of deliberate policy operated by the city and by government. Edinburgh had no large staple industry such as cotton, shipbuilding, woollens or steel, and its diversity and complementarity guaranteed stability and local prosperity. Rodger's magisterial book *The Transformation of Edinburgh: Land, Property and Trust in the Nineteenth Century* (2001) makes that key point. His later article with Rebecca Madgin (2013) developed the argument that there were key moments in the city's political and economic history which set it on a different and non-industrial path. Rodger (2005: 88) has elsewhere written:

> Edinburgh was the quintessential instance where 'the talk of the bourgeoisie, not the smoke of the factory, was the defining characteristic of the modern city economy', but significantly the presence of the chimney, warehouses, mills, malt houses and other physical features in the industrial landscape were central to the daily experience of the majority of the citizens of the capital.

Focusing on the period 1860 to 2010, Rodger points up the contradictions in perceptions and reality. It was long true that professional employment was disproportionate in Edinburgh, one person in six, twice the national average, and heading a league table of professional employment in over twenty towns and cities between 1861 and 1951. It was, furthermore, closely connected to particular forms of production: 'and provided a steady demand for furniture and fine art, prints and pianos, and generally underpinned the consumption-based industries in the city. In turn, this supported highly skilled, craft-based firms and sustained a substantial labour aristocracy' (Madgin and Rodger

2013: 510). This makes the point nicely that forms of production and consumption, and of social stratification, are synergic and relational. It also conferred on Edinburgh a metropolitan role 'which gave the Lothian economy its structural similarity to the South East of England, and that mixture of professions, commerce, personal services and consumer good industries such as printing and publishing' (Clive Lee 1983: 22; quoted in part in Madgin and Rodger 2013: 511). The city also had the benefit of spreading its economic activities across diverse industries, and being beholden to none in particular. Note, too, that women were much more likely to be employed in single industries: in Edinburgh's case, domestic service, and in Dundee's, the jute industry (see Table 3.4).

Recall John Heiton's comment that 'in Liverpool or Manchester, who can compete with the blazon, "'Twas cotton that did it"; in Sheffield, "'Twas steel that did it"... in Dundee, "'Twas tow [rope, i.e. flax/jute] that did it"; in Glasgow, "'Twas pig-iron that did it"; in Leith, "'Twas Dantzic wheat that did it?" (Heiton 1861: 282). This dependence on single industries is picked up by Madgin and Rodger (2013: 509) as follows:

> civic esteem was often synonymous with the wealth generated through industry: 'cottonopolis', 'juteopolis', 'worstedopolis' and 'coal metropolis' defined Manchester, Dundee, Bradford and Cardiff more precisely than historic buildings. Elsewhere in the British urban hierarchy, towns were firmly identified by a single industrial product – Sheffield steel, Stoke pottery, Burton brewing.

Edinburgh's advantage lay in its diversity of industries; its disadvantage, that one or more of many could be chosen as *primus inter pares*, and the rest demoted or simply airbrushed out of

Table 3.4 Percent employed in largest single occupational category, 1861–1951: males (females in brackets)

	1861	1911	1951
Edinburgh	13 (52)	15 (39)	14 (20)
Glasgow	17 (36)	24 (21)	28 (23)
Dundee	26 (37)	28 (49)	19 (31)
GB	24 (37)	13 (35)	20 (12)

Source: Adapted from Madgin and Rodger 2013, table 2, 514; original source: Censuses of population, 1861, 1911 and 1951.

the picture, which was ultimately the fate of manufacturing. Furthermore, Edinburgh had the trappings of a capital city: 'These capital city functions, with their superior courts, national assemblies and institutional headquarters became deeply embedded in the city and influenced fundamentally its economic structure and social ecology' (Madgin and Rodger 2013: 509–10).

And so Edinburgh was re-imagined, and thus reinvented, as a *non*-industrial city; a place of panorama, panoply and history. Even the Merchant Company, who might have known better, reproduced this view in its report of 1919:

> Edinburgh has no serious claim at present to be considered as an industrial or commercial centre . . . Its striking picturesqueness and historical associations attract visitors from all countries. Its qualifications used to be summarised as Beauty, Beer and Bibles. [Edinburgh] prints and brews, and builds, and works in rubber and metals, but it has no great key industries. (Cited in Madgin and Rodger 2013: 515)

If the city's own merchant class could not express its support for indigenous manufacture, one could not expect those furth of the city to do so. And so 'the political will was weak, and the response to the problems facing the local economy in the 1930s was lacklustre' (Madgin and Rodger 2013: 516).

Abercrombie's Edinburgh

In the post-war period, the Abercrombie Plan, or to give it its full title, *A Civic Survey and Plan for the City and Royal Burgh of Edinburgh*, prepared for the town council by Patrick Abercrombie and Derek Plumstead (referred to hereafter as 'Abercrombie 1949') was an iconic document. It shaped what came before in terms of reinterpreting history, as well as setting the agenda for what came afterwards. This was no ordinary plan, but included a massive social survey of the city, published in 1949, and driven by the requirements of the 1947 Town and Country Planning Act. Its maps and photographs give us an insight into how the city was in the post-war period, as well as its concerns. It provides a unique document and historical statement of Edinburgh in the post-war period.

Much of the Plan did not come to pass, notably its enthusiasm for building roads on stilts through the centre (a proposal which, nevertheless, was to make a comeback twenty years later – see Chapter 8), and especially the triple-decker road through Princes Street, and the downgrading of Waverley station in favour of Haymarket. Its 'faults to correct' are interesting in that they reveal the concerns of the time, at least as the planners saw them. These were: 'the increased development of a nearby coalfield' (in the south-east corner, centred on Newcraighall), 'the mounting volume of traffic', the 'recent and incoherent urban sprawl requiring rationalisation for neighbourly life', 'a new conception of living standards in the old quarters', 'a desire for a more regular distribution of open space', 'an adequate diversification of industry', and 'the accommodation for a festival' (Abercrombie 1949: 1).

It is possibly not a coincidence that 'colliery encroachment' figures as the first-mentioned 'fault', and that in particular, 'the dread danger of "Black Country" development of Midland infamy to guard against' (1949: 29). Those are strong words, and betray a fear of contamination by the iconic coal industry in the surrounding Lothian coalfields. Coal mining died out on the Edinburgh/Midlothian border in the late 1990s; in 1997, Monktonhall, opened as a super-pit in the early 1950s, was closed. Mining in the Esk Valley ran under the Forth, with onshore coal seams mined in Newcraighall, and The Jewel,[12] as well as Midlothian. Here was another, industrial, Edinburgh far removed from the douce, bourgeois city of professions and the culture industries.[13]

Abercrombie, in his 1949 Plan, was unsettled by the presence of industry in Edinburgh and commented that 'there is also an industrial element which conflicts and it is suggested must ultimately be eliminated', notably from the Old Town (Abercrombie 1949: 2). The Plan argued for the segregation of industry from residential areas (even 'elimination'), and its resettlement in new industrial estates and in the 'chief existing industrial areas, Leith, Dalry and Gorgie, remodelled for greater efficiency' (Abercrombie 1949: 3). These were the days of moving large numbers of industries, as well as people (around 190,000 will have to be moved, declared Abercrombie) in a post-war culture in which people were expected to do what they were told, because it was considered to be for their own good. The tone of the report can be gauged from this revealing comment (Abercrombie 1949: 18) to be found below a map of 'sub-standard living conditions':

> Experience teaches us that one condition leads to another until complete deterioration occurs. Industry often seeks to establish itself in outmoded areas [*sic*] and hastens the process of 'blight'. No family can exist healthily in an atmosphere of smoke, grime and noise. Overcrowding the land reduces the access of light and air for and recreation space among the homes: bad internal planning as reflected in the lack of sanitary accommodation prevents cleanliness. Such conditions are too a great burden for the family and result in malnutrition, ill-health, disease and child delinquency.

Such statements tell us much about the mores and prejudices of the times,[14] and are bolstered by accompanying photographs of 'slums'. Today we are highly sceptical about the social theories lying behind the statements, notably that poor housing somehow 'causes' child delinquency, rather than being its correlation. Abercrombie pointed out that in 1932, Edinburgh had an industrial insured worker population of 19 per cent, roughly half that of Manchester, and three-quarters of Glasgow's, but only slightly below the figure for GB as a whole. On that basis, the report concluded that Edinburgh was not an 'industrial city', and in a curious form of logic commented: 'before the war, Edinburgh was not tending to become an industrial city. That is to say, though there was industrial development, by comparison, it was less than the average for the country as a whole' (Abercrombie 1949: 50). There was little attempt to situate the city's industrial sector, except to divide it into industrial zones as follows: special ('to accommodate noxious industries'); general ('heavier type of factories and warehouses'); light; service; and 'neighbourhood services'. It is clear from Abercrombie's Plan that industry was seen as a problem for the city, not a solution, despite the zoning; 'on no account should the city encourage a big industrial expansion within its own administrative area' (Abercrombie 1949: 38).

It would be unfair to accuse Abercrombie of being entirely 'anti-industry'; it had its place. After all, the planners were keen on zoning, confining industry to the 'chief industrial areas of Leith, Dalry and Gorgie – remodelled for greater efficiency' (Abercrombie 1949: 3), but there was little comprehension of its significance in the city; it was seen as a nuisance rather than an asset, and at odds with the policy of zoning. Then there is the curious logic that because Edinburgh had a *lower* proportion of industrial workers than the country as a whole, it was therefore *not* industrial. Much more attention was paid to the transport system, and the planners were much taken by overpasses and underpasses, as well as by tunnels. The three-decker road system on and under Princes Street was described as 'a wonderful opportunity for a feat of engineering and of architectural achievement' (Abercrombie 1949: 54). There was a plan for 'the gradual transformation of the New Town from residential to office, shop and industrial [*sic*] use' (Abercrombie 1949: 57), and removing the fruit and vegetable market from Market Street, described as a 'conglomeration of market vehicles and baskets of vegetables' (Abercrombie 1949: 59). The latter was to come to pass in due time (moving to Chesser in Gorgie on the city's west side), but the New Town reverted to residential use, much in demand and reflected in rising property prices.

It is somewhat unfair to apply the standards and expectations of the twenty-first century to Abercrombie's Plan of 1949. Its 'four prevailing evils' were of their (post-war) time: 'outmoded or sanitarily unfit dwellings, overcrowded dwellings upon the land, overcrowded families within dwellings, and the mixing of homes and industry' (Abercrombie 1949: 83). The Plan, however, provides key insights into what kind of city the planners envisaged, and that did not include much of an industrial future. Although much of Abercrombie's Plan did not come to pass – thankfully, as regards roads on stilts (through Holyrood Park) or in tunnels (beneath Princes Street) – it set the frame for the downsizing of industry despite its desire for 'an adequate diversification of industry', and the city's reinvention as a primary place of commerce and culture. The Festival was new to the city (starting in 1947; see Chapter 4), and 'accommodating the festival' described as a 'change to provide for, especially urgent in their impact upon an ancient and venerated shrine' (Abercrombie 1949: 1). That shrine-like description of the city, and its 'heritage' qualities became the dominant perception in the decades to come. The argument here is that the Abercrombie Plan set the frame for much of the development (or lack of it) in the following years.

Twenty Years On

At the end of the 1960s, Edinburgh Corporation, as it then was, commissioned a report on Edinburgh's economy: present and future prospects, from academics Norman Hunt and Harry Nicholls.[15] It reflected concern that the city was losing the place, that during the 1950s the rate of economic growth was less rapid than in GB, although it had picked up at the end of the decade. In 1962, Edinburgh's unemployment rate at 2.1 per cent was well below that of Scotland's (4.9 per cent), and just below that of GB. It is clear, they said, that 'despite the contrary view commonly held, Edinburgh was to a large extent an industrial city' (Hunt and Nicholls 1968: para. 11: 3). Industries contributing to its strong economic position included: biscuits and confectionery, electronics, wholesale bottling, electrical machinery, printing and publishing, the drinks industry (other than brewing), motor repairs, and cardboard boxes and cartons (para. 14). Nevertheless, there was a distinct possibility of stagnation in the Edinburgh economy unless industrial growth was deliberately planned and made provision for. This would 'avoid Edinburgh's becoming a museum piece with a colourful past' (Hunt and Nicholls 1968: para. 17: 6). This was a distinct possibility because the introduction of the selective employment tax (SET) in 1966 by the UK Labour government was aimed at taxing services, in which Edinburgh excelled, to aid manufacturing exports. Furthermore, the development of an industrial park at South Gyle had been blocked by the Secretary of State for Scotland in 1968.

Hunt and Nicholls concluded:

> It may be questioned whether an economy which is as desperately in need of growth as Scotland's can afford to run the risks of stultifying that growth by deliberately curbing growth where it seems to be endemic [such as Edinburgh] and trying to force it into 'unnatural' areas of development. (Hunt and Nicholls 1968: para. 68: 56).

Edinburgh was the only part of Scotland excluded from 'regional incentives' on investment grants, the regional employment premium, and selective employment tax. The concern in particular was that areas like Livingston, recently declared a New Town in 1962, and West Lothian generally, as well as Fife, benefiting from the opening of the Forth Road Bridge in 1964, would leech industrial employment away from Edinburgh: and so it proved, with incentives, grants and land, available as close to the city as Newbridge, aided by building a city bypass in 1981. As Madgin and Rodger (2013: 520) pointed out:

> [T]he decision by the government in 1966 to exclude Edinburgh from Development Area status ensured that investment grants for 'footloose capital' rewarded firms that relocated beyond the city's boundaries with subsidies at double the rate available in the capital city. Furthermore, the Regional Employment Premium introduced during the 1960s to foster industry in depressed areas also disadvantaged Edinburgh since it favoured labour-intensive firms with a large payroll – features uncharacteristic of the industrial economy of Edinburgh.

Edinburgh's problem was that, perversely, the city had low unemployment and high economic growth without an incentive regime and development grants; while industrial sites, and manufacturing in particular, were in short supply within the city boundary. We have already seen that the major loss of manufacturing employment in the city took place between 1961 and 1981; Hunt and Nicholls's fear of Edinburgh becoming a museum with a colourful past was all too real. Indeed, the stage was set for the invention of 'Festival City', and the tourist economy, presented as the 'natural' order of things, aided and abetted by aggressive promotion of place. In Madgin and Rodger's words (2013: 512):

> By manipulating its own image, and continually emphasizing the historic and picturesque, the myth of Edinburgh as a non-industrial city was invented and nurtured. In fact, a policy of anything-but-industry. So successful was this process of reinvention that the myth grew that Edinburgh had *never* been industrial. Marketing slogans such as: 'Edinburgh's "Inspiring Capital"' or 'Glasgow's Miles Better' . . . are marketing devices loosely framed on future expectations of development and have, as the Edinburgh evidence shows, subverted resources and planning strategies in the process. (Madgin and Rodgers 2013: 528)

And so industry was airbrushed out of Edinburgh's story.

EDINBURGH: CITY OF MONEY

There is, however, another story to be told about Edinburgh. As Bob Morris astutely observed: 'Manufacturing tended to be ignored in Edinburgh's self-image, in part because of the greater social prestige of the lawyers and bankers' (Morris 2010: 15). Edinburgh is existentially a city of lawyers and bankers, but how did that come about? In particular, how did it become, in Ray Perman's telling title, *The City of Money?*[16] To make sense of that, we need to delve into its history. In large part it was fortuitously timed. True, Edinburgh was, until 1707, the capital of an independent Scotland, with the apparatus possessed of capital cities, and that undoubtedly helped.

The story begins, naturally, with the banks, now fallen on harder times: Bank of Scotland ('the auld bank') founded in 1695, and the Royal Bank of Scotland (1727). So why did Edinburgh and its banks have such financial autonomy?[17] Put simply, the auld bank managed to get going before the Bank of England (1694) was properly established, and in any case, the Union was more than a decade in the future. The year 1695 was not a great year to start a bank; a failed harvest, four years of continuous dearth, rocketing grain prices. Scotland suffered from the English Navigation Acts, aimed mainly at the Dutch, but effectively destroying Scottish trade and commerce. There was at the time virtually no paper money, and bullion was trundled about in carts.

Scots were quite keen on money, and they pledged as much as half their wealth to finance. The auld bank raised more than half a million pounds Scots in less than two months, and while the rich provided most, there was a wide spread of subscribers, or 'adventurers' as they were known. There was competition from the Company of Scotland, better known as the Darien Company, founded by William Paterson, 'a polished and experienced salesman', with all that implied. Large shareholders provided less than 3 per cent of the total raised, with 70 per cent coming from subscribers with £200 or less, and half with less than £100. Perman observes: 'It was an impressive demonstration of the breadth of appeal that the venture inspired amongst those who did have surplus wealth in a period of "Dearth and Want"' (Perman 2019: 10). The Company of Scotland had more shareholders than either the Bank of England or the East India Company. Famously, Paterson had had a hand in setting up the Bank of England but had fallen out with his fellow directors. He inveigled a run on the auld bank, which was seriously undercapitalised, but he lost the battle, and the 'cautious faction' on the Company of Scotland scored a victory. The auld bank was usually in some financial trouble but was saved by the 1707 Union which recapitalised the Scottish economy and boosted paper money, most obviously by paying 'The Equivalent', a capital sum of almost half a million pounds.

By 1728, the auld bank was solidly profitable, but bank wars broke out with the upstart Royal Bank of Scotland, which had strong Hanoverian and Whig ties in contrast to the auld bank's alleged Jacobite leanings. The Royal Bank bought up large quantities of Bank of Scotland banknotes and tried to cash them in, which it was legally entitled to do. The auld bank dragged its feet, and even tried to pay in sixpences. At one stage, the bank was down to its last £585 (worth about £1.6m in today's income value[18]) in cash, but recovered.

There was, though, more to Edinburgh money than the two banks. Lawyers played a big part in the development of finance, and so did kirk ministers, and professors of mathematics. Alexander Webster, better known for carrying out the first Scottish census in 1755 by writing to his fellow ministers, and who was himself an evangelical, was exercised as to how to maintain the widows and orphans of church ministers. Colin Maclaurin, Professor of mathematics at Edinburgh, collected mortality statistics to calculate how many ministers were likely to die each year and how much their dependents would need. Maclaurin used actuarial maths to calculate the price and valuation of annuities. Thus, the Scottish Ministers' Widows Fund was born – 'Scottish Widows', for short.

The Edinburgh banks largely ignored Glasgow, and rather than financing the tobacco trade, it operated the other way round with western banks established on profits from tobacco. The Edinburgh banks ran an anti-competitive cartel against the western upstarts but were unable to suppress competition for long. They petitioned the House of Lords on the grounds that there was quite enough banking capacity around as it was. The auld bank even objected to the new Commercial Bank using 'of Scotland' in its title and fought rearguard actions against all-comers. By the middle of the nineteenth century, Edinburgh had been outflanked by Glasgow, but many of the west of Scotland banks were seriously under-capitalised. The collapse of the Western Bank, in particular, generated resentment in the west: 'it was a clash of cultures – of modern risk-taking Glaswegian entrepreneurs against the entrenched reactionary vested interests of Edinburgh' (Perman 2019: 195).

Edinburgh, 'City of Money', had three dimensions: the banks; the insurance/assurance industry (Scottish Widows joined by mutuals); and the investment trust industry. These were closely entangled. The expansion of North America spawned investment opportunities in railways (always risky), and real estate. In the final quarter of the nineteenth century, a slew of trusts were created by the likes of Robert Fleming and William Menzies: Scottish American Mortgage Co. (1874), North British American Mortgage Trust (1875), Edinburgh American Land Mortgage Co. (1878), Scottish Investment Trust (1887), and many more: 'Investment trusts were fairly established as a popular choice for individual investors and Edinburgh was to make them a speciality' (Perman 2019: 215).

By 1884, two-thirds of overseas investment by British investment companies (valued at around £20m) came from Scotland: 'enthusiasm for investing overseas seemed undimmed' (Perman 2019: 216). Evidently, there was more profit to be had abroad than at home. The lack of indigenous investment was, in any case, a matter of profit, not patriotism. By the end of the 1920s, out of 209 UK trusts, seventy-nine were in Scotland, and the majority in Edinburgh.

Financial services were Edinburgh's bread and butter, and a complex network operated with cross-shareholdings and shared directors despite the animosities. Companies adopted a veneer of respectability. The Bank of Scotland was 'led' for fifty years by the Earl of Stair (1870–1903) and Lord Balfour of Burleigh (1904–21). The aristocracy sat at the head of table and met in the House of Lords, while professional elites met in the New Club on Princes Street or, when in London, at the Caledonian Club. However, 'with a board of titled amateurs above them, the General Managers were omnipotent in their banks' (Perman 2019: 228). There was a 'gentlemen's agreement' that Scottish and English banks would stick to their own territory, but there was nothing to stop them looking for business abroad. Perman characterises Scottish banks as follows:

> Scottish banking was insulated by the era of gentlemanly capitalism. Deals concluded verbally seldom needed writing down and hostile takeovers were unthinkable against honourable men, who came

from the same backgrounds, shared the same attitudes and were members of the same clubs. (Perman 2019: 230)

By the mid-1960s, scandals broke out (in truth, not very scandalous in terms of what was to follow in the twenty-first century). Sir Alastair Blair who chaired three investment trusts and was board member of the Bank of Scotland and Scottish Widows, was socially indicted for having the temerity to pay incentives for business. As a result, 'dinner invitations were withdrawn and there was said to be "much weeping" among the women of the Ivory family at their ostracism' (Perman 2019: 237). Much worse: Sir Alastair was shunned in the clubhouse of Muirfield golf club, and had to eat his dinner at a table on his own.

The 'Big Bang' deregulation of 1986 is usually given discredit for ending 'gentlemanly capitalism', but it was happening long before that. By the 1970s, the spotlight was back on the banks. Barclays, the English bank, had owned a one-third stake in the Bank of Scotland, and sold it in 1984. Tom Risk, a good name for a banker, contacted the ubiquitous Robert C. Smith, chair of Standard Life. Perman (2019: 241) observed:

> Quietly, in a typically Edinburgh way, the two Glaswegians arranged that Standard Life would acquire the Barclays stake for £155m and provide a safe haven against the fear of takeover. One insider called it 'a squalid Edinburgh stitch-up', but it showed that some vestiges of gentlemanly capitalism remained.

The Royal Bank of Scotland (RBS) was more than a trifle staid by this time. It had fourteen grades of staff between the lowliest clerk up to the executive, 'people at the top [who] jealously guarded their privileges – chauffeured cars and "the mess" – a suite of dining and reception rooms on the third floor of HQ where senior managers were waited on by liveried staff' (Perman 2019: 245). If the banks were in trouble, fund managers were riding high. Whereas in 1982, they had £500m 'under management', by 2008, this had risen to more than £55bn, a staggering increase of over 1,000 per cent. Insurance companies and mutuals did not fare as well. In 1979, Edinburgh had been the headquarters to three of the ten largest life companies in the UK: Standard Life, Scottish Equitable and Scottish Widows. Scottish Equitable was gobbled up by Dutch company Aegon, and Scottish Widows by Lloyds TSB. Only Standard Life resisted the pressure to demutualise, but at considerable damage to its assets and values. In 2017, it merged with Aberdeen Asset Management, and the following year sold its insurance business to Phoenix of London, becoming simply an asset management company. In this way, Edinburgh's links with independent life assurance companies, started back in 1815 with Scottish Widows, was broken.

Around the year 2000, Edinburgh was the second most important financial city in the UK, with two of the top ten European banks; seven large life assurance companies; a substantial fund management sector; and a legal apparatus sustaining that finance industry. Twenty years later, much of that has gone, though it retains fund management investments and the cadre of professional institutes: banking, chartered accountancy, and law. To cap it all, RBS decided (in February 2020) to change its name to NatWest, except in Scotland where the old name survived; badging being everything these days.

How did Edinburgh come to be the only city in the UK to resist the pull of London? Answers: two banks set up in this erstwhile capital, the auld bank well before the Union, and thus escaping control from the Bank of England.[19] The Bank of Scotland and the Royal Bank of Scotland were in a curious competitive alliance all the way down to the banking crisis of the twenty-first century. In the aftermath, it became difficult to tell who owned what. Consider this ownership description of the Bank of Scotland in 2017: 'Halifax is a division of BoS plc, which is a direct subsidiary of HBOS, which is a holding company, which is a direct subsidiary of Lloyd's Bank plc, which is a direct subsidiary of Lloyds Banking Group plc' (in Hearn 2017: 131). That merger between Halifax and the Bank of Scotland (hence, HBOS) fell apart in less than a decade, and out of that wreckage emerged once more 'The Bank of Scotland', but it manifestly is not the creature it once was. The Royal Bank of Scotland has a similarly convoluted recent history, and while headquartered in Scotland still, it is a brass-plate HQ, and effectively ceased to be a 'Scottish' bank some years ago.[20] Rebadging RBS in England as 'NatWest' simply confirms that. Both banks still issue their own banknotes in an era where non-cash e-transfers are becoming the norm.

The rise and fall of the Scottish banks might seem to be a familiar elegy for indigenous Scottish industry.[21] The significant clusters of businesses around the Scottish banks are no more. The network of Scottish business interests had been held together by three banks, the Bank of Scotland, the Royal Bank of Scotland, and, in the west, the Clydesdale Bank,[22] each with their own clusters of related companies and spheres of influence (see McCrone 2017a, Chapter 6).

The Scottish banks, however, carried out key roles in the wider Scottish financial industry, and especially as this affected the Edinburgh economy. They attracted ancillary industries of money management and investment; and the city housed distinctive institutions of law, church and key professions. And while the broad picture is one of declining influence, there are exceptions to this story.

Baillie Gifford as an investment management company was formed in 1908, still has its headquarters in Edinburgh, and manages assets of around £260bn. It is, significantly, owned by the partners who work in the company. Scottish Mortgage Investment Fund, managed by Bailie Gifford, was an early investor in Tesla, the Californian electric car company, in 2013. By 2021, they had made £21bn for investors. Fund manager James Anderson explained why he first bought Tesla, at a time when many experienced investors thought it was hugely overvalued at $6 a share (*The Guardian*, 24 January 2021):

> To us it was, frankly, clear even back half a dozen years that the underlying technologies from batteries, to solar to eventually self-driving were progressing and would continue to do so. We thought (and simply observed) that Tesla was already past the technological and practical challenges to a good degree and that execution and finance were the practical issues. What we needed was time. Not many investors can have that luxury and necessity.

Anderson concluded: 'This leads on to a core belief: that our purpose as investors is to assist beneficial, transformation change. Isn't this the point of capital allocation? If we do this our results for shareholders will look after themselves' (*The Guardian*, 24 January 2021).

The banking and finance industry in Edinburgh may be a shadow of its former self, but it is still a significant player in the city, and truth to tell, the world; which helps to explain why it is a major employer in Edinburgh.

CONCLUSION

In his essay on his native city, Robert Louis Stevenson wrote about Edinburgh[23]:

> Beautiful as she is, she is not so much beautiful as interesting. She is pre-eminently Gothic, and all the more so since she has set herself off with some Greek airs, and erected classic temples on her crags. In a word, and above all, she is a curiosity. (Stevenson, *Edinburgh: Picturesque Notes* [1878]: 1)

Edinburgh is difficult to read. What you see is not always what you get. It does not present itself as an industrial city, even when in mid-twentieth century, most people, men at any rate, were employed in manufacturing. Edinburgh was not iconically defined by a single industry: as shipbuilding in Glasgow, cotton in Manchester, engineering in Birmingham, steel in Sheffield. That was its good fortune, as well as its problem. We could make a case for defining the city around printing and publishing, but there were too many competing interests to so define it singularly. It had the legacy of being a city of government, and to quote Stevenson again: 'Edinburgh has but partly abdicated, and still wears, in parody, her metropolitan trappings. Half a capital and half a country town, the whole city leads a double existence' (Stevenson [1878]: 2).

Nevertheless, as Hunt and Nicholls pointed out, it is clear that 'despite the contrary view commonly held, Edinburgh was to a large extent an industrial city and a relatively prosperous one' (Hunt and Nicholls 1968: 3). No longer, at least, industrial. That feature of the city had virtually gone by the early 1980s, reinforced by the dubious distinction of being too affluent to receive development grants and financial inducements. It might have, to use Bob Morris's words, de-industrialised with good grace, but it had little option. Planners and policy makers set about reinventing Edinburgh, and in Richard Rodger's words: 'Edinburgh traded on the reality of its knowledge-based professional classes, and on its striking historical environment. This was, however, a partial account and was built on the denial of its industrial record' (Madgin and Rodger 2013: 529). While the Abercrombie Plan of 1949 did not banish industry from the city, it did little to encourage it. It would be corralled into areas such as Dalry, Gorgie (and Sighthill) and Leith. Its perimeter would be protected from the depredations of the coal industry which threatened a northern Black Country on its south-eastern boundary. No matter that coal-mining would be dead by the late 1990s, killed off by geological as well as by political fault-lines in the 1980s. Between 1995 and 2008, there was a further loss of manufacturing jobs of the order of 63 per cent, compared with only 49 per cent in Glasgow. Thus, comment Madgin and Rodger (2013: 525), 'Edinburgh lost more jobs than Clydeside, South Yorkshire, Wigan, Hull, Stoke-on-Trent, Sunderland, places normally associated with de-industrialisation'. Edinburgh's problem was that the process of de-industrialisation was virtually invisible, and that the city did not define itself, nor was defined as, a place of manufacture. In any event, it had a complex service economy to fall back on and develop, and almost serendipitously a cultural history to exploit. The stage, quite literally, was set for Festival City, a status more serendipitous than planned, as we shall see in Chapter 4.

NOTES

1. Taken from minutes of the meeting on 21 March 1914.
2. Ibid.
3. McVitie's, owned ultimately by a company in Turkey, announced in May 2021 the closure of its factory in Tollcross, Glasgow. See <https://www.bbc.co.uk/news/uk-scotland-scotland-business-57084762>.
4. The 2011 Census is the latest we have at the time of writing. The one in 2021 was postponed by Scottish Government because of Covid-19, even though the Census went ahead in England and Wales. For a critical view of this decision, see <https://www.audit-scotland.gov.uk/report/the-202021-audit-of-national-records-of-scotland>.
5. The source of these data is Nomis, the data source provided by the Office of National Statistics: <https://www.nomisweb.co.uk>.
6. ONS defines 'elementary' occupations as those which involve simple and routine tasks which mainly require the use of hand-held tools and often some physical effort: <https://onsdigital.github.io/dp-classification-tools/standard-occupational-classification/ONS_SOC_hierarchy_view.html>.
7. 15 per cent, compared with 25 per cent in Scotland, and 24 per cent in GB.
8. ONS defines such occupations as follows: 'The main tasks involve the operation and maintenance of complex equipment; legal,

business, financial and design services; the provision of information technology services; providing skilled support to health and
social care professionals; serving in protective service occupations; and managing areas of the natural environment. Culture,
media and sports occupations are also included in this major
group. Most occupations in this major group will have an associated high-level vocational qualification, often involving a substantial period of full-time training or further study. Some additional
task-related training is usually provided through a formal period
of induction': <https://onsdigital.github.io/dp-classification-tools/
standard-occupational-classification/ONS_SOC_hierarchy_view.
html>.

9. Especially administrative and secretarial jobs (minus 30 per cent),
compared with minus 21 per cent in skilled jobs.

10. The massive rubber works at Fountainbridge. Gutta percha
became better known to generations of school children as 'gut-
ties', an eponym for gym shoes, also known in politer society as
plimsolls, but also simply as 'gymmies'.

11. By the turn of the century, it was hard to imagine this site, now
made up of modern tenemented housing, ever having been the site
of an iron foundry.

12. Now remembered as a bus terminus for the number 5.

13. The film maker Bill Douglas produced a remarkable trilogy, starting with *My Childhood* (1972), followed by *My Ain Folk* (1973)
and *My Way Home* (1978). The first was centred on austere life in
the pit village of Newcraighall, and I was privileged to attend its
first screening in the University's George Square Theatre, attended
by many of the villagers who had been extras in Douglas's film, and
who provided a running commentary throughout. Duncan Petrie's
book *Screening Scotland* (2000) uses a clip from *My Childhood* as
the book cover, and discuss Douglas's work in context.

14. Take, for example, the sexist statement that 'the housewife does
not wish to travel daily a ten mile return journey to buy day to day
necessities in Princes Street' (p. 31), an argument used in favour
of suburban shopping centres, referred to as 'neighbourhood
services'.

15. Norman Hunt, the lead author, and Professor of business studies at Edinburgh University had previously written an article for
the *Glasgow Herald* in September 1962 on Edinburgh's industrial
employment, and was invited to develop it, which he did with his
departmental colleague, Harry Nicholls. Their report was commissioned by Edinburgh Corporation, and was followed by a report by
the town planning officer, T. T. Hewitson, 'Edinburgh's Economy,

1966–71: A Study of Recent Economic Trends Completed by the Town Planning Department-Research Section', 1972.

16. I was pleased to review Perman's book *The Rise and Fall of the City of Money: A Financial History of Edinburgh* (Edinburgh: Birlinn, 2019) for *Scottish Affairs* (29(2), 2020, pp. 285–91). My account here is based on my review, 'The discreet charm of the Edinburgh bourgeoisie'.

17. Contrast the fortunes of the Bank of Scotland with the Bank of Ireland, established by Royal Charter of the Parliament of Ireland in 1783. The Bank of Ireland, like the Scottish bank, was a commercial, not a state bank, only becoming the banker of the Irish government after the founding of the Irish Free State in 1921.

18. Using <https://www.measuringworth.com/index.php>.

19. The Bank of England was established de facto as the English government's bank in 1694, one year before the Bank of Scotland, and was privately owned by shareholders until it was nationalised in 1946 by the Labour government under Clement Attlee.

20. The fall of the Royal Bank of Scotland is told in Ian Fraser's excellent book *Shredded: Inside RBS: The Bank that Broke Britain* (2014; updated in 2019), and of the Bank of Scotland in Ray Perman's *HUBRIS: How HBOS Wrecked the Best Bank in Britain* (2012).

21. This is a tale well told, and presciently, by John Scott and Michael Hughes in *The Anatomy of Scottish Capital* (1980).

22. The Clydesdale Bank, based in Glasgow, was taken over by the (English) Midland Bank in 1920, and sold to National Australia Bank in 1987. By 2016, it was floated on the London Stock Exchange, and acquired by Virgin Money under the holding company CYBG (Clydesdale and Yorkshire Banking Group). Virgin Money retain the right to issue Clydesdale banknotes, while rebranding its activities, and shops, as Virgin Money. At the end of September 2021, Virgin Money announced the closure of its branches in twelve Scottish towns.

23. The version of Stevenson's essay cited here is published by Valde Books (n.d.). The essay was first published 1878.

4

Treading Angels: Edinburgh and its Festivals

And another thing. In August the city grows,
Groans more, and weighs more. It shows.
Bus stops, taxi stances, sprout linguists endlessly
Who all speak a common language called
Waverley

(mac Neil 2000: 100)[1]

How did Edinburgh come to be 'festival city'? Consider this opening comment in the 2018 report by the consulting company BOP: 'Edinburgh is an undisputed world leader as a festival city. The innovation and momentum of its Festivals inspire people from local audiences through to international cultural peers.' (BOP Consulting 2018: 2). The report continues:

> Edinburgh's identity as a festival city has been built over the past 70 years to its current position as an acknowledged world leader. Its individual festivals are leading cultural brands in their respective fields; collectively, they attract audiences in excess of 4.5 million and have an economic impact of £313 million annually. (BOP Consulting 2018: 3)

We have grown used to cultural boot-strapping in the modern world, as cities reinvent themselves to put distance between themselves and their industrial past. Bilbao has its Guggenheim museum, a catalyst for cultural regeneration. Glasgow, Edinburgh's near-neighbour is, these days, miles better, and has reinvented itself as city of culture.

The competition, though, is a cut-throat business. The consulting company BOP called its 2015 report *Thundering Hooves*, 'metaphorically named after the sound of the competition catching up with Edinburgh', but 'Edinburgh is the undisputed world leader as a festival city', and no amount of catch-up by other places will alter that, it argues. Still, by 2018, that 'the' has become 'an', just in case any other place has pretensions to the cultural crown.

This chapter will examine how Edinburgh has been 'branded', and with what effect; examine the origins of the 'official' Festival; look at 'festival adjuncts', better known as the Fringe; the role of the Traverse Theatre; and what it all means in terms of living with these things. In the classical 'you'll have had your tea' mode Edinburgh is infamous for, we might agree with the anonymous citizen who commented: 'I quite liked the Festival, I even enjoyed it. All in all, we were none the worse for it.'[2]

BRANDING PLACE

The origins and development of Edinburgh as 'festival city' is a form of modern branding, an ongoing process of 'place-making', of cultural boosterism. Indeed, the Edinburgh Trams Story (Chapter 9) is a central feature of this process of re-invention, as if it was always meant to be 'the festival city', notwithstanding thundering hooves. There are, or have been, numerous 'festivals': the official festival (Edinburgh International Festival, EIF), the Fringe, the Tattoo, Film, Science, Jazz and Blues, Art (singular), Book, Storytelling, Mela (somewhat defunct or at least in abeyance) and the Winter festivals (aka Christmas and Hogmanay). All are not equal. The Fringe dominates, accounting for just under half of attendances ('trips', in the jargon of economic development consultants, SQW). A further 10 per cent 'trip' to EIF, 10 per cent to Capital Christmas (at least they did so in 2005 when SQW did the study), and 7 per cent to the Military Tattoo; thus, four festivals account for around three-quarters of 'trips'.

This urge to enhance reputations was picked up by BOP Consultants in their reports of 2011, 2015 and 2018, documents short on economic evidence but long on rhetoric. BOS employed high-blown marketing, replete with the language of pathways, stakeholders, toolkits, sustainability, well-being and 'core Festival outcomes'. There are also 'logic models' of the 'Edinburgh Festivals Evaluation Framework'. The report asserted that: 'Local residents take great pride in the Festivals and the value they provide to Edinburgh as a city', and, further-more, festivals had a 'noticeable impact on people's all-round well-being, which is in line with other cultural and heritage events research' (BOP Consulting 2011: 4). These are big claims, for anyone living through festival periods in August pre-Covid when the city doubled its numbers of 'residents' may doubt that, still less that there is 'increased self-esteem and curiosity', 'build-ing social capital' and establishing 'new social networks'.

In any case, getting at the opinions of 'local residents' is surely harder than simply sifting out those 'locals' who attend festival events. Undeterred, the 2015 BOP report ups the ante in terms of zeitgeist: 'a new form of leadership is emerging in the city and the nation . . . a more open and collaborative approach, based on a fully engaged partnership across the private, public and voluntary sectors which is rooted in mutual respect and shared ambition' (BOP Consulting 2015: 2). All becomes grist to the mill; the Scottish Government's 'commitment to equalities and social justice' (there's another zeitgeist); 'the festival's ability to lead . . . is demonstrated by their environmental strategy and the creation of Creative Carbon Scotland' (6). There are bizarre con-tradictions: promoting the 'green festival city' is surely incom-patible with 'working closely with Edinburgh Airport' (cited on the previous page of the report) and the carbon emissions of aircraft. All ideas are pressed into service, 'creative and cultural ecosystems' (and the 'wider events ecosystem'), social network theory, logic models and the rest.

Grand claims are made in the 2015 report: 57 per cent of respondents said that the festivals were events that 'bring(s) the community together'; 89 per cent of local festival-goers agreed that 'the Festivals increased people's pride in Edinburgh as a city'; and a whopping 94 per cent of respondents agreed that 'Festivals are part of what makes Edinburgh special as a city'.

The bases for such claims are audience surveys of around 29,000 people attending the festivals, and over 1000 'delegates'. The methodology – 'for overall sample size, audience surveys received a very high response rate' – but no precise figures or breakdown of such are given, still less issues of sampling. We could simply dismiss such claims as the marketing hype com-monly used in culture industries, but the whole shifts the focus towards the assumption that most people are happy with the cultural strategy apart from a few curmudgeons. Not everything gets prizes, however. The Tattoo, undoubtedly 'the Festival' for many people, gets viewed critically: 'The Tattoo's main vision is to promote the military in the eyes of the public', so it cannot be expected 'to primarily deliver against outcomes to do with community cohesion' (BOP 2011: 14). That may be so, or not, but one wonders how we might tell.

Furthermore, such data seem to imply a longstanding commitment by the city and its people to the idea of 'festival city'. There are a few caveats along the way: that 'there is no guaranteed template for a successful leading festival city that can be sustained over time' (BOP Consulting 2011: 19), and 'Edinburgh's cultural budget appears lower than comparator cities on the basis of per capita spending' (29). Clouds are on the horizon; thundering hooves are on the chase. The implication: too much is at stake to pull back now. But was it ever thus?

How did Edinburgh come to be this 'festival city' in the first place? Has there been backsliding on the part of city fathers and mothers? Has local capital fallen down on the job? Does, for example, a proposed bed tax (transient visitor levy to give it its proper name) indicate that Edinburgh citizens and politicians are less than happy with the city doubling in size in the month of August? Where, then, did all this festivaling come from? Whose idea was it in the first place?

FESTIVAL DREAMING

Writing in 1997, Iain Crawford, sometime director of publicity for the Edinburgh Festival, began his account, which he called *Banquo on Thursdays*,[3] as follows: 'The Edinburgh Festival began fifty years ago as a strange amalgam of cultural banditry, civic enterprise and idealism, an intriguing – even bizarre – but singularly effective combination' (Crawford 1997: 1).

The official account of the Edinburgh International Festival (EIF) was written by Eileen Miller in 1996, covering the years between 1947 and 1996. There had been festivals in Edinburgh before, she points out; in 1815, there was a five-day six concert affair, a grand occasion, organised by the lord provost with the Duke of Buccleuch as president.

> The festival opened on 31 October 1815 with a morning concert in Parliament House. By 8 o'clock the streets were thronged with

carriages, chairs and pedestrians, and a patrol of dragoons was required to preserve order in the High Street. On entering the building the patrons were confronted by the spectacle of such eminent personages as the Lord Provost, the Earl of Moray, Sir William Forbes, Lieutenant-General Wynyard and the Lord Advocate acting as stewards, and the Earl of Dalhousie, Sir George Clerk of Penicuik and George Hogarth collecting tickets at the door. (Miller 1996: xii)

The festival was built around performances of Handel's music, and 'the princely sum' of £1500 (about £100,000 at 2018 prices) was handed over to the Royal Infirmary and other charitable institutions. The next festival was in 1819 under presidency of the Duke of Atholl (a programme of Handel and Mozart). This time, £1232 (£89,000 in 2018) went to charities. Decidedly an aristocratic affair like its 1815 predecessor, the traffic arrangements around St Giles tell us a lot about the clientele:

All carriages going to Parliament House are to line up the High Street and to enter Parliament Square keeping close to the houses on their left and to put down their company at the piazza on the south side of the square to drive round the statue, keeping close to the wall of the High Church, when they are to turn up Lawn Market and go off by the Mound. They are to take up the same order. The entry by the Lobby of the Writers' Library will be reserved exclusively for those who come on foot or in chairs, and no carriages will be allowed to enter the area in the Lawn Market before the Public Libraries. (Miller 1996: xiii)

Were the twentieth-century festivals built on similar social credentials? Were they gatherings of the Great and Good? They turn out to be but pale reflections. Back to Crawford's 'strange amalgam of cultural banditry, civic enterprise and idealism'. The centre of British cultural festivalry was Glyndebourne Opera, whose general manager was Rudolf Bing. In Eileen Miller's words:

According to Glyndebourne legend the idea for the current Edinburgh International Festival was born on a clear night in 1942. The English soprano, Audrey Mildmay, and Ronald Bing, the General Manager of the Glyndebourne Opera, were walking along Princes Street after a performance of Gay's *The Beggar's Opera*. Audrey is said to have looked up at the moonlit castle and given voice to an idea, that had first occurred to her a few years earlier in Salzburg, that the Scottish capital would make a wonderful setting for a festival. The truth was rather more prosaic and was inspired more by the necessity of find-ing a solution to Glyndebourne's monetary problems than a desire to establish an Edinburgh Festival. (Miller 1996: 1)

Others place the encounter between Bing and Mildmay in 1939,[4] but either way, it is a 'piece of amiable fiction' (Crawford 1997: 1). Bing's first choice was Oxford, but neither it, nor Cambridge, showed much interest. The British Council was minded to establish a post-war festival of the arts somewhere in the UK, and Harry Henry Wood who was the Scottish represen-tative on the Council wrote the following in *The Scotsman* on 7 August 1946:

> Certain preconditions were obviously required of such a centre. It should be a town of reasonable size, capable of absorbing and enter-taining between 50,000 and 150,000 visitors over a period of three weeks to a month. It should, like Salzburg, have considerable scenic and picturesque appeal and it should be set in a country likely to be attractive to tourists and foreign visitors. It should have a suffi-cient number of theatres, concert halls and open spaces for the ade-quate staging of a programme of an ambitious and varied character. Above all, it should be a city likely to embrace the opportunity and willing to make the Festival a major preoccupation not only in the City Chambers but in the heart and home of every citizen, however modest. Greatly daring but not without confidence, I recommended Edinburgh as the centre and promised to make preliminary investi-gations. (Cited in Crawford 1997: 2)

Wood suggested Edinburgh on the grounds that 'the city had suffered little bomb damage, had great natural beauty, a colour-ful history and close proximity to the sea and the Scottish Highlands' (Miller 1996: 2). He sought the support of 'prom-inent Edinburgh citizens' including Lady Rosebery, the editor of *The Scotsman* James Murray Watson, the playwright James Bridie, and the judge Lord Cameron. Manifestly, the Town Council was central. Lord Provost John Falconer[5] was keen, though Bing thought him 'not too well informed of the things I was talking about' (Crawford 1997: 2). Above all, he was up against Bailie Stevenson who was in charge of the city's parks and halls, who told Bing that the project could not be enter-tained or supported by the lord provost or the magistrates (Miller 1996: 2). Wood circumvented the bailie, meeting instead with the lord provost and the city treasurer, Andrew Murray (the successor lord provost), and the city chamberlain, John Imrie (who controlled the money). There was support from the Chamber of Commerce, the Hotels Association of Edinburgh, the railway companies, and theatrical and musical associations. An interim festival committee was formed in November 1945, and a sum of £1000 (around £40,000 at 2018 prices) for expenses was agreed. The committee included the manager of Howard and Wyndham theatres (who at the time owned the King's), the director of the Royal Scottish Academy, Sheriff (later Lord) Cameron and the playwright James Bridie (Osborne Henry Mavor). Bridie observed:

> Your Edinburgh project is a magnificent one and I sincerely hope it may come to fruition. At the same time you have managed to stir up interest in Edinburgh, a city which prides itself on not being interested in anything at all . . . but I cannot help feeling that a good deal more vital energy than I have hitherto found in contemporary Edinburgh will be required before anything really happens. I hope you will not think this discouraging. It is only fair to say that I am a West of Scotland man myself and that between the West and the East there is a great gulf fixed. It is difficult for anyone living outside Scotland to understand the nature of this gulf but it is nevertheless a fact. (Miller 1996: 3–4)

Crawford later observed that Glasgow never understood 'how the weakling infant [the Edinburgh Festival] which was half an idea in 1945 should have grown to the mature age of half a century' (Crawford 1997: 3). The festival notion 'was regarded by level-headed Scots folk as an act of consummate folly and pretentiousness of a kind fairly typical of a capital city often regarded (outside Edinburgh) as too big for its brogues' (Crawford 1997: 3). Indeed, Glasgow's one-time lord provost (1949–52), Sir Victor Warren, Progressive and explosives manufacturer, had turned down an invitation to Edinburgh's Festival, opting instead to go to the local circus: 'I sincerely hope that when a National Theatre comes to be built it will be built in Glasgow, where the population is and where the theatre-and art-loving communities are' (Miller, 1997: 25). Warren got his wish (when National Theatre of Scotland was created in 2006), but long after he had departed this earth.

By September 1946, the town council had, unanimously, approved the provost's proposal for a three-week festival in the late summer of 1947, and a Festival Society was established as a company limited by guarantee. Bing was confirmed as director; he thought it would be worth a High Mass in St Giles with which to begin the festival, and had to be disabused of the notion by Wood, lest a modern-day Jenny Geddes set up in the pews armed with stool. The festival would be run by Bing from the Glyndebourne offices in London. The town council voted £20,000 (around £800,000 at 2018 prices), and a further £20,000 came from 'citizens' including the Earl of Rosebery who donated his winnings from a recent Derby win.[6] The Arts Council (of Great Britain), formerly the Committee for the Encouragement of the Music and the Arts (CEMA), who 'were somewhat reluctant at the outset' (Miller) under the influence of John Maynard Keynes eventually gave a grant of £20,000 over two years.

Lord Provost Falconer may not have been up to Rudolf Bing's speed on the arts (Bing patronised him as 'an awfully nice little man') but, according to Crawford, Falconer 'handled the delicate matter of finance with consummate skill'. He continued:

> Owing to the generosity of Edinburgh citizens, we have been promised £20,000 – not a guarantee but a gift to the Festival Fund . . . with all the dexterity of an expert salesman producing a gold brick from his Gladstone bag – he [Falconer] went on to let them in on it. 'I propose to ask the City of Edinburgh to take a share in this work, which would certainly benefit the city and also to contribute £20,000, which should give us enough to stabilise a Festival Fund so that the Festival may get firmly established. If one estimates 10,000 persons for 3 weeks at say £4 a week, it gives £120,000 coming into the city in all at one Festival.' (Crawford 1997: 5)

Said Crawford: 'It was irresistible, a beautiful piece of "You can't afford not to join us" salesmanship . . . a splendid piece of fiscal legerdemain.' He continued: 'there have been some dents in the enthusiasm down the years but citizens have almost lived down the snide fable that everybody leaves Edinburgh during the Festival and rents their houses to foreigners' (Crawford 1997: 5).

Given what EIF was to evolve into in its quest for financial support, John Falconer's introduction in the first festival souvenir programme stands out: 'May I assure you that this Festival is not a commercial undertaking in any way. It is an endeavour to provide a stimulus to the establishing of a new way of life centred round the arts' (Miller 1996: vii). It is a far cry from what EIF (and cultural life generally) later became.

There were many critics, and not only on the town council. Hugh MacDiarmid, in full rant, thought it 'a luxury entertainment, jamborees of the well-to-do and cosmopolitan extravagance' (Crawford 1997: 8). The early, and perennial, complaint, was that there was too little Scottish content in the festival. Bing wanted Bridie's play 'Knox', but the Old Vic theatre company judged it to be 'too wordy, very historical and not sufficiently dramatic' (Crawford 1997: 8).

It was not the greatest of times to mount a festival, given post-war austerity. The organisers thought it might be not only a civic folly but 'more akin to certifiable lunacy' (Crawford 1997: 3). It was not a good omen that, at the end of March 1946, the Theatre Royal at the top of Leith Walk burned down, never to be rebuilt. There was a shortage of residential accommodation, and Lady Rosebery urged the citizenry to put people up in their homes: 'Ten thousand offers of accommodation are needed. People must be told more' (Crawford 1997: 4). There were claims that 6000 beds were made available in flats and houses to accommodate visitors. Bing worried that 'the sombre Scottish capital could acquire the necessary "festival spirit" as understood in the European festival centres' (Miller 1996: 8). Membership of the Festival Club (a £1 fee, costing about £40 in today's money) could be had at the Assembly Rooms and Music Hall in George Street. The weather came, unexpectedly, to the festival's aid:

> During the day Edinburgh had probably never seen so many brightly coloured summer frocks and at night, long after the theatres and restaurants had closed, Princes Street was still thronged with people, many in full evening dress, enjoying the cool night air and admiring the magnificent vista of the castle on one side and the elegant New Town on the other. After the grim years of war Edinburgh had suddenly come alive. (Miller 1996: 8)

Crawford elaborated:

> Plastered poets ululated behind the potted palms at the Festival Club in the elegant Assembly Rooms in George Street, where drink was sold until the un-Scottish hour of one o'clock in the morning . . .

and people kissed each other in the street, pretending it was an old Edinburgh habit or that they were insouciant continentals who couldn't tell the difference between Edinburgh and Paris. (Crawford 1997: 13)

Another hurdle to be overcome was the ban on floodlighting the castle. The minister for fuel and power (the Scottish MP, Mannie Shinwell[7]) had decreed that this was wasteful during post-war austerity. People rushed to donate some of their coal allowance to offset the cost, and the minister relented, allowing the castle to be floodlit for four nights from dusk to midnight.[8] On the subject of light, the festival was happy to employ the so-called Fiery Cross to announce the Enterprise Scotland 1947 exhibition at the Royal Scottish Museum, first 'raised to summon the clans to repel the Roman invaders and last used in 1745 to call clansmen to support Bonnie Prince Charlie'. It perversely drew attention to the lack of Scottish material at the 'official' festival, a running complaint for the next half a century. In 1948, Tyrone Guthrie directed a version of *Ane Satyre of the Thrie Estaites*, for which the Scottish playwright Robert Kemp cut the script to a manageable two and a half hours. The play had not been performed for almost 400 years, and there was the problem of a suitable venue. Guthrie later wrote:

> We visited big halls and wee halls. Halls ancient and modern, halls secular and halls holy, halls upstairs and halls in cellars, dance halls, skating rinks, lecture halls and beer halls. Darkness was falling, I was beginning to be acutely conscious that I had led them all on a wild goose chase. Then spake Kemp in the tone of one who hates to admit to something unpleasant: 'There is the Assembly Hall . . .'. (In Crawford 1997: 17)

Both Kemp and Guthrie had family links with the Kirk, 'and may have feared more from its strictures than was justified. There were no problems, no attempts at censorship of the often bawdy text, no inhibiting restrictions on use. Only one condition was made – that no nails be hammered into the Moderator's throne' (Crawford 1997: 17). An apron stage in sixteenth-century style jutted out in front of the moderator's chair. Seats didn't sell too well until reviews came out, and when they did, *The Thrie Estaites* was a sell-out, the first great original triumph of the Edinburgh Festival. Queues of people were turned away. 'In a strange and deeply satisfying way Scotland had discovered something about itself it had not known before. Only boasted about' (Crawford 1997: 19). Luminaries of the Scottish stage such as Duncan Macrae, Bryden Murdoch and Moultrie Kelsall were accompanied by Cedric Thorpe Davie's music.

The Fringe on Top

The festival had a significant offspring: the emergence of what were called 'festival adjuncts'. Robert Kemp observed: 'Round the fringe of official Festival drama there seems to be more private enterprise than before' (Crawford 1997: 16), and so the Edinburgh Festival Fringe came into being. Six theatre companies, both amateur and professional, who arrived uninvited, hired their own halls and staged a selection of plays which added to the variety of drama on offer during the period' (Miller 1996: 11). These included Glasgow Unity Theatre in Robert McLellan's *The Laird of Tortwatletie* and *The Lower Depths* (translations of a Gorky play into Scots); Christine Orr Players in *Macbeth* (where Crawford did his turn as Banquo on a Thursday); Bridie's *The Anatomist* by Scottish Community Drama Association; Strindberg's *Easter* by Edinburgh College of Art Theatre Group; Pilgrim Players (London) did T. S. Eliot's *Murder in the Cathedral* and *The Family Reunion*; and a medieval morality play, *Everyman*, across the Forth at Dunfermline Abbey.

The 1948 Festival sold 237,000 tickets, more than in 1947, despite traditional Scottish weather (said the manager of the King's Theatre, 'ah can't justify the heating being on in August' (Crawford 1997: 19)). Nevertheless, the Festival had a deficit of £10,500, half that of the previous year. The town council had agreed a contribution of £15,000 over three years (around half a million pounds at today's prices) for the 1949 Festival, and the Arts Council a grant of £3000 (worth around £100,000 today).

Critics came from all sides. The conductor Thomas Beecham had previously said that 'The people of Scotland are damned fools to throw away £60,000 on a musical festival' (reported in the *Dundee Courier* of 20 February 1948); worse still, 'the money is thrown away on foreigners'. Beecham later recanted, conducting Handel's *Fireworks* on the castle esplanade – the prelude to the Tattoo – wearing a requisitioned tin helmet, which the military ensured he signed for. Hugh MacDiarmid thought the whole thing a fool's errand:

> Scotland through EIF has gained the whole world with the usual effect on its own soul. I have always been opposed to the notion that cultural advance can be secured by giving any body of people all the culture of the world on tap – and none of their own . . . This false eclecticism is perhaps the outstanding fault of the Edinburgh Festival. (Miller 1996: 19)

Bridie replied: 'Hugh MacDiarmid, the poet, is one of the glories of Scotland . . . Hugh MacDiarmid, the pamphleteer, is just plain daft' (Miller 1996: 19).

Rudolf Bing was released from his contract in order to spend more time with Glyndebourne, after the council insisted that he be directly responsible to it, which helped to bring about the break. Somehow, the Edinburgh Festival had made it through the first three years of infancy.

By all accounts, the festival had come about through considerable sleight of hand, notably that of Lord Provost Falconer (that 'awfully nice little man'). As chief air raid warden during the Second World War, he had grown used to flying and falling obstacles. A lawyer to trade, he was provost from 1944 until 1947, succeeded by Andrew Murray, also a supporter of the festival, and Liberal in politics (Falconer was a Progressive, the 'non-political' confection of Tories and Liberals which Murray had a large hand in stitching together). Politics mattered because council funding was the financial backbone of the festival, and yet, as we have seen in Bailie Stevenson's comment, not everyone approved of perceived profligacy. A succession of town councillors made their reputations by opposing culture especially if it involved 'filth'. Indeed, 'filth' took an annual starring role in successive festivals.

Whose Festival is it Anyway?

Undoubtedly, the festival was formally the town council's property. The articles of association specified that all 'members present and future of Edinburgh Town Council' would automatically become members of the Edinburgh Festival Society Limited (Bartie 2013). Furthermore, the Society's chairman, *ex officio*, would be the lord provost. There were, in any case, tensions between Glyndebourne and the (UK) Arts Council, dominated by John Maynard Keynes. Angela Bartie commented: 'Bing wrote in his memoirs that Sir John Christie, Glyndebourne's owner, did not personally get on with the chairman of the Arts Council, Lord Keynes, and this was why Glyndebourne did not receive support from the Arts Council' (Bartie 2013: 3). It was not until September 1946 that 'the Arts Council formally agreed to be associated with the venture and offered a grant of £20,000. This came after some prompting' (Bartie 2013: 3).

The post-war period was the high noon of British cultural and political centralism, and Keynes reflected that he was 'tetchy about the Arts Council in Scotland and preferred a policy of centralism (in London)' (Bartie 2013: 4). Keynes, however, while leaving his stamp on CEMA, died suddenly in spring 1946, and before the Arts Council was incorporated under Royal Charter. The Scottish Covenant to have home rule for Scotland was growing, but not signed until November 1949, but there were already stirrings. Comments Bartie (2013: 29):

> There was . . . a very palpable fear that involving the Scottish Committee of the Arts Council would lead to a more nationalistic festival, like the Scottish Theatre Festival envisioned by (James) Bridie in October 1946. Some members of the Arts Council's Scottish Committee were considered 'too nationalistic and difficult to work with' by the London office.

In any case, Bridie had been involved in talks about a more northerly festival, possibly in Perth, commenting that he looked forward to 'the time when Perth will invite [Scottish theatres] to co-operate in making Perth a Scottish Salsburg'[9] (quoted in Bartie 2013: 4). Bridie had a powerful ally in Tom Johnston, the legendary Scottish Secretary of State, who mandated Bridie to be 'Scotland's man' when he, Johnston, was appointed as chairman of the Scottish Committee of CEMA. Euan McArthur, who examined the relations between Scotland, CEMA and the Arts Council between 1919 and 1967, observed that:

> Cultural nationalist feelings were expressed consistently by Scottish Committee members, but although sometimes linked to political aspirations, the Committee's determination to secure its ambitions, if at all possible, within a British structure is striking. Separation was only contemplated under direct pressure. Hostility within CEMA's Council to Scottish nationalism was marked by a general failure

to distinguish between its political and cultural aspects. (McArthur 2013: 109)

In truth, it would have suited the Scottish Committee to nuance the distinction as appropriate, just as it suited Tom Johnston as Scottish Secretary of State to play the Scottish card when necessary. Being considered 'too nationalistic and difficult to work with' by CEMA in London had its advantages. Mary Glasgow, secretary general of the Arts Council, in a letter to Keynes had commented that the Edinburgh Festival organisers 'do not seem to have decided properly whether it is to be a Festival of British Art for foreigners or of International art for everyone. (Probably, it will be, in fact, a Festival of Scottish art, although the Lord Provost disclaims that suggestion)' (quoted in Bartie 2013: 5). Mary Glasgow[10] took the view that the Scots exaggerated their cultural differences for political reasons (McArthur 2013).

The answer, with hindsight, is that the Edinburgh Festival evolved, and arguably, the tensions, down through the next fifty years, are not only discernible but productive, giving the festival a cultural edginess: all things to most people. Even the Kirk got into the act. The Elm Row Community Centre, gifted to it anonymously, became the Gateway Theatre, and in due course the Assembly Hall was the venue for *The Thrie Estaites* spectacular, as long as the moderator's chair was treated with suitable decorum (remember: no nails). Comments Angela Bartie, 'For Edinburgh, the Festival was a chance to create a new post-war identity as the "cultural resort of Europe" and reclaim its position as the "Athens of the North", a place of major cultural and spiritual importance' (Bartie 2013: 9).

So whose festival was it? Strictly speaking, the town council's, on the grounds that the majority funder called the tune. The Arts Council's element was welcome, but not central. In any case, as Bartie comments, 'just as CEMA had been a force for "cultural conservatism", so the Arts Council developed a reputation for funding only art that was established and generally conservative (and usually London based)' (Bartie 2013: ch. 3). By 1952, the Arts Council had stopped funding the Edinburgh Festival directly, and its funding contribution came instead from the Scottish Committee's budget. The Edinburgh Festival Society (EFS) had control over the content, with the artistic director setting the programme, which was approved by the Programme

Committee, 'composed of representatives of cultural organisations, members of the Town Council and other interested parties who had helped to found the Festival' (Bartie 2013: ch. 3).
There wasn't much that was 'Scottish' outwith the stereotypes
of 'regimental sword dances, Scottish folk dances and bagpipe
music' (Bing's preferences, and safely predictable). James Bridie
was especially critical of the absence of Scottish-based drama
and theatre.

Keeping the Shows on the Road

Bing was followed as director by his assistant, Ian Hunter (from
1950 until 1955), but he followed the Bing line. He had a better
'ear' than Bing for Scottish sensibilities, but his Scottishness was
of the 'Fettes' variety (his obituary in *The Guardian* described
it as 'the Edinburgh public school that fitted Scots for English
careers'). The obituary tells us more about the writer than about
Hunter – 'with his Scottish background, Hunter was able to
guide Bing through the minefields of Edinburgh philistinism and
disapproval'. Scots are conventionally stereotyped as 'dour', or
at best 'canny', and throughout there is the sense that Scots (and
Edinburgh) did not deserve anything as grand as the Edinburgh
Festival, and, furthermore, they didn't pay enough for the privilege. Another obituarist, this time in *The Glasgow Herald*,
described Hunter 'as a grand elitist in the days when elitism in
the arts was something to be sought after and admired' (quoted
in Bartie 2013: ch. 3).

Trying new things was left to 'festival adjuncts', and it suited
both 'official' and 'Fringe' as it became known to make up for
the cultural shortfall of the former. Bartie (2013: ch. 3) observes:

> balance was derived from the observation that the majority of plays
> being performed on the official stages were written some 'three cen-
> turies ago' while the semi-official plays were all modern plays and,
> furthermore, that of the eight theatre groups that turned up [at the
> first Edinburgh festival in 1947] six were Scottish.

'Political' plays were on the fringe, notably through Glasgow
Unity Theatre productions (Bing had told Unity that 'No
Scottish theatre is up to standard' (Bartie 2013: ch. 3)). Glasgow
Unity was both Scottish and left-wing, committed to 'people's
drama', and had received Arts Council association status in

1946. Its artistic director Robert Mitchell was told the following year that this status was suspended 'as from the commencement of the [1947] Festival period' (Bartie 2013: ch. 3), and Unity had to find its own funding. There were tensions between James Bridie's and Unity's conception of theatre, and Unity disbanded in 1951. However, comments Bartie, 'by defying the Festival organisers and very publicly mounting a challenge to the exclusion of Scottish theatre from the new Edinburgh International Festival, Glasgow Unity helped to create a cultural force that today is bigger than the official festival' (Bartie 2013: ch. 3).[11]

Glasgow Unity Theatre set the pace for 'political' theatre, to be followed by the Edinburgh Labour Festival Committee (ELFC) which set up 'a People's Festival', first held in August 1951. Martin Milligan, Communist Party member and one of the organisers, noted that the International Festival 'has a "Keep Out" notice posted for the working people of the city in which it takes place. This takes the form, first, of high prices, and second, of a ludicrously cultivated air of "snootiness"' (Bartie 2013: ch. 3). Changing its name from ELFC to the People's Festival, there were (misleading) claims that the Fringe was founded by the same. Tensions emerged soon enough between the different fractions, notably the STUC which considered the People's Festival a Communist Party front, as did the Labour Party, while the local Labour Party and Edinburgh Trades Council continued its support.

He who Pays the Piper

The Edinburgh Festival had long existed on a wing and a prayer. Lord Provost Falconer had been praised for 'a splendid piece of fiscal legerdemain' (Crawford 1997: 5) to get the 1947 Festival rolling, but his assurance to council (in the first souvenir programme) that 'this Festival is not a commercial undertaking in any way' was not sustainable in the longer term. By 1948, the deficit of £10,500, even while half that of 1947, became the *modus vivendi*. Council funding was central to the festival, but also its Achilles heel: not unreasonably, councillors thought they had bought a say, and proceeded to add to off-stage performances. In 1948, the council agreed a contribution of £15,000 over three years (around half-a-million pounds at

2018 prices), and the Arts Council chipped in £3000. By 1951, when Ian Hunter took over from Rudolf Bing, opera alone was budgeted at £35,000 (about £1m: 2018) but turned out to cost almost £3000 over budget and was duly capped by the council at £35,000.

The main problem for the Festival Society continued to be finance, with opera the main drain. Audiences were running at about 80 per cent capacity in the early 1950s. When Robert Ponsonby was appointed in 1956 to succeed Hunter, having been his assistant, £15,000 of the budget came from the council, and £7,500 from the Arts Council (respectively, £300,000 and £178,000 at 2018 prices), and the search for commercial sponsorship began in earnest. Opera in particular was costly, and the issue of a purpose-built opera house (which became the longest-running production known as the 'hole in the ground', the Poole's cinema site in Castle Terrace[12]) proved beyond the council (plans from 1948 put the cost of an arts complex at £10m (about £340m in 2018 prices: think Edinburgh Trams, or Holyrood Parliament building). When Ponsonby took over as director in the mid-1950s, the council budget was increased to £25,000 (about £600,000 in 2018 terms), this required a quid pro quo:

> At the same time it asked for an increase in the number of town councillors on the Festival Council and Executive Committee. The Society agreed and the number of town councillors on the Festival Council from one-third to half the total number, and the Executive Committee to a total of 12 comprising the Lord Provost, 6 town councillors and 5 non-town councillors. (Miller 1996: 44)

It was impossible to avoid the politics. Iain Crawford observed that: 'Edinburgh Tory councillors were always very impressed by the kind of Eton and Scots Guards background which Ponsonby offered . . .' (Crawford 1997: 43). Furthermore:

> a great many of [the general public] were still highly suspicious of the Festival . . . as an elitist plot to foist alien culture on a baffled bourgeoisie. They could not quite understand how it happened or why it was rated a success and would really have preferred if the City's contribution had been spent on new public lavatories in Leith.

Lord Provost Sir John Banks considered the festival 'an interesting but rather troublesome interlude in Edinburgh during the summer season' (Crawford 1997: 43). Ponsonby found relations with council to be trying. He commented (Crawford 1997: 54):

> It's never been very good. Not because the directors have not been Scottish but fundamentally because the local authority aspect of Edinburgh has always been unimaginative, concerned with immediate and obvious topics and traditions whereas the Edinburgh Festival was an imaginative stroke of genius, really. The committees expressed a generally philistine indifference towards artistic aspirations and policies.

In 1960 Ponsonby resigned because 'I could see no way out of the trap of local authority money to support things which I knew the Festival had to do' (Crawford 1997: 54). He was succeeded by Lord Harewood (1961–5) who, commented Crawford, had a serious reputation in the music world, 'having overcome suspicions of being merely a royal dabbler' (Crawford 199: 61), and, thought Crawford, appealing 'to the ingrained snobbery in the city' (Crawford 199: 61).

The incoming lord provost (Ian Anderson Johnson-Gilbert) launched an appeal for public support, claiming that the festival brought in 34,000 overseas visitors, 19,000 North Americans, and 57,000 from the rest of the UK. Crawford commented: 'In 1978 when I was involved in seeking sponsorship for the Festival, one major Scottish Princes Street store which must have taken several thousand pounds a day during the Festival offered £400' (Crawford 1997: 58). James Bridie's son, Ronald Mavor (known, curiously, as Bingo), claimed that the city's share of funding was less than three-farthings (three-quarters of an old penny) on the council rates. Tyrone Guthrie, who had directed *The Thrie Estaites* in 1948, 1949, 1951 and 1959, 'declared that he would have no truck with haberdashers' (Crawford 1997: 48), an allusion to the perceived domination of the council by shopkeepers.

Notwithstanding, councillors who paid the piper wanted to call the tune. Magnus Williamson, a Labour member, observed:

> We want a bigger control of Festival affairs by the business people of Edinburgh and the Corporation. There comes a time in every organisation when there must be a wind of change. That time has almost been reached in the Festival Society. The Society should be run by the Corporation, helped by a number of 'artistically clever' people. The present rather arty-crafty collection of people on the Society

who have given us a great deal of assistance in the past should be replaced by new people. (Crawford 1997: 65)

Ponsonby's unwitting claim to fame had been to usher in 'Beyond the Fringe' (Jonathan Miller, Alan Bennett, Dudley Moore and Peter Cook) to fill an unexpected late-night slot for the official festival (not the Fringe) at the Lyceum Theatre. Crawford commented: 'What Bernard Levin was later to christen "the annual Ritual of the Grudging of the Money" was hardening into a Festival Rite' (Crawford 1997: 65).

By 1963, the Festival Society faced its worst-ever financial crisis, with an overdraft of £22,500 (just under half a million pounds at 2018 prices). The Earl of Harewood, who had succeeded Ponsonby, turned it into a surplus of £35,000 (about £700,000 in today's money), the first time the festival had seriously balanced its books. By this point it must have become clear that splashing out on big prestigious projects tended to provoke major deficits. Nineteen sixty three was also the year when a nude actor on a trolley was wheeled across the McEwen Hall, little noticed at the time, much commented by those who were on the look-out for 'filth' even, perhaps especially, when they weren't actually present.[13]

Edinburgh festivals had a good line in moral outrage emanating from local councillors, notably Councillor John D. Kidd ('my big mouth is necessary if the country is to remain sane') who played the role from the late 1960s into the 1970s. His successor as outraged-of-Edinburgh was Moira Knox, Tory councillor for douce Davidson's Mains who retired from active service in the late 1990s. Brian Pendreigh who wrote her obituary (2016) in *The Scotsman* observed: 'She could generate ticket sales like few other performers, without ever putting on a show at the Festival.' Said one Fringe administrator: 'She will be sadly missed. She has generated more copy for errant Fringe companies than anyone else.' The *Glasgow Herald* headlined their obituary: 'Councillor and Public Decency Spokeswoman': Edinburgh's own Mary Whitehouse.[14]

In 1965, the council increased its grant to the Festival Society by 50 per cent to £75,000, and two years later cut it back by the same amount. The incoming director Peter Diamand threatened to resign. The grant was restored by Lord Provost Herbert Brechin (a butcher, not a haberdasher) who said the Society would be unwise to count on an increase for 1969. Councillors were getting in on various acts. Baillie Theurer attended Richard Demarco's exhibition: 'At the opening the eagle eye of Bailie Theurer, a member of the Festival Council, detected one or two four-letter words in an exhibit . . .' (Miller 1996: 71). The offending part was removed, and, naturally, great publicity ensued for the exhibition. Lord Provost Brechin was a particular bête noire during Peter Diamand's tenure. Comments Iain Crawford, on the SNO's production of *The Flying Dutchman*:

> The only critic to withhold his praise was Lord Provost Brechin. On Scottish Opera's first night the year before he had irritated everyone by closing the Circle Bar in the King's Theatre to hold a civic reception. In 1968 he booked a block of seats for the European burgomasters and other municipal chain-wearers he had invited to the festival, then cancelled the booking at the last moment and took his international group for a sail down the River Clyde instead. The rain which poured down on the burgomasters' nautical bash was greatly enjoyed vicariously by opera enthusiasts everywhere. (Crawford 1997: 93)

When Brechin held a civic reception for USSR State Orchestra in the 1968 Festival at the point of the Soviet invasion of Czechoslovakia, only three councillors attended. By the end of the 1960s, box office receipts (which ran at 83 per cent capacity) were the best they had been for more than a decade, and the deficit was reduced from £52,000 to £9,500. Florence Opera had used Italian PR to decorate the Kings Theatre with flowers, and perfume. Alas, the flowers were mistakenly sent to another King's Theatre – in Glasgow. Furthermore:

> the perfume was greatly appreciated by the ladies although a group of Edinburgh matrons (who had formed a queue at the box office to purchase tickets for the forthcoming pantomime) surprised at being accosted by a bevy of sexily dressed young ladies, with typical Edinburgh suspicion refused the offer of a small gift. (Miller 1996: 74)

Another 'criticised excursion' was made by Lord Provost James McKay and a censorious posse from the Festival Council who sent themselves on a moral inspection tour to the Deutsche Oper am Rhein at Frankfurt to attend a Sunday performance of Prokoviev's *The Fiery Angel* to see if it was fit for genteel Edinburgh consumption (Crawford 1997: 103).

In 1964, the city had collected £11m in rates, and in 1969, £21m; the Festival contribution went from £75,000 to £80,000 (around 0.67 per cent). Criticising the festival turned out to be an all-party council affair. Labour (under convener Peter Wilson) objected to the proposal to raise the grant to £100,000, and wanted it reduced. Wilson said: 'I think Edinburgh is well to the fore in the world as a sewage preservation society,'[15] Cllr Kidd, true to form, proposed that the new sports centre at Meadowbank should be used as an opera house. Said the long-suffering Peter Diamand:

> The city and the citizens of Edinburgh will continue to be a splendid host to the artists and to the visitors – not the boastful flashy sometimes oppressive kind – more in that cautious yet reliable spirit in which one Edinburgh citizen summed up his feelings last year: 'I quite liked the Festival, I even enjoyed it. All in all we were none the worse for it.' (Crawford 1997: 106)

Not to be outdone by Labour, the Conservatives on the regional council (two-tier local government had been introduced in 1975) recommended cutting the festival grant to £50,000. Miller (1996: 93) comments:

> A political row blew up when a "Festival spokesman" was reported to have said that the Conservatives did not appear to be interested in the Festival. Then on top of this came the devastating announcement that the Region was withdrawing its grant to the Festival completely.

Edinburgh District Council, the lower tier of local government, proposed to increase its grant to £190,000 on condition that it took all twelve local authority seats on the Festival Society Council, which the Society acceded to. There was controversy over funding of the opera, Carmen (later bailed out by BP). Three Labour councillors (Jimmy Kerr, David Brown and George Monies) wrote to the *Edinburgh Evening News*:

> We are absolutely incensed by this colossal squandering of public money – squandering which has only come to our notice because we managed to uncover some secret documents of the Festival Society which the public have never been allowed to see. In the interest of the ratepayers of Edinburgh and the people who are subsidising the

Festival, we feel it is our duty to tell them the facts which the Festival organisers would prefer to remain unknown. (Miller 1996: 93)

To make matters worse, the Tories on the council accused them of making a pre-election attack on festival in a bid to 'capture the moron vote' (Miller 1996: 94).

In Peter Diamand's final year as director (he had lasted twelve years), Edinburgh District Council came up with a grant of £300,000 (about £1.5m in 2018 terms). Fund-raising among business came to little: 'Letters appealing for funds had been sent to large business concerns in Scotland with disappointing results. Out of 151 letters sent to prospective new donors, 9 made donations amounting to £4875[16] and 58 refused to contribute at all' (Miller 1996: 95). Diamand summed up his tenure as follows:

> in the first place the difficulty was lack of funds, lack of an opera house, and the general weight of the Festival Council being dominated by the Town Council and the many philistines among them who were looking at the box office rather than any kind of artistic innovation or risk. (Crawford 1997: 146)

He went on:

> all this stuff about people being afraid to go to cultural events – they're afraid to go to the Usher Hall and afraid to go into the King's Theatre – and you must make it easy for them. It's all nonsense. They're not afraid – they're just bloody well not interested. And why shouldn't they be? I am uninterested in many things. (Crawford 1997: 147)

Regime Change

Diamand's successor was John Drummond (1979–83). Miller (1996: 112–13) commented:

> John Drummond was perhaps the most multifaceted of all the Festival Directors and his five Festivals were by far the most finely balanced, almost equal emphasis being given to all the art forms. With his championship of Scottish companies, artists and particularly his poetry and prose recitals such as a series on Gaelic culture *Dualchas* [tradition, in Gaelic], he was the first Director to give Scottish arts and culture a truly prominent place in the Festival . . . Drummond also succeeded in breaking down the barriers between

the official Festival and the Fringe, a factor that had troubled both Harewood and Diamand, but neither had found a solution to the problem. But his greatest contribution was in making the Festival more acceptable to the ordinary people of Edinburgh.

It is not clear on what basis Miller makes this judgement, for Drummond managed to get his publicity officer to resign (the same Iain Crawford who later wrote his account of the Festival), and he alienated the director of the Royal Scottish Museum, as well as the festival's programme director. Neither was Drummond averse to railing against Edinburgh's bourgeoisie, when, one imagines, they would have been a better bet than the city's shopocracy:

> The class of people who want the benefit of the Festival without con-
> tributing are in fact the Edinburgh professional classes, particularly
> industry and commerce. All those people sitting around St Andrews
> Square and up and down George St and banks and insurance com-
> panies think it's jolly nice to have a Festival, but actually do very
> little for it. (Crawford 1997: 172)

By the 1980s, the principle of appointing Festival directors seemed to rely much more on going for opposites rather than clones. Frank Dunlop was a theatre man (Drummond's pen-chant was for dance and ballet). Dunlop inherited a deficit, which he had not known about, of £175,000 (about half-a-million pounds: 2018), expressing the view that if he had known he would have declined the job, given that it was the largest on record. The district council gave an additional £70,000, and Scottish Arts Council £10,000, but the Festival Society still had an overdraft of £22,000. To make matters more difficult, a rad-ical Labour council took control of the district council in 1984 opposed to 'ingrained elitism'. Referring to carping attacks on councillors' philistinism, George Kerevan, the culture convener, replied that these 'proved that there was an arts establishment in Edinburgh', adding 'we declare war on it; we will abolish it; we will democratise it' (Miller 1996: 116). Labour councillors wanted all local authority places on the Festival Society to go to them, so as to enforce the party line.

This, together with Labour's threats to close down the festi-val, had an intimidating effect on the non-town council mem-bers who were very nervous about disagreeing with the Labour group or even putting forward any view that might run counter to Labour policy; no member wanted to be responsible for the festival's subsidy being cut. As a result, Dunlop found himself without the support or backing of the council (Miller 1996: 118).

Dunlop's efforts at appeasing the council were eased when community events around the city suffered from low attendances. In the words of Dunlop it 'proved once and for all that the "activists" were wrong' (Miller 1996: 120). Dunlop resigned in 1991, and his

> frustration and anger at his long-running feud with the District Council surfaced when, on the eve of his departure, he gave an interview to *The Scotsman* in which he accused some of the Labour leaders of major interference and an anti-Festival attitude during his eight years in charge. It was not a case of his not being able to get on with the city fathers, but 'there [*sic*] not being able to get on with me'. (Miller 1996: 137)

Late in Dunlop's charge, the penny began to drop, that the arts were becoming an important means of economic regeneration. The other place, Glasgow, by this time miles better, had won the accolade European City of Culture in 1990. Crawford (1997: 206) observed:

> This Damascene conversion had been prompted, one councillor admitted, by the success of *The Scotsman* campaign after last year's funding shortfall, which had demonstrated public support for the Festival by raising 90k. It could also have been brought on by the Policy Studies Institute's report on Glasgow which had found the arts to be a good buy and that tourism generated by arts attractions sustained more than 4000 jobs in Glasgow and that every arts job had helped create 2.74 other jobs in the wider economy and enhanced tourist beds figures.

Dunlop had tried to encourage collaboration with Glasgow prior to this. Commented Miller: 'There was no doubt that Glasgow's success was a severe blow to Edinburgh's pride and caused the District Council to reconsider its attitude to the arts and, in particular, to the funding of the Festival' (Miller 1996: 133). There had long been surprise that Edinburgh 'the weakling infant' (Crawford 1997: 3) had stolen a march.

After the stormy tenure of Frank Dunlop, the appointment of Brian McMaster ushered in a period of calm, and he survived in the job for fifteen years, beating Diamand's tenure by three years. Miller (1996: 138) observed: 'After the outspoken, erudite, multi-faceted Drummond and the flamboyant, puckish and equally forthright Dunlop the appointment of the small, bearded, self-effacing Brian McMaster with the general air and appearance of a senior civil servant startled many people.'

McMaster moved all staff to Edinburgh from London, and appointed the consummate Joanna Baker as director of marketing and public affairs. Edinburgh District Council upped its grant from £600,000 in 1989, to just under £1m in 1994. Lothian Region came back with £350,000, Scottish Arts Council, £735,000, and there was a major increase in sponsorship to over £1m. McMaster's reign also saw the end of 'the hole in the ground' which was sold to a property company on the condition that the site incorporated a new theatre: which became the Traverse, with two auditoria. The Empire Theatre on the southside, first a music-hall, then a bingo parlour, became the Festival Theatre, and a venue for opera. The Empire was sold to the Council for £2.6m in 1991, and cost £11m to refurbish. Edinburgh District Council provided half, and the rest came from Lothian Region, Scottish Arts Council, Scottish Tourist Board, Historic Buildings Council, and the private sector. It opened in 1994 with Scottish Opera's *Tristan und Isolde*.

The stability provided by Brian McMaster (for whom the description 'quiet, dapper and self-effacing' was tailor-made) and Joanna Baker (marketing and publicity director since 1992, and managing director from 2006 to 2018), together with a more stable funding regime, almost all from the public purse, meant that the festival was in better shape than for some time. McMaster, who managed fifteen years, was followed by Jonathan Mills's eight years, and Fergus Linehan became director in 2015 with his contract lasting until 2022.

SUPPORTING CASTES AND NOISES OFF

What of claims that Edinburgh is the Festival City par excellence? We might quibble with how many 'festivals' Edinburgh actually has, but the Fringe attracts almost five times the audiences of the official festival. The Fringe is the closest thing to a free market in culture –put on a show and people come, or they don't – although the arrival of cultural entrepreneurs

('The Big Four') capturing the big venues made it more of a cartel than a free market. We saw earlier that 'festival adjuncts' muscled in regardless, and that while overtures were made concerning better complementarity (even on start and finish dates), they have melded into each other. The Fringe is, in the words of Wikipedia, 'an open access (or "unjuried") performing arts festival meaning there is no selection committee, and anyone may participate, with any type of performance'.

The important thing to remember is the symbiotic relationships between the various 'festivals'. The 'official' festival (EIF) might take the credit for being the mainstay, but, as Jen Harvie observes: 'it is misleading to consider the cultural effects of the EIF as though it occurred in hermetic isolation, separate from the events and resources that have grown up around it' (Harvie 2003: 21). There was no question that Festival and Fringe merge together. Back in 1959, when the Fringe Society was formed[17] – to publish the programme, to create a box office, and to give companies advice on halls and accommodation – 'a suggestion by Mr Imison [Oxford Theatre Group] that the proposed society should attempt to gain recognition by the Festival Society did not go down well with other delegates. "We don't want recognition" was the general consensus of opinion' (Moffat 1978: 43). Alistair Moffat, who was Fringe director from 1978 to 1981, commented (Moffat 1978: 44):

> As a direct result of the wishes of the participants, the Society had been set up to help the performers who came to Edinburgh and to promote them collectively to the public. They did not come together so that groups could be vetted or invited in some way controlled artistically. What was performed and how it was done was left entirely up to each Fringe group. Essentially that is how the Fringe Society operates today.

The most recurring criticism of the Fringe has been that it is too large and unwieldy. Some (such as the director Gerry Slevin) wanted the number of venues/halls licensed: 'these could be balloted and everyone would be much happier' (Moffat 1978: 50). Critics such as *The Scotsman*'s Cordelia Oliver thought the Fringe was growing 'grosser each year like a fat old cat going to seed and not giving a damn' (Moffat 1978: 111). (One might reply: If no one came, bought tickets, then the cat would have wasted away; and Slevin's suggestion of vetting would surely

have started a rammy in one of Edinburgh's many graveyards.)
Frank Dunlop likened the Fringe to a 'third-rate circus', 'smug
and self-satisfied', and 'reminiscent of a modern Tower of
Babel of the arts' (Harvie 2003: 22). Michael Billington wrote
in *The Guardian* ('Why I hate the Fringe', 25 July 2002) that
the Fringe had become 'overweening, grotesquely outsized
and highly commercialised', and that was before domination
by the Big Four. Notwithstanding, as Owen Dudley Edwards
observed: 'each [Festival and Fringe] is now unthinkable without the other, and each is in part the product of the other'
(Harvie 2003: 22).

For good or ill, the Fringe has evolved. Fringe directors follow
'professional' routes. For example, at the time of writing, the
current director (Shona McCarthy) has come from 'Derry, City
of Culture'; her predecessor, Keith Mainland, from Melbourne
Festival; and his predecessor, Jon Morgan, from Contact Theatre
in Manchester. Arts entrepreneurs have created 'super-venues',
notably the so-called Big Four, Bill Burdett-Coutts (Assembly
Rooms), Chris Richardson (The Pleasance), Karen Koren (Gilded
Balloon), and Ed Bartlam and Charlie Wood, of Underbelly. In
2013, the Summerhall Arts Hub opened as a year-round venue
at the former Dick Vet School at the University of Edinburgh.

The scale of the Fringe has grown hugely: between 1973 and
2017, there was a nine-fold increase in the number of shows;
a thirty-eight-fold increase in performances; and a twenty-one-
fold increase in ticket sales (at 2.5m in 2017). Arguably, the
Fringe is the tail which wags the Festival dog, and audiences
shift seamlessly from one genre to the other without worrying
too much about which 'festival' they are in.

'Up a Winding Staircase'

Then there is the Traverse, which opened in 1963 in a former
brothel/doss house in the Old Town known as Kelly's Paradise.
The former *Scotsman* theatre critic Allen Wright described
it as: '"up-a-winding staircase-in-a-17th century-Edinburgh-
tenement-you-will-find-the-most-exciting-theatre-in-Britain"
type of theatre'. This is a tale beautifully told by Wright's successor, Joyce McMillan (in her book *The Traverse Theatre Story*,
1988) who observes: 'If it wasn't the first intimate theatre in
Britain, it certainly was the only one in Edinburgh, a focus for

the avant-garde interests and bohemian impulses of a small but considerable swathe of the Edinburgh bourgeoisie' (McMillan 1988: 10).

The Traverse (probably the director who named it meant 'Transverse' – two raked banks of seats at either end of the stage – but the name became 'too famous to change') was set in the (official) festival context. McMillan commented (1988: 10):

> The city of Edinburgh seems to have experienced that tension [1960s] in a particularly acute form. Paralysed in dour provincial respectability from September to August, it was nonetheless galvanised, for three weeks of the year, by what was then quite unrivalled as the world's greatest and most exciting arts festival.

The academic philosopher, Stanley Eveling, who moonlighted as playwright and, later, as TV critic for *The Scotsman* described it thus:

> the thing about the Traverse at the beginning was that it was more like an anti-theatre than a theatre . . . then it got famous for putting on plays, and everyone thought it must be a theatre, then. But the original idea was that people came to the place not to see but to live. The play was the centre, but just the centre, of a more generalised thing that was happening to them. They were being liberated, that's what. Then they would straighten their ties and fix their hair and go back to their nice Edinburgh flats. But it had an effect . . . (Quoted in McMillan 1988: 32)

The Traverse became notorious, especially among critics who made a point of not going there. Councillor John D. Kidd, 'the leading scourge of permissiveness', pronounced that 'he didn't approve of drama as such' (McMillan 1988: 40), which, one imagines, came as a surprise to few. 'Filth on the Fringe' became a by-word. Brian Meek, journalist and Tory councillor, and a worthy successor to Councillors Kidd and Knox, admitted: 'I didn't actually see the show . . .' (McMillan 1988: 39). Joyce McMillan's point is that the Traverse, now safely ensconced in a two-auditorium complex in the financial district, has been at the confluence of a number of creative tensions in its fifty-odd year history, similar indeed to that of festival and Fringe: between experimental freedom and orthodox management; between cutting-edge radicalism and more conventional structures of British theatre; between the active creation of new work and making space for that created elsewhere; between Scottish and UK/international aspirations; and between the city of Edinburgh and its festival(s). In short, the Traverse 'was the Fringe venue that got away, the crazy, youthful, one-off venture that somehow became a permanent theatre' (McMillan 1988: 98).

CONCLUSION

What does all this cultural activity add up to? On reflection, it was happenstance that brought 'Festival City' about. Recall James Bridie's comment that Edinburgh was a city 'which prides itself on not being interested in anything at all'. If Glyndebourne had found somewhere closer to the English Home Counties – Oxford, Cambridge, Cheltenham, for example – the Edinburgh Festival would not have happened. In truth, for much of its modern history, Edinburgh was not that kind of place. Rather, '(b)y manipulating its own image, and continually emphasizing the historic and picturesque, the myth of Edinburgh as a non-industrial city was invented and nurtured' (Madgin and Rodger 2013: 512).

Furthermore, Edinburgh has been reinvented as festival city, aided and abetted by cultural re-imagining and re-branding. This has not been the result of some grand plan, still less funded by private capital. The festival story has relied on public capital, mainly council grants, supplemented by Scottish Arts Council, and latterly by Scottish government. Complaints that Edinburgh commerce was happy to reap benefits but not put its hand in its pocket, abound. Recall, too, John Drummond's comment that 'All those people sitting around St Andrews Square and up and down George St and banks and insurance companies think it's jolly nice to have a Festival, but actually do very little for it' (Crawford 1997: 172). Providing audiences in this most bourgeois of cities is as far as it goes. The official Edinburgh Festival is a publicly funded event, paid for out of council and public coffers. As such, it tells us little about 'who runs Edinburgh' apart from the obvious fact that the council does. Private commerce funds concerts and events, and Lord Provost Falconer's admonition that 'this Festival is not a commercial undertaking in any way' has long fallen by the wayside. The rest has become improbable, but entertaining, history.

NOTES

1. I am grateful to Neil for his permission to quote this stanza.
2. Attributed to a comment by Peter Diamand, festival director from 1965 to 1978 (Crawford 1997: 106).
3. Crawford explained that, in one of the earliest Fringe performances of Macbeth, he played the part of Banquo, 'a role which allowed me to sneak away after the first scene in Act IV to cull a few more gossip pars [sic] from the Festival Club. I stood in for a well-known Edinburgh actor . . . who worked in a bank which kept him late on Thursdays' (p. 6). Hence, Crawford played 'Banquo on Thursdays'.
4. George Bruce attributes the 1939 claim to Lionel Birch who wrote for the magazine *Picture Post* (Bruce 1975: 18).
5. Lord Provost Falconer was the grandfather of Charlie Falconer (ennobled as Baron Falconer of Thoroton), the Labour politician and lord chancellor in the Blair government of 2003.
6. One of the Earl of Rosebery's horses, Ocean Swell, had won the Derby and Jockey Club Cup in 1944 (Bartie 5/17).
7. Shinwell was at the time MP for Seaham in county Durham, a seat he won from Ramsay MacDonald in 1935.
8. A symbolic gesture, as burning piles of coal at the castle walls would have added to the problems of air quality in Auld Reekie.
9. Scotland had its own Salsburgh, a former mining village near Shotts in Lanarkshire close to the M8, and an unlikely candidate for an arts festival on the scale envisaged.
10. Mary Glasgow had been a junior inspector with HMI before joining CEMA. Despite, or because of, her surname, like her boss J. M. Keynes, she held strong views about what she took to be Scottish special pleading.
11. Recall the early figures given by BOS Consultants that 47 per cent of 'Edinburgh festivals' audiences are associated with the Fringe, and only 10 per cent for the official EIF, a ratio of roughly 1 to 5.
12. The campaign to building an opera house on the Castle Terrace site began in earnest in 1961 (under the Earl of Harewood), but was formally rejected in 1975 by Edinburgh council (thirty-two to twenty-seven voted to abandon the scheme). It was revived in modified form in 1984, and passed by the council by thirty votes to seven. It was cancelled when Labour took control of the council in 1984, and in 1988 the site was sold to Scottish Metropolitan Property to build a financial centre, but incorporating the new Traverse Theatre.
13. The Edinburgh poet Robert Garioch included it in his poem 'Embro to the ploy'. 'A happening, incident, or splore/affrontit them that saw/a thing they'd never seen afore/in the McEwan Haa/a lassie

in a wheelie-chair/wi naething on at aa/just like my luck! I wasna there/it's no the thing ava, tut-tut/in Embro to the ploy.'

14. Mary Whitehouse founded the National Viewers and Listeners Association (NVLA) to combat 'filth' on TV and elsewhere. She died in 2001. As far as Edinburgh was concerned, Mary Whitehouse was England's Moira Knox.

15. At the time, there was controversy about processing and disposing of the city's sewage at Seafield near Leith. One hesitates to say that the problem has been solved.

16. An average of £541, not much more than the notional £400 that Iain Crawford extracted from one shop in 1978.

17. By 1954, an Edinburgh printer, C. J. Cousland, had put together the first programme listed.

5

Are You One of Us? Status in the City

Consider the jokes about Edinburgh. They are about reserve, snobbery and meanness ('East Windy, West Endy'; 'fur coat and no knickers'; 'You'll have had your tea?'; 'Queen Anne front; Mary Anne back'[1]). Behind them one can sense a process of decision-making which implies a city in which status matters rather than simply social class. Status is about social and cultural power, rather than about money and wealth, although it would be foolish to treat these as distinct spheres. Recall the comment by John Heiton with which we began this book: '"Look you, sir. Your city is a very fine city, but it swarms with castes". The American was right: Our beautiful Modern Athens is in a swarm of castes, worse than ever was old Egypt or is modern Hindostan' (Heiton 1859: 1). Edinburgh: as a city of castes, verging on the conspiratorial.

THE SOCIAL WORLDS OF EDINBURGH

In this chapter and the next, I will consider these spheres, first, those who inhabit the shady social worlds, based indubitably on wealth, but discreetly manifest, underplayed and often unspoken. In Edinburgh, you don't flaunt it. This is the world of clubs, associations which you do not join without an invitation, and without knowing who else is a member. If you have to ask to join, then you're not their sort of person. Fuelling this world, the story goes, is a complex hierarchy of schools, many, but not all, in the private sector. If Edinburgh is a city of castes, then the question what school did you go to? becomes the key to open doors, and we will examine that in Chapter 6. There is, however,

Figure 5.1 Talking Edinburgh; courtesy of the Robert Blomfield collection

a complex relationship between rhetoric and reality. One might believe that Edinburgh is a hierarchical and closed society – it has myth-status – but we cannot take that for granted, at least in the times we live in. Past and present are in a curious relationship: we cannot rule out that once upon a time the city's caste-like culture was more important than it is now, while accrediting the myth of caste with considerable power to define the situation as all too credible. But myths have a habit of living on and dragging out in their after-life.

The World of Clubs

First, we will explore the world of clubs and associations, by picking out a few which come up in Edinburgh conversations. There is, above all, the New Club: commented one academic colleague: 'Ah yes, the New Club – one of the delights of living in Edinburgh is the belief that there is some conspiracy which runs the place – the New Club is top item.' He puts his finger on a key point: the *belief*, in his words, 'some conspiracy', that this is where key decisions are made. But there is more to Edinburgh than the New Club, which we will explore later in this chapter. There is the Merchant Company of Edinburgh which runs many of the private schools in the city. In exploring municipal politics in Chapter 2, we found that Edinburgh's merchant class had a hold on its politics for much longer than elsewhere. Only in the 1970s did its hegemony end, although it has had a long after-life. So the nexus between merchantry and schooling is worth exploring.

Examine the connection between the city's politics and the merchant class, and you come across the High Constables of the City of Edinburgh. Ask Edinburgh citizens about the High Constables, and many will know little or nothing. They will, probably, not confuse the organisation with 'real' constables, the police force at Fettes Avenue, once called Lothians and Borders, and now Police Scotland. Those with whom it rings a bell will think of men in pin-stripe suits and lum hats[2] parading up and down the Royal Mile carrying silver batons on ceremonial occasions: the Kirking of the council, welcoming the queen to Holyroodhouse, marking the beginning of the Edinburgh Festival in St Giles,[3] and, revealingly, the Kirking of the master of the Royal Company of Merchants, who happens to be, despite the sexist title, HRH Princess Anne. How one gets to be a High Constable is not at all clear.

Furthermore, there is much to play for. There is the Honourable Company of Edinburgh Golfers, so-called but based at their private golf course at Muirfield at Gullane in East Lothian.

The company began playing golf on Leith Links in 1744, inventing, as they went, the thirteen rules of golf, before moving out to Musselburgh old course in 1836. This they found too crowded and public for the likes of members of the Honourable Company,[4] so in 1891 they built their own – private – course at Muirfield, which has become a mainstay of the British Open golf tournament. It achieved a degree of notoriety in 2016 when members voted by insufficient margin (two-thirds was required) to admit women as full members. A year later they tried again, and this time succeeded, though few women were lining up to join.

The male domination of clubs and associations has long been a feature. The High Constables of Edinburgh only admitted women in 1997, and that at the insistence of the City of Edinburgh Council with which it has a symbiotic, if shadowy, connection. The New Club sought, one is tempted to say manfully, to admit women as full members for some years before successfully doing so in 2010, although they could be associate members from 1970, but only with the support of their husbands. 'Ladies', for that is how they are designated in the New Club, were mere appendages of their husbands. In the list of New Club members for 2008,[5] for example, it is quite common to find women subsumed under their husbands: thus, 'Mrs ABC Brown' (to invent a fictitious person) is the wife of member 'ABC Brown', seemingly having lost their identities entirely, in this respect their own first names as well as their so-called 'maiden' names in the process; proof if needs be as to how identities were entirely subsumed on marriage.[6] It is, then, not a coincidence that the High Constables of the City of Edinburgh, the Honourable Company of Edinburgh Golfers, and the New Club, belatedly admitted women (or in their parlance still, 'ladies') to membership at or around the beginning of the twenty-first century. Women, needless to say, were not storming the club house to join any of these organisations (very few applied to join Muirfield when it became 'open'). It reinforces the point, however, that Edinburgh at least historically has been a closed, male, world (wearing 'the old school tie'), and this was reinforced by the gender segregation of Merchant Company schools until gender politics, but above all, economics, demanded co-educational schools.

Elites in Edinburgh

It would be easy to assume that Edinburgh is 'elitist' if we simply focused on certain organisations. Let us, then, begin with a more general review of elites in Edinburgh, which, of course, assumes that we know what an 'elite' is. We are in the world of *Who's Who*, the eponymous listing of biographical data on 'influential people' which has been published annually since mid-nineteenth century. Scotland has its own cut-down version, *Who's Who in Scotland*, which I used for the years 1986 and 2019 (McCrone 2021) to make a comparison of how Scottish elites, so defined, had changed (or not) over time.[7]

The data are based on those giving Edinburgh as their normal place of residence, which does not preclude having another house elsewhere. The first feature to notice is that a much higher proportion of Scottish elites now live in Edinburgh than thirty years ago: 27 per cent in 1986, but 39 per cent in 2019[8]; more than three times the proportion living in Glasgow, the bigger city. Living in the capital is now a more significant feature. It is still a male elite: a gender ratio of 4 to 1, compared with almost all male (95 per cent) in 1986. It is also disproportionately a legal elite: 40 per cent of the Edinburgh-based elite are lawyers in 2019, compared with one-third in 1986. The other major increase is in the Edinburgh-based political class, up from 5 per cent to 16 per cent, reflecting the creation of the Scottish parliament in 1999. There are, however, among the administrative class, proportionately fewer based in Edinburgh, a proportion which almost halves, from 35 per cent in 1986 to 19 per cent in 2019; whereas the Edinburgh-domiciled business class is fairly stable, 25 per cent in the earlier period, and 21 per cent in the later. Law, business and politics make up over three-quarters of members of Scotland's elites living in Edinburgh, a much higher concentration than in 1986.[9]

There have also been major shifts in where the Edinburgh-based elite were educated. Almost half (48 per cent) attended Scottish Education Authority schools,[10] compared with just over one-third (36 per cent) in 1986. Even among those educated privately, there has been a fall in those who had attended Edinburgh day schools (the likes of Heriot's, Watson's and so on), and a rising proportion attending such day schools elsewhere in Scotland.[11] This reflects the opening up of the Edinburgh-based elite to those educated outwith the city, but above all at education authority (EA) schools elsewhere in Scotland. In other words, the Edinburgh-based elite in 2019 is drawn much more from those publicly educated in Scotland, something reinforced by post-school education, where far more went to university elsewhere in Scotland (the proportion educated at Oxbridge fell from 19 per cent to 12 per cent).

What do these data suggest about elites resident in Edinburgh?

- A much higher proportion now live in Edinburgh.
- The Edinburgh-based elite is far more likely to be 'state' educated at education authority schools, especially those furth of the city.
- In short, it is a much more diverse and 'meritocratic' elite than hitherto (at least, taking 1986 as our benchmark), state-educated, with about one-third educated at Edinburgh University, and 20 per cent at Glasgow.

Curiously, however, in terms of given recreational activities, 'traditional' pursuits such as golf, fishing and shooting are more salient among the Edinburgh-based elite in 2019 than in 1986. Thus, 'golf' is by far the most mentioned recreational pursuit (37 per cent, compared with 34 per cent in 1986), while 'country pursuits' such as fishing and shooting see a rise from 17 per cent to 24 per cent. It appears, then, that golf, fishing and shooting are, taken together, more significant (at 61 per cent) than they were in 1986 (51 per cent). We can speculate as to why, but the best guess is that these pursuits are places to do business and meet significant people, whether on the golf course or the grouse moor.[12] These data are, of course, indicative, but they suggest that while the composition of the Edinburgh-based elite is more open in social and educational terms, its leisure pursuits are, if anything, narrower and more traditional, suggesting that spending leisure time in social company matters in terms of networking.

IN THE COMPANY OF MERCHANTS

Thus far, we have focused on the characteristics of Edinburgh members of elites as described in *Who's Who in Scotland* in 1986 and 2019. This is something of a deck-clearing exercise, for it helps us see how these may or may not have changed. We now turn to the Merchant Company of Edinburgh which, historically, has dominated political and economic life in the city.

The Merchant Guild was formed in 1260, in the words of historian Rosalind K. Marshall, 'Anxious to protect their monopoly, fend off illegal competition and give each other mutual support' (Marshall 2015: 7). By the 1530s, the Edinburgh merchants controlled 80 per cent of Scotland's foreign trade, and through Leith as the main gateway to Europe, had considerable wealth, municipal influence and royal patronage. This irked local craftsmen in particular who objected to the restraint of trade imposed by the Merchant Guild's trading monopoly, and formed their own Incorporated Trades (goldsmiths, masons, tailors, candlemakers and the like). In James VI's time, while merchants provided the lord provost, four bailies, the treasurer and dean of guild, of the eighteen councillors, eight were to be craftsmen, and both groups represented in parliament. By 1681, the Merchant Guild, fearful of losing power, sought and were granted a royal charter, and the Merchant Company of Edinburgh was founded. In the early days, women were also members, often widows who had taken on the business on the death of husbands. After 1701, however, there were no more women members until the twentieth century (Marshall 2015: 14–15). By then, the Merchant Company had three main expenditures: the Widows Fund (established in 1827); helping elderly and infirm tradesmen 'who had fallen on hard times and were unable to work' (Marshall 2015: 35); and above all, setting and funding Merchant Company schools, for which the Merchant Company is today best known in the city, and which I will discuss in the next chapter.

The power and influence of the company can be measured by the company it kept, such as those attending the annual dinner held on 6 December 1902: the lord provosts of Edinburgh and of Leith (separate burghs, of course, until 1920), the local MPs, the president of the Royal Scottish Academy, the chairman of the Northern Lighthouse Board, the chief inspector of schools, the dean of guild, the president of the Scottish Chamber of Agriculture, the secretary of the Carnegie Trust, the moderator of the Edinburgh High Constables, the lord justice general (as guest), the minister of South Leith parish church, the ex-president of the Royal College of Physicians, the president of the Society of Solicitors in the Supreme Courts of Scotland (better known by the initials SSC), the chairman of Leith Chamber of Commerce, and the chairman of the Scottish Trade Protection Society. It was clearly a grand occasion for the great and good as reported in *The Scotsman* newspaper. A toast was made, in surprisingly national(ist) terms, to the lord justice general as follows:

> At the back of our belief in our College of Justice was our respect for our Scottish system of laws which was strongly rooted in the history of our country, and carried back in our minds to the days when the best minds of Scotland were in touch with the intellectual power of the great Latin races of Europe in a bond of sympathy which the English never felt.

In reply, the lord justice general said: 'Everyone associated with the College of Justice appreciated the approbation of such a body as the Merchant Company, so representative of the men who were in the van of the commerce in the city'. The president of the Royal Scottish Academy observed that 'there was a good deal of similarity between the Town Council and the Merchant Company not only because of their antiquity, but because of their connection with various public trusts'. The master of the Merchant Company sounded a note of caution, however, observing that the company 'had become somewhat parochial, and they had closed the doors to a great many good men in the city because they were not merchants', and furthermore, 'some people might say they were going back a little by excluding ladies from the Merchant Company'. The point was reinforced by Lord Provost James Steel in reply, that he 'was sorry that there were so few of the large merchants of the city who come forward to give their services in the Town Council' (*applause*), and said that he believed 'that if a man liked to set his mind to it he could carry on his own business and yet attend to that of the city' (*more applause*).

These comments were straws in the wind for the Merchant Company. In 1914, it was reporting that 'the Company has lost the power of enforcing membership on unwilling entrants; it has also lost the penal powers it once exercised' (*The Scotsman*, 21 March 1914). It was no longer

> a compact association of members with identical and limited interests, but includes merchants, bankers, traders, principals or agents

engaged in any department of commerce, trade, manufacture or handicraft, architects, engineers or surveyors, managing directors, managers and principal officers of banks, insurances or other companies.

In short, the Merchant Company represented 'many various and sometimes antagonistic interests'. Nevertheless, it concluded:

The Company is not merely a company of merchants. It is the Company of Merchants of the City of Edinburgh and nothing that concerns Edinburgh or the district included in the definition should be a matter of indifference to it. In everything that concerns the welfare of this district as a whole the Company has a direct responsibility.

Such was how the Merchant Company saw itself. All this might seem ancient history, but by the final quarter of the twentieth century (1974), Rosalind Marshall was reporting that the membership had reached a record total of 791 members. As a former master of the company had remarked a few years before: 'a high membership was not an important objective in itself, but a token of the Company's stature and significance in the city' (Marshall 2015: 129). Much depended on the importance of family dynasties; Marshall commented:

As well as the Macmillans [director of Melrose's tea firm, and grandson of its founder in 1901], Salvesens [shipping and whaling], Archers[13] [Leith merchants], successive Crabbies [Leith wine and spirit merchants], Dowells [auctioneers], Thins [booksellers], Yerburys [photographers]. This was in part because it was traditional for sons to join fathers in the family business in those days, and in part because they were encouraged to become Company members because of the contacts and prestige that it brought them.

KEEPING THE PEACE: THE HIGH CONSTABLES OF EDINBURGH

Then there is the Society of High Constables of Edinburgh, whose only visible presence in the city these days is on parades associated with the city council. You will recognise them by their dress, described in Wikipedia as follows: 'The uniform of the High Constables is that of morning dress, a black top hat, pinstripe grey trousers and a black morning coat. On non-ceremonial occasions the High Constables may wear a lounge suit and bowler hat' (https://en.wikipedia.org/wiki/High_Constables_of_Edinburgh). The High Constables began as a police force in the city, described by the nineteenth-century historian and town clerk James D. Marwick as follows: 'During the 16th and early part of the 17th centuries, Edinburgh was the scene of frequent and often sanguinary tumults . . . a casual meeting on the streets might at any time give rise to a tulzie[14] [brawl]' (Marwick 1865: 32). Their role was to apprehend 'suspected persons, apprehend those wearing pistols or dagges [daggers], break up affrays at any time of day or night, check bounds or apprehend vagabonds, sturdy beggars or egyptianes [gypsies]'. The Old Town was, according to Marwick (1865: 38) citing contemporary sources, frequented by beggars who

> lie all day on the causey of the Canongate, and with shameful exclamations and cursing not only extorts almous but by their other misbehaviour fashes and wearies . . . sae that hardly ony man of whatsomever quality can walk upon the streets nor yet stand and confer upon the streets, nor under stairs, but they are impeshit [impeded] by numbers of beggars.

The Constables, comprising 'merchantis and craftismen in equal measure', were required to maintain the curfew ('ten hours bell'), examine weights and measures ('Mrs Black the tobacconist gave us all the trouble she could'), armed only with 'short batons for their pockets as long as they paid for them out of their fines' (the city's legendary meanness has a long history). Constables were also required, in 1750, not only to 'inform himself of all beggars or infamous persons, and all *priests and Jesuits, or other persons keeping private masses*'. They were required to 'be in attendance at executions, fires and riots', but it is not clear what being in attendance meant – probably not actually putting out fires or quelling riots. Following a proper police force being established in 1805, by 1810 the society was given permission to use the title 'High Constables of the City of Edinburgh'. Clearly, the less power they had, the more gold chains and regalia they wore, including silver batons and caskets to hold ceremonial keys.

Today, how you get to be a High Constable is not at all clear, and one presumes that the merchants/craftsmen split is no longer observed. Marwick, writing in 1865, noted that despite the city council being empowered to appoint constables, the practice was to permit the society to name its own members, expressed in circumlocutory terms in a 1828 document, that this

> affords the strongest proof of the expediency of such a practice, and as that practice has existed so long, the present members of the society conceive that a privilege has thereby been conferred and acquired by the High Constables, which they feel it to be their imperative duty to maintain. (Marwick 1865: 250)

One important activity, described by Marwick (1865: 290), was holding dinners for the great and good:

> (T)he society has always shewn the most generous hospitality, not only to the magistrates, sheriffs and other official personages, but to a large circle of distinguished citizens. In the notices of these convivial meetings, are recorded many familiar names, whose frequent presence on such occasions attests at once the hospitality and high respectability of the society.

Marwick attests to 'frequent festive meetings', the most important of which were the annual election dinner, the supper (later changed to dinner) on the anniversary of the birthday of the reigning sovereign, and the moderator's farewell dinner. How were they funded?

> Towards the expense of these entertainments, the sums received from the government for taking up the militia and jury lists, the fines levied from defaulters, and such portion of the allowance from the city as was not required for actual and necessary outlays were applicable, but the excess of cost was still large, and had to be borne by the constables individually. (Marwick 1865: 290; with reference to 1862 minute book)[15]

The dinner guests bear remarkable similarity with those attending Merchant Company dinners described above.

Marwick's 1865 'sketch' (running to more than 400 pages) is as much as we learn about the High Constables. A glimpse into its current practices was given in 1997 when the city council insisted that the society admit 'lady members'. In 2019, the first lady moderator, Jacqueline Easson, was elected, described as a senior partner in the employment agency Macploy, and having been a past governor of George Watson's, a Merchant Company school. There is no current public record as to who

High Constables of the City of Edinburgh are these days, but it is reasonable to speculate that the society is still an important nexus between the city council and the Merchant Company, and that the overlap between the society and the Company is strong, despite the absence of elected members of the City of Edinburgh Council. It reinforces the impression that there are non-elected notables who wield informal influence, and make conspiracy hypothesis at least plausible. Which brings us to the New Club.

A CLUB OF ONE'S OWN

If you are interested in who runs Edinburgh, you will be told often enough that you cannot avoid the New Club. It is easy to miss because its entrance at 86 Princes Street resembles a wooden wall, and you would not know that the Club was there, and that is by design. Built in the late 1960s, it replaced a much grander building which the Club, as it is simply known, had owned since 1837.

The Club itself was formed in 1787, an idea conceived at the Caledonian Hunt Ball in Kelso in 1777. The Caledonian Hunt is described in the Club's latest history (McCrae 2004) as 'an association of noblemen and country gentlemen who shared a common interest in field sports, races, balls and social assemblies' (McCrae 2004: 1). Initially drawn from the landed gentry of Roxburghshire, who held balls in the assembly room of New Cross Keys Hotel in Kelso, membership expanded across lowland Scotland, and Edinburgh was the obvious place to meet. Coincidentally, the New Assembly Rooms were opened in Edinburgh's George Street in 1787, and the landed gentry took advantage, committed to the construction of 'polite society', which meant learning how to behave – elocution, dancing and 'rules of good deportment'. 'It was a new club, part of an emerging new polite society. In 1787 the New Club was an appropriate name and so it has remained' (McCrae 2004: 27).

Its initial membership – of 110 – was drawn from the aristocracy, landed gentry and Edinburgh's legal establishment. To be sure, the New Club was part of a general fashion of clubs in Britain, dedicated to fostering polite society by means of assembly, dinners and drink. Many such clubs were political, but, commented Harry Cockburn who wrote (one of) the New

Club's histories, the majority were of social origin, 'coteries of friends meeting for dinners and suppers'.

Clubs came and went; there was a Shakespeare club founded in Edinburgh in 1830, but it survived only for a few years. A University Club was formed in the city in 1864 at 127–8 Princes Street; its trustees were virtually all lawyers. By mid-twentieth century, it had amalgamated with its New Club neighbour, the latter being the last club standing, at least of social repute. The New Club started at Mrs Bayle's Tavern in Shakespeare Square at the east end of Princes Street, and by 1809 acquired a house on St Andrews Square. The club secretary, Lieutenant Colonel Montagu Wynyard, who wrote the first club history in 1900, commented that by 1815,

> It appeared . . . to a majority of the meeting (24 to 20) that a dining-room was a greater need than a billiard-room, and the room erected for a billiard-room was converted into a dining-room and fitted and furnished as such 'at great additional expense to the Club'. (Wynyard 1900: 17)

The New Club has had a succession of histories: first, Lieutenant Colonel Wynyard's in 1900, Harry Cockburn's in 1938, followed in 1988 by Sir Alastair Blair's *Annals*, and finally, Maurice McCrae's account (with plentiful photographs) in 2004. Cockburn was critical of Wynyard's: 'Colonel Wynyard knew little or nothing of Edinburgh in the old days, or of social conditions in Edinburgh, or of Scottish family history' (Cockburn 1938: 156). Cockburn's account tells us much about which rooms were used for which purpose, the arrangements for smoking, and the extent of the drinks bill, but far less about the composition of the membership. Much is said about leisure pursuits, including billiards and pool, and in 1839 twenty members protested against cards being played on Sundays, 'contrary to the principles and objects of the Institution, and which if not checked, is calculated to bring it into disrepute' (Cockburn 1938: 74). There were fierce objections to the 'the damned railway' being built in Princes Street Gardens in 1845. Blair's later history (1988) has more to say on membership, and is more entertainingly tongue-in-cheek, while ending on a moral tone: 'in the hope that the Club will long continue to be a stronghold of Scottish integrity, courtesy, good behaviour and high moral standards, as an example to others in this modern permissive age' (Blair 1988: 124).

Does the New Club Matter?

Why bother with the New Club in trying to puzzle out who runs Edinburgh? It is overtly a social, not a political, club. Its latest historian, Maurice McCrae, commented that in Victorian times, it remained 'firmly apolitical' (McCrae 2004: 45), and refused to host a 'political' dinner: 'Then, as now, it was not the practice for the political persuasion of the members of the New Club to be either noticed or recorded' (McCrae 2004: 45). Alastair Blair describes the club in the 1930s: 'life in the New Club in those old days was like living in a large country house except that it was an entirely male establishment' (Blair 1988: 3).

The New Club presents itself as a social, not a political, establishment, and both Blair and McCrae claimed that the Club is open to (almost) all. Blair described the membership in the round as follows: 'Throughout its first 150 years [1787–1938] the New Club attracted to its membership the best-known men in Scotland – noblemen and country gentlemen . . . and soldiers and sailors and other adventurers, beside a few eminent Edinburgh citizens *from all walks of life*' (Blair 1988: 3) (italics are mine). Maurice McCrae took a similar line in his 2004 history of the New Club: 'in keeping with the intentions of its founders, the membership of the New Club is still drawn from those in a position to advance the interests of Scotland as individuals and leaders *across the spectrum of Scottish life*' (McCrae 2004: 53) (again, italics are mine). The import of both sets of remarks is clear: the New Club is open to all, and reflects Edinburgh, and even Scottish, society as a whole. Without examining the membership, however, this seems highly unlikely, unless one defines 'the spectrum' very narrowly. On the other hand, in the late 1970s, *The Scotsman* diarist made the jest that: 'election to the New Club depended on possession of the following assets: a decent job with Standard Life, education at a good school and the letters TD [Territorial Decoration[16]] after one's name, the holder having been "something in the army"' (McCrae 2004: 100). Being 'open to all' becomes a statement of belief and not of evidence.

What are Clubs For?

Why bother with the New Club, or indeed any club? If it is ostensibly a 'social' club, dedicated to dining, playing billiards, or pool, reading, playing cards, resting and drinking, why assume that it matters as regards running the city in which it is located? The sociologist C. Wright Mills once observed that 'clubs do two things: they signal achievement and create communities' (cited in Matthew Bond 2012: 617). Mills was writing at a time (the 1950s) when studying power locally was much more common than it is today, and the classic urban power studies by Dahl, Polsby and Hunter were in their heyday (as we saw in Chapter 1). Mills characterised the distinctive qualities of elite club membership as follows:

> To the outsider, the club to which the upper-class man or woman belongs is a badge of certification of his status; to the insider the club proves a more intimate or clan-like set of exclusive groupings which places and characterises the man. (Bond 2012: 615)

Note that Mills allows for the involvement of women, but correctly characterises such clubs as in essence a *man's* world. In terms of the New Club, women, or 'ladies', that crucial but ill-defined sub-set of females, have played simply a walk-on, decorative, part, as we shall see later.

Matthew Bond[17] makes the key point about social clubs, that club membership is not a status symbol as such, but requires the need to 'fit comfortably into personal social settings' (Bond 2012: 615); social clubs are sites of leisure and escape; you are not compelled to join. 'It is the existence of choice, whether exercised or not, that allows the study of social clubs to inform us about mutual dependencies between status and other social orders' (Bond 2012: 615). Crucially, you need to know how to behave. Being private clubs, they have the legal right to 'elect' whom they wish, and to run their affairs within the law (having an abundance of lawyers is helpful). Dirty linen need not (and should not) be washed in public, and the annals of the New Club are replete with discretionary words of admonition, and the threat of expulsion, without the law having to be involved.[18] Unless, that is, it is 'staff' who are prosecuted for theft, to discourage others.

The annals of the New Club are much given over to matters of dress and deportment: notably, the wearing of ties and jackets, by men,[19] for women were less of a problem (only if they wore trousers, and certainly not jeans) for there were so few of them admitted, and only as 'associate' members, as the accompaniments of husbands. Matthew Bond's concluding comment is key: 'It is precisely because clubs are exclusive institutions that are not open to all members of the elite that permits them to preserve their distinctive qualities and to maintain identity over decades as most of the country changed' (Bond 2012: 631). It is the careful process of vetting, and 'election', which determines who is 'one of us'. Thereafter, members, by and large, know how to behave.

Staff, that is, employees, are another matter. Most are in the category of faithful retainers, as befits Blair's description of life in the New Club in the 1930s as akin to living in a large country house. 'Inebriated staff' such as two stokers and one plateman were dismissed forthwith in 1949. Fraud (known in the legal trade as 'heavy defalcation') such as liberating the wine cellar led to instant dismissal. Supply and demand of labour could be tricky, as during the Second World War when a high-handed, inebriated member who had been rude to the night porter had to be reminded that 'these days staff were even more difficult to recruit than members' (Blair 1988: 49). The AGM of 1943 recorded the chairman, General Sir Archibald Cameron's comment that 'senior staff and those with some years' service were very loyal and accepted hard work readily, but the lower, fluctuating, staff were of a very different calibre' (Blair 1988: 8). Above-stairs staff ('managers') were key to 'proper behaviour'. In the 1970s,

> the managers recorded their disapproval of a few members who had been seen in slovenly clothing in the Dining Room, and let it be known that for those members who might be in need the Hall Porter kept a spare tie and the valet a spare jacket. (Blair 1988: 94)

Changing Members

As we might expect, the membership of the New Club is drawn from a narrow clientele, as befits a club founded by noblemen and country gentlemen. Broadening out membership is the result of keeping a watchful eye on fee income. Currently (2020–1), the full fee is £880 for those living within twenty-five miles of

Edinburgh, with fees for those furth of twenty-five miles ranging from 37 per cent to 77 per cent of the full fee. Associate members (that is, spouses and partners) pay one-third of the full fee. Broadly speaking, the New Club fee is not out of line with those of London clubs most of which have fees of £1000 to £1500 per annum.[20]

Starting out with 110 members in 1787, the New Club had about ten times that number (1052) a century later, which was as high as it got until mid-twentieth century. Membership in the inter-war years was at its lowest level since the 1840s, so 'it was made easier for the sons of members to join and new group subscriptions were introduced for officers serving in Scotland' (McCrae 2004: 49); as befits a club founded by landed gentry. In 1933, a resolution was passed to admit as extraordinary members all officers of the regular army quartered in Edinburgh on payment of regimental mess subscriptions (Cockburn 1938); such fees were twenty-four guineas for the cavalry regiment, twelve guineas for the Royal Artillery, and twenty-eight guineas[21] for the infantry battalion. Furthermore,

> In conformity with tradition the Club continued to grant Honorary Membership to distinguished persons – members of the Royal Household, staff of the Lord High Commissioner, the Moderator of the General Assembly of the Church of Scotland, and important Foreign Visitors – during periods when they would be in residence in Edinburgh. His Majesty King George VI granted his Patronage in 1937, as his father King George V had done on his accession. (Blair 1988: 2)

In 1948, 'His Royal Highness [Prince Philip] graciously accepted the Club's invitation to become an Honorary Member' (Blair 1988: 16), and became the Club's Patron in 1952 until his death in 2021.

Nevertheless, in the inter-war years, 'the number of the aristocratic members remained unchanged (between 78 and 81) but the proportion of the members listed as "landowner" fell from almost 50 per cent to less than 13 per cent' (Blair 1988: 48). To keep up membership levels, efforts were made to make the New Club more open to 'Edinburgh's young business and professional men, entrepreneurs, bankers, merchants, accountants, doctors and solicitors' (Blair 1988: 49). Such an appeal was not especially new, for in the Victorian period the 'overwhelming

majority of members belonged to the new, expanding and pros-
pering upper middle class' (Blair 1988: 44). By mid-nineteenth
century, around one in five members were titled, twice that proportion were landed gentlemen who added their landed properties to their names, one in five were in the army or the navy,
and the same proportion were mere 'Esquires'. Alastair Blair
observes that

> solicitors were not included in the membership though judges and
> advocates certainly were: physicians were few and far between: the
> members had no wish to meet socially with the 'plumbers' they and
> their colleagues might consult for troublesome problems and ail-
> ments. (Blair 1988: 3)

A curious observation, even allowing for the fact that the
social status of the medical profession has improved in the last
150 years. Actual plumbers, of course, would have little chance
of being elected. The New Club, however, has never allowed
its association with monarchy, military and land to lapse, while
ever-mindful of the importance of money.

Membership numbers recovered after the Second World War,
notably when the New Club merged with the University Club in
1953, which brought in a greater number of academics, scientists
and literary men.[22] Lawyers (the University Club's trustees were
virtually all lawyers) dominated both clubs. By 1987, the nobil-
ity and landed gentry were outnumbered, with lawyers being
the largest professional group among elected 'ordinary' members. By this period, lawyers, churchmen, medics and academics
were about 40 per cent of those elected, and an equal proportion
from banking, finance and commerce (McCrae 2004: 53). The
siting of the New Club had a particular appeal to the legal establishment. A former sheriff principal for Lothians and Borders
who wrote a chapter on lawyers in MacCrae's book commented:
'Until some years ago [writing in 2004] the Club was a popular
place for lunch for judges, sheriffs and advocates on a Friday if
their cases finished early' (O'Brien,[23] in McCrae 2004: 101).

Since its amalgamation with the University Club in the mid-
1950s, New Club membership has been fairly stable, reaching
just under 1300 in 1978. Thereafter, there was an increase in
numbers, to 2160 in 2003, with the admission of 'associate members' who represent about 20 per cent of club membership. Despite claims that Club membership represented

'the spectrum of Scottish life', half of the population were simply ruled out of election; for they were female. It was not until 2010, over 200 years since the New Club was founded, that women could be elected in their own right, or rather as 'Ladies', a social not biological category.[24] To adopt the nomenclature, 'ladies' were admitted as associate members in 1970s (designated as 'Ladies Day'), which meant that they were appendages of their husbands.

'Ladies' had long presented problems for the New Club. Lieutenant Colonel Wynyard's 1900 history notes that in 1859, it was proposed 'to have a room set apart for the reception of ladies, but after considerable discussion, the motion was withdrawn' (Wynyard 1900: 45). 'Ladies' were not excluded entirely. They could come as adornments on special occasions, for example:

> Ladies admitted to the New Club in 1903, were admitted again in 1920 to view the parade to mark the coronation of George V. In 1922, a proposal that ladies should be allowed to dine on the occasion of the Club Ball just failed to command a majority. There was a long delay until ladies become associate members of the New Club in 1970. (McCrae 2004: 46)

Alastair Blair suggested that 'the crux of the problem . . . was the inability of anyone, at the time of the merger [with the University Club] to evolve the creation of a Ladies Annexe' (Blair 1988: 51). This, and much else, was patently special pleading, as if accommodating 'ladies' (still less, women) was a matter of extreme technical difficulty, rather than a matter of institutional misogyny. Thus, Blair observed that 'Lady Day' (25 March 1970) when 'lady associate members' might be elected, 'involved the Committee of Managers with a host of new problems' (Blair 1988: 78).

The truth of the matter was that the New Club was a gentlemen's club with all that entailed; an escape from domestic surroundings, when men ('gentlemen') could 'be themselves'. In 1969, 257 'ladies' could become associate members, but 'their husbands had applied on their behalf' (McCrae 2004: 120). Prior to that, 'ladies' were ornamental accessories:

> After the amalgamation with the University Club in 1954, there was an evening party along the lines of a Victorian soirée with a band playing incidental music. This proved to be a great success; everyone was in evening dress, or mess or hunt uniform and ladies

were bedecked with jewels, tiaras being much in evidence. (McCrae 2004: 122)

When they were admitted after 1970, there was controversy over 'ladies' wearing trousers, and in 1986, 'the managers recorded their displeasure' when one came in jeans. 'The managers' (who included the redoubtable Miss Tweddle, 'lady assistant secretary' from 1972 to 1993) could always be relied upon to maintain standards on behalf of members, who no doubt might claim that this would offend 'the managers', rather than themselves. 'Ladies', until 2010, could only be an associate member if their husbands applied (the formally unmarried but partnered presumably could not apply in any case), and they had to include other 'ladies' 'as proposed signatories. In 1982 a ceiling of 375 associate members was introduced, but there were anomalies. 'After a divorce, could the former wife remain an associated member? Answer No' (Blair 1988: 102). How the Club handles same-sex marriages (leaving 'partnerships' aside) is another question in search of an answer.

Anecdotage

Recall C. Wright Mills's observation that clubs 'create communities'. A key function of creating and maintaining communities is the telling of stories. The social anthropologist Anthony Cohen has observed that the key feature of communities is not what they look like to us (outsiders) but what they look like to their members (Cohen 1985: 20). Cohen's point is that 'community' is symbolically constructed by its members, and reinforced in the telling. He gives the example of 'Erte's greatcoat', a tale told on Whalsay in Shetland about a reclusive character, Erte, whose shabby greatcoat held the secrets of his life, and both metaphorically and practically, was a repository of its keys. The point of the story, told on important occasions, was not that the listeners had not heard it before, but that they had heard it so many times. It functioned to reinforce 'community', for it cannot be understood outwith the symbolic context, and, crucially, validates the community and its members. Cohen observed:

> Members of a community can make virtually anything grist to the symbolic mill of cultural distance, whether it be the effects upon it of some centrally formulated government policy, or matters of

dialect, dress, drinking, marrying or dying . . . People construct their community symbolically, making it a resource and repository of meaning. (Cohen 1986: 17)

So much resides in the skill of the story-teller. The tale has to be told in a 'knowing' way, tongue-in-cheek. Alastair Blair's 1988 New Club *Annals* fits the bill. Here is one such, knowingly told (Blair 1988: 16):

> It was about this time [in 1948] that the late Hon. Henry Douglas Home, while staying in the Club for a period of Army duty, had to look after a female tawny owl wished upon him by a cousin who had adopted it but had now gone off with her naval husband to Malta. He told the tale, in his own inimitable style in his book 'The Birdman' published by Collins in 1977. He kept the owl, in secret, in his bedroom in the Club, and took her daily with him in a box, wherever he went, in Edinburgh or elsewhere. He smuggled food to her from wherever he ate, including the Club dining-room. Such surreptitious purloining of tasty scraps, during a time of food shortages, was occasionally observed by fellow-members, who realised that Henry was hiding something somewhere. The owl sat on his bed-rail at night, and of course answered calls of other owls in the outer world. One evening Henry was called from his room to the telephone and the bird escaped. She took up her position, balancing rather nervously, on the stair bannister. An elderly resident, somewhat inebriated, swooned on seeing her and cut his head open. Henry picked him up with the re-assurance that the apparition was not a monster, simply a tame tawny owl. But for a long time this elderly member was convinced that the bedroom floor was haunted by a vulture.

The point of the story, of course, is not that members can keep tame birds in their bedrooms, nor that strong drink makes you hallucinate, but that it celebrates the eccentricity of both keeper and inebriate, and says: we're that kind of club. As a club historian, Alastair Blair had an eye for that sort of community tale.[25] The fact that the New Club had a number of bedrooms, and even members who lived for decades on the premises,[26] encouraged the practice.

There is more than a whiff of P. G. Wodehouse (known to chums as 'Plum'; this is a world of nicknames) in all of this, akin as it was to public schools, or at least closed communities for whom tale-telling was a key reinforcing of 'who we are' and often built around 'characters'. The story is frequently told since

1907 'of a member coming into lunch, deep in thought, who revolved round with the door and walked away luncheon-less' (Cockburn 1938: 164).

Indeed, the Club's relation to new-fangled technology (such as revolving doors) marks out the eccentricity, that 'modern' appliances take some getting used to, the point being that members are deemed to live 'in another world'. The New Club took pride in being an early pioneer of the water-closet in 1787. In 1881, 'it was proposed that the Club should have a telephone but it was declared by a high official of the Telephone Service that the telephone would never be used much in this country' (McCrae, 2004: 143). Nevertheless, one was installed in 1886. In more modern times, the new-fangled microwave was introduced because

> complaints were still being received about vegetables being of variable quality. After a visit by the Secretary and the Chef to the Open Arms, Dirleton, and Grey Walls, Gullane, the Sub-Committee took on hire for three months a microwave oven. This proved very successful for vegetables. Later on, the Club purchased it outright. (Blair 1988: 106)

What does it all amount to? That the New Club had a complex relationship with modernity and technology; that it strove to retain traditional practices until new and (reluctantly) better ways of doing things emerged; and that eccentricity was accommodated as long as things did not go too far. In short, anecdotage has its functions in creating and reinforcing the certification of membership and community. There are, of course, rules (and the Club has a formal set periodically updated), but if you have to look it up in the rule-book, perhaps the New Club is not for you, even if you wished to join. You have to be a certain kind of chap.

The Politics of the New Club

Recall Maurice McCrae's observation that 'Then, as now, it was not the practice for the political persuasion of the members of the New Club to be either noticed or recorded' (McCrae 2004: 45). In strict regard, the New Club does not do 'politics', and sets its face against association with formal party matters. McCrae himself says that the Club is 'fairly apolitical'; note the

'fairly', because it is manifest that in its practices and culture it
has a particular view of the world, reflected in the character of
its membership. Consider, for example, Rule XI (2002):

> The managers shall have power to admit as Honorary Members:
>   For Life, Princes of the Blood Royal.
>   For such periods as they may think fit, any gentleman in atten-
> dance on Members of the Royal Family, the Senior Representative
> of each of the three Services in Scotland, and in exceptional circum-
> stances such other persons as the managers may decide.

Monarchy and military are central to the honorific status of the
Club. That curious phrase, 'Princes of the Blood Royal', would
appear to rule out the current head of state though not her late
husband who became patron, and 'Blood Royal' seems oddly
quaint, and at odds with ostensible blood mixing which the
British monarchy has indulged for a century or more.

Alastair Blair's earlier (1988) history is more overtly 'political' than McCrae's (2004). Harold Wilson's Labour government
of 1964 is dubbed 'socialist'; and its later manifestations in the
1970s are held responsible for inflation. Thus, 'with the election
of a Labour government in 1974 the Managers had no doubt
that inflation would rise steeply' (Blair 1988: 89); and later, 'by
the end of 1981 the worst period of inflation had passed and the
Conservative Government was successfully reducing the inflation rate year by year' (Blair 1988: 92).

One doubts that inflation happened quite in this way, but
these are revealing comments. A few pages later, Blair refers
to the New Club's 'most distinguished ordinary member, Lord
Home of The Hirsel, KT, whose political career, mostly at the
Foreign Office, from 1931 onwards, but a year 1963–4 as Prime
Minister, was second to none' (Blair 1988: 99). That is a revealing, and contentious, judgement, unlikely to be shared by many
political historians. Blair's history ends with the aspiration that
the New Club 'will continue to be a stronghold of Scottish
integrity, courtesy, good behaviour and high moral standards,
as an example to others in this modern permissive age' (Blair
1988: 124).

These are, manifestly, 'political' statements in their own
terms, and revealing of the Club's cultural zeitgeist. It does set
its face against overt non-social practices, because, to re-quote
C. Wright Mills, 'to the insider the club proves a more intimate

or clan-like set of exclusive groupings which places and characterizes the man' (in Bond 2012: 615). Certain spheres are not for display or to be set out formally. After all, Rule 1 states: 'The purpose of the Club shall be the association of members primarily for social purposes.' Blair again: 'Early in 1982 one of the managers complained that the Club was becoming too commercial, members having no inhibitions as to discussing business matters quite openly' (Blair 1988: 118). This was 'vigorously resisted' by the members at the time, and a motion to amend Rule 1 was withdrawn. In essence, rules are 'procedural', not 'behavioural'; how members are elected, running the AGM, and so forth. Members are assumed to know how to behave as befits membership of the New Club.

There is, of course, nothing to stop members talking about what they like, but setting aside place and time to have business meetings (other than as pertain to running the Club) is out of order. McCrae noted that having a business room on the premises encouraged its use for business. Said the Club secretary in the 1960s, somewhat tongue-in-cheek, 'there must be somewhere where members can interview prospective gamekeepers' (McCrae 2004: 153). So the New Club does not allow 'politics' (or 'business') as such but such practices imbue its very existence. Its values are deeply conservative, though not formally Conservative. It is a haven in a fairly hostile world into which members can retreat and 'be themselves', while knowing that other selves share a similar world-view. It would a straightforward matter to have social conversations with one's peers (and even Peers).

In the context of our question – 'who runs Edinburgh?' – there is patently no New Club view, nor can one conclude that New Club members themselves run Edinburgh, although individually they are likely to wield considerable economic, social and cultural power in their own right. While in many ways, the New Club is *in* Edinburgh but not especially *of* it (recall its earlier history as a social base for landed gentry), one imagines that starting a conversation on who runs the city would be highly productive and illuminating.[27]

The New Club is a place of formal informality, where no discussion is off-limits if it arises 'naturally': after all, it is a *social* club in which members can talk about what they like. It occupies that symbolic space between home and business, and is not constrained by discussion over lunch or dinner in a public restaurant where the need to be discreet is paramount. Claims that membership is drawn from 'all walks of life' or 'the spectrum of Scottish society' are not to be taken literally, but are indications that the Club is a place of ease and familiarity, populated by people 'like themselves'. The boundaries are policed such that excluding 'politics' or 'business' in formal terms does not mean these are not topics of conversation subject to eavesdropping.

CONCLUSION: KNOWING WHO YOUR FRIENDS ARE

To many, even its citizens, Edinburgh is a secretive place in which what matters is who you know. We are dealing here in plausibilities, for the more secretive an organisation is, the more likely people are to think that it runs things. The perambulations of the High Constables might seem like a performative feature of the city, another entertainment, perhaps, at festival times, and it may be no more than that. The Merchant Company of the City of Edinburgh may once have been an organisation of considerable power and influence when economies were highly local, and who you knew was a matter of business success or failure, if not one of life and death. The Honourable Company of Edinburgh Golfers may indeed simply play golf, but knowing who your golfing friends are might well come in useful beyond the eighteenth tee. The New Club may be a secret place behind closed doors (if you could work out where the doors are on Princes Street), and may simply be a locus for likeminded folk to drink and dine. Edinburgh, however, conveys a sense, more than most, of decisions made behind the hand, largely because organisations such as these are closed; the outsider (like the author) has no way of finding out who the members are, and hence, what their influence might be in running things.

This is a world, by repute, of freemasonry, at least in the metaphorical use of that term, of secret associations between men set up to help each other, and if necessary, to employ subtle signs of membership. Freemasonry, with a capital F, is something else, and may well operate in Edinburgh which reputedly houses the oldest lodge extant in the world: Lodge of Edinburgh (Mary's Chapel) No. 1, dating from 1599, once in South Bridge, now at 19 Hill Street. Periodically, the media gets interested in Freemasonry,[28] mainly because it employs esoteric rituals, and rather more darkly, helps out its own, the antithesis of getting there on merit (or indeed cost). We have no way of knowing whether Freemasonry as such is a significant force in politics, business and social life in the city.[29]

Edinburgh, arguably, is especially prone to conspiratorial views because historically the 'old school tie' mattered so much. The hierarchy of 'independent' schools, many run by the Merchant Company, were deemed to provide significant cultural capital to be traded in the job and business markets, when local economies were more self-contained than they are today. Hence, we will explore the Edinburgh schools system in the next chapter.

NOTES

1. These, of course, are not unique to Edinburgh, but seem particularly apposite.
2. Lum hats are top hats, so described in this Wikipedia entry: <https://sco.wikipedia.org/wiki/Lum_hat>.
3. But also at the Catholic Cathedral in York Place, and the Jewish Synagogue on the Southside, so as not to be thought sectarian.
4. The Honourable Company of Edinburgh Golfers took out a patent on their name with Edinburgh council in 1800.
5. The list of members of the New Club is not available to non-members. The 2008 list was lodged in National Library of Scotland (NLS) by Iain Gordon Brown along with other papers on the New Club, to whom researchers, such as the author, are grateful. As the former principal curator of manuscripts in the National Library of Scotland, Dr Brown clearly knew the value of such documents.
6. In recent years, however, women have recovered their identities and names in New Club lists.
7. Described by the editor as follows: This first (1986) edition contains 5,000 biographies of people from all walks of Scottish life, including politics and public service, law, religion and education, business and finance, science and medicine, the arts and sport. It should be emphasised that the title of the book means what it says, and that prominent Scots living outwith Scotland are not included. Entries are arranged in alphabetical order, according to surname. Each entry contains full name, education and career, publications, recreations and address.
8. By way of comparison, in 1986, 8 per cent of elites lived in Glasgow, and in 2019, 11 per cent.
9. In 1986, it was fewer than two-thirds (63 per cent).

10. 'Education authority' schools is the correct descriptor rather than 'state' or 'public' schools.
11. The likes of Glasgow High School, Robert Gordon's in Aberdeen, the High School of Dundee, and Dollar Academy in Clackmannanshire.
12. Giving a 'recreation' in the *Who's Who* entry was more common in 1986 than in 2019: in the former, 85 per cent of the Edinburgh-based elite did so, while in the latter period it had dropped to 64 per cent. Among Scottish elites as a whole, 68 per cent gave a recreation in 1986, compared with 59 per cent in 2019. Those residing in Edinburgh plainly were more likely to give recreations in their *Who's Who* entry.
13. A good example is the Archer family. By 1997, the Master of the Merchant Company was Gilbert Baird Archer whose long and successful business career had included terms of office as President of the Edinburgh Chamber of Commerce, Deputy President of the British Chamber of Commerce, Master of the Worshipful Company of Gunmakers, and Moderator of the High Constables of the Port of Leith, and Deputy Lieutenant of Peeblesshire.
14. Marwick defines tulzies as 'broils [*sic*] or street combats of the day'. The term is best known as the title of Robert Burns's poem 'The Holy Tulzie' (1784), which mocks a dispute between two ministers about parish boundaries. The letter 'z' is a yogh, written as a 3, resembling a lower-case z, and remains in surnames such as 'Menzies' and 'Dalziel' (pronounced 'Menyies' and 'Dalyell').
15. Among their lists of dinner guests are: the Earl of Errol, the Lord High Constable of Scotland, Lord Melville, Baron Clerk Rattray, Baron Sir Patrick Murray, Lord Advocate Maconochie (after-wards Lord Meadowbank), Principal Baird, Sir Henry Jardine, the Right Honourable W. Dundas MP, Professor Wilson, Dean of Faculty (afterwards Lord) Moncreiff, Lord Advocate (afterwards Lord) Jeffrey, Solicitor-General (afterwards Lord) Cockburn, Sir John (afterwards Lord Chancellor) Campbell, Sir James Gibson-Craig, Sir Thomas Dick-Lauder, Leonard Horner, Lord Advocate (afterwards Lord) Murray, Lord Advocate (afterwards Lord) Rutherford, Sir William Allan, Principal Lee, Drs Inglis, Brunton, Dickson, Peddie, Grant, Alexander, Lee and Hanna, Dr Abercromby, George Combe, Charles Cowan MP, Major-General Walker, Commander of the Forces, N. B., George Harvey, and others.
16. According to Wikipedia, the Territorial Decoration (TD) was a military medal of the United Kingdom awarded for long service in the Territorial Force and its successor, the Territorial Army. This award superseded the Volunteer Officer's Decoration when the

Territorial Force was formed on 1 April 1908, following the enact-
ment of the Territorial and Reserve Forces Act 1907, which was a
large reorganisation of the old Volunteer Army and the remaining
units of militia and Yeomanry. However, the militia were transferred to the Special Reserve rather than becoming part of the
Territorial Force. A recipient of this award is entitled to use the
letters 'TD' after their name (post-nominal).

17. Bond was examining the club affiliations of members of the House
of Lords, but his key points have much wider implications.

18. 'In June 1947 a member who had the misfortune to be convicted of
a minor breach of the very stiff currency regulations, wrote asking
whether he must resign from the Club. The Committee decided
that his conviction should be ignored' (Blair 1988: 15).

19. Alastair Blair records: 'a little discipline had to be applied at the
1984 and 1985 Balls to prevent the removal of jackets by some of
the younger members' (Blair 1988: 109).

20. For fees for comparable London clubs, see <https://www.thehand-
book.com/londons-best-private-members-clubs/>.

21. Roughly £1,900 at 2020 prices: <https://www.measuringworth.
com/index.php>.

22. The University Club had been founded in 1864. Its prime mover
was Sir Lyon Playfair, Professor of Chemistry at Edinburgh
University.

23. Sir Frederick O'Brien was a former sheriff principal for Lothians
and Borders.

24. Accordingly, I will use quotation marks around 'Ladies', except
when it is used in quotations, to indicate that it is entirely a social
construction; much like the term 'race'. Its significance lies entirely
in its social/cultural usage, not in its facticity.

25. Alastair Blair is described as KCVO, TD, WS.

26. One such was Ivor Guild who joined the New Club aged twenty-
six, and lived in a 'Club flat' for fifty years. He recorded his
'Memoir of Half a Century' in McCrae's edited 2004 history
(Chapter 9).

27. The author, not being a member of the New Club, can only assume
this to be the case.

28. BBC Scotland, for example, ran a couple of programmes in March
2018 on Scottish (and Edinburgh) Freemasonry: <https://www.
bbc.co.uk/news/uk-scotland-43385303>.

29. The author has no inside knowledge of Freemasonry, although he
has been on the receiving-end of curious handshakes in the city
over the years.

6

What School did You Go To?
Education and Status in Edinburgh

Take part in any social occasion in Edinburgh, and sooner or later someone will ask you this question. The same one is asked in the west of Scotland – but that is about religion – which foot you kick with, is the cruder version. In Edinburgh, this is a question about social class, or more precisely, social status. It is a question not about what you earn, but about your connections and social networks, and possibly even your values. It seeks to place you in the scheme of things, the degree to which you are well-connected. If you reply, like this author, that you were not educated in Edinburgh, then the question is quickly judged to be irrelevant. It is really about being educated in the city and where you fit in socially.

Why should it matter so much? Because around one-fifth of secondary school pupils in Edinburgh attend 'private' schools, a much higher percentage than other Scottish cities. How we describe such schools is a vexed question (hence the quotation marks around 'private'). Perhaps the most common epithet is 'Independent' schools, in juxtaposition to 'public' schools, but arguably neither of those terms is helpful. Because such schools have charitable status, they are able to offset costs against tax – a bone of political contention – and, one might aver, they are as a consequence not truly 'Independent'. The term also implies that other schools are 'dependent' (on state funding). Then there is the distinction between 'public' and 'private' schools, but that distinction is bedevilled by its misuse in England, where 'public' means no such thing. In any case, in Scotland 'public school' is literally etched in to the stonework of many primary schools to render a nonsense such a descriptor for what are in essence 'private' schools. The preference in this article is for 'fee-paying' which has the merit of being a categorical term, at least since the mid-1970s when 'grant-aided' schools were abolished; to be discussed later. On the other side, the term 'education authority' schools has the merit of being self-descriptive in terms of

Figure 6.1 Climbing the ladder; courtesy of the Robert Blomfield collection

how they are governed – by the local authority. So throughout this chapter, the terms 'fee-paying' and 'education authority' are preferred.

PAYING THE FEES

If we take as a rough rule of thumb that one in five senior school pupils in Edinburgh attend fee-paying schools, then by definition four-fifths do not, and substantial numbers attend old senior secondary education authority schools (the likes of Boroughmuir, Royal High, James Gillespie's, Trinity and Broughton). Furthermore, fee-paying schools are considerably stratified by levels of fees charged.[1] Thus, 'Merchant Company' schools such as Stewart's-Melville/Mary Erskine (one wonders who dreamt up 'ESMS' as a brand name[2]), and Heriot's (never a Merchant Company school) charge similar fees for day pupils (2021–2 figures): to wit, ESMS (£13,038 for senior pupils), Heriot's (£13,970), and Watson's (£13,551). St George's School for Girls charges £15,288, and Edinburgh Academy, £15,342. Considerably higher fees (given here for boarding pupils) are charged by Loretto (in Musselburgh) at £36,195; Merchiston Castle (marketing slogan, 'Boys First!') at £35,880, and Fettes, modelling itself as a 'public' school on the English model of the same, at £36,495. These latter three schools are geared to taking boarders (as well as some day pupils). Comparators outwith Edinburgh have fees on a par with the Edinburgh 'day' schools: the Glasgow cluster of fee-paying schools are Hutcheson's (£13,149), Glasgow Academy (£13,224), the High School of Glasgow (£14,211), and St Aloysius RC (Jesuit) school (£14,130). Aberdeen's Robert Gordon's school charges day pupils £13,995, the High School of Dundee £13,650, and Dollar Academy in Clackmannanshire £14,571. Boarding schools such as Glenalmond (£38,100) and Strathallan (£36,036), both in Perthshire, and Gordonstoun in Moray (£40,050) compete with the likes of the Edinburgh contingent (Loretto, Merchiston Castle and Fettes). We would expect, then, that this variable market would attract different social clientele. Most of the fee-paying schools have gone co-educational, with the notable exceptions of St George's (girls) and Merchiston Castle (boys).[3]

The caste-quality of fee-paying schools lies deep in their history. Geoffrey Walford, who wrote about the Scottish assisted-places scheme in the late 1980s, provided a succinct history:

> The Merchant Company of Edinburgh has played a major part in the provision of private education in Edinburgh, and hence in Scotland, for nearly 300 years. George Heriot's Hospital, a charitable institution for the education and welfare of fatherless boys and run by the Town Council and City Ministers under the terms of a bequest, opened in 1659. In 1694 The Merchant Company found that it had received a similar bequest from Mary Erskine for them to establish and run a corresponding hospital for orphaned girls. It opened the Merchant Maiden Hospital in 1695, and further bequests led to the establishment of the Trades Maiden Hospital in 1704 and George Watson's in 1734. It also accepted the management of Daniel Stewart's Hospital in 1860. (Walford 1988: 144)

The 1860s Argyll Commission on Scottish schools was critical of the 'endowed hospitals', and, as Robert Anderson commented:

> (I)n 1870 the residential hospitals were turned into large fee-paying day schools for the middle class; a small core of foundationers survived, but no longer lived in. Heriot's was to follow the same path in 1885, after years of controversy, and amid charges that the poor were being despoiled of their rights. (Anderson 1983: 174)

Such claims rest on judgements about precisely whose Heriot's 'faitherless bairns' were being catered for, and Anderson is of the view that the Merchant Company schools in particular were catering for the offspring of the merchant class suffering from 'genteel impoverishment'; 'the boys mostly went into shops and merchants' and lawyers' offices, and the girls became teachers or governesses' (Anderson 1983: 174). Heriot's, in the 1860s, had 180 boys 'living a somewhat cloistered life, and educated free by a well-qualified staff' (Anderson 1983: 173), most subsequently apprenticed to a trade, with a few receiving a bursary to go to university. Comments Anderson: 'Heriot's offered real opportunities of social mobility through the quality of its teaching and the existence of university bursaries, and those opportunities were prized by the city's working and lower middle classes' (Anderson 1983: 174).

Eton of the North

Nonetheless, 'the vagueness of the benefactors' intentions often gave the trustees the power to indulge their private views' (Anderson 1983: 175), none more so than those of William Fettes, former lord provost, who died in 1836 leaving his fortune (£166,000, or over £15m at 2018 prices): '(F)or the maintenance, education, and outfit of young people, whose parents have either died without leaving sufficient funds for that purpose, or who, from innocent misfortune during their own lives are unable to give suitable education to their children' (Anderson 1983: 175). It is likely that Fettes himself envisaged a 'hospital' on the lines of George Watson's, but his trustees thought Edinburgh over-provided for in that respect, and were minded to found a 'Public School' on the English model (hence, 'Eton of the North').

Fettes's money might have supported fifty foundationers drawn from such classes as would use a hospital school, a set-aside soon lost as Fettes (the school) moved rapidly upmarket. Fettes's trustees did not quite get away with it, and the Radical Liberal (and lord provost) Duncan McLaren alleged a misuse of funds left ostensibly for the welfare of Edinburgh. McLaren thought that 'the history of Fettes demonstrated both the selfishness of the professional classes, as opposed to the "mercantile" classes to which he belonged, and the evils of "close" bodies like the Fettes trustees compared to popular representation' (Anderson 1983: 192). McLaren sought to break up Fettes into something resembling Heriot's, but did not succeed. 'When is this transfer from poor to rich to stop?', he asked rhetorically (Roberts 2009: 26). Nevertheless, 'the campaign against Fettes had been a powerful one. It was supported by the town council, and in the parliamentary debate which was the last attempt at opposition three of the city's four MPs spoke against the scheme' (Anderson 1983: 26). As late as the 1960s, the school was required to sell eighteen acres to allow Telford College to be built, as well as fourteen acres for the Police HQ (known simply as 'Fettes' for those who know their Ian Rankin novels), and in 1965 after a public enquiry, it was forced to sell fifteen acres to enable Broughton High School to be built. Evidently, Fettes school was a major landowner to be reckoned with on the north-west side of Edinburgh.

Day Schools

So too, by irony, was Heriot's whose trustees made judicious purchase of land, and the trust was feu superior for much of the New Town such that 'as the city expanded, rents and feu-duties poured in' (Anderson 1983: 177). Thus, the income of Heriot's rose from £4,389 in 1800 (about £350,000 at 2018 prices, to £18,546 in 1871 (worth £1.7m today). Heriot's trustees were street-smart enough to develop 'outdoor schools', and by 1868 had about thirteen in the city, educating more than 3,000 pupils.[4] Comments Anderson: 'The Heriot's free schools were efficient and popular, but the creation of the school board made their position anomalous, and they were prime examples of that "indiscriminate" free education of which experts disapproved strongly' (Anderson 1983: 177). Endowments were used to buy land, in turn ploughed into bursaries for sundry faitherless bairns and foundationers.

George Watson's was reformed in 1868, day pupils being sent to the High School. By 1870, five large fee-paying schools had replaced the old hospitals, notably Watson's (for boys), Daniel Stewart's, the Edinburgh Institution for Young Ladies (formerly the Merchant Maiden), and George Watson's school for girls in George Square. The headmaster of the Edinburgh Institution saw the writing on the wall. The Merchant Company's system:

> does much more to cheapen the highest secondary education to those who need no cheapening, than to render it accessible to people in humble life. It is much more a boon to ladies and gentlemen than to working men. £10 a year for a girl, and £6 for a boy, are sums that cannot be paid by working people. (Anderson 1983: 181)

Outdoor schools on the Heriot's model were transferred on the recommendation of the Balfour Commission in the 1880s to the local public school board, and hospitals became fee-paying day schools, with most endowments ending up in scholarships and bursaries. Schools, notably those like James Gillespie's lacking substantial endowments, were transferred from the Merchant Company to the school board in 1908. Comments Anderson: 'Public opinion came to regard [endowed schools] as "independent" and to reject "political interference" in their affairs, a development which would have surprised the 19th century reformers' (Anderson 1983: 250).

To focus on fee-paying day schools is to over-simplify the plethora of such establishments. At the 'top end' were those directly modelled on English public schools, the first such being Glenalmond (1847), founded by Episcopalians (including William Gladstone): in Anderson's words, 'expensive and exclusive . . . a somewhat exotic import to the Scottish scene' (Anderson 1983: 20). The aristocracy sent their sons to England before the opening of 'public' schools such as Glenalmond and Fettes. The rector of Edinburgh's High School was critical of the aristocracy, and of Fettes in particular, describing it as 'an institution . . . opposed in the strongest manner to what is best in Scotland and Europe' (Anderson, 1983: 67). The High School had its own critics, and those wanting an education in Latin and Greek 'to promote classical learning', such as Walter Scott, Francis Jeffrey and Henry Cockburn, helped to found the Edinburgh Academy in 1824 near the Water of Leith on the city's north side. Today, a co-educational school, the Academy charges a premium fee of £14,121, marginally more than St George's.

Educating Ladies

Educating boys at school was the norm; referring to 'public schools' in Scotland goes all the way back to the Reformation. Girls deemed worthy of an education historically had home governesses (thus, in private). The Scottish Institution for the Education of Young Ladies was founded in 1833 in Queen Street (known, unsurprisingly, as 'Queen Street'), and later became Mary Erskine's. A bewildering array of girls' schools came and went. Thus, St Denis's (an allusion to its French origins) occupied as many as six houses in only thirty-three years from 1855; a bus went round the town in the morning picking up pupils. Cranley's started as Brunstane School, then moved to Merchiston/Polwarth. St Serf's was at Albany Street, then moved to Abercromby Place in 1882. Other establishments included the Trades Maiden Hospital (1704), Bell Academy, Grange Home School, Craigmount School (1874) in Dick Place, Strathearn College (1908, for cookery and domestic science), Miss Gamgee's School in Alva Street (1895), St Hilda's in Liberton, St Trinnean's (made famous by Ronald Searle as St Trinian's, latterly based at St Leonard's in the Pollock Halls of Residence), the Ministers' Daughters College at Esdaile in Kilgraston Road, St Margaret's Ladies College on twin sites at Newington and Morningside (travelling between them made easier by the south-suburban railway line), and George Watson's Ladies College at George Square. Catholic nuns ran a school at St Catherine's convent in Lauriston, St Margaret's in Whitehouse Loan, and at Craiglockhart; the latter building was made famous as a reha-bilitation centre for soldiers suffering shell shock in the First World War (recuperating war poets such as Siegfried Sassoon and Wilfred Owen), and from 1920 until 1981, was a Catholic teacher-training college. Lest we think that nuns (of the Catholic Order of the Sacred Heart) were above this sort of thing, one former pupil of Craiglockhart school told author Alasdair Roberts: 'Mary and I both had slight Fife accents when we first went, and we weren't allowed in the school plays until we got rid of them. No dialects were permitted, so we had elocution lessons which cost extra' (Roberts 2007: 189).

The doyenne of them all was St George's, which began at Melville Street in the West End, moved to Ravelston, and finally to Murrayfield in 1901. St George's was essentially a 'political' foundation, and its founders were prominent in the campaign for the admission of women to Edinburgh University, and more generally to women's suffrage. In 1867, special classes were arranged by sympathetic (male) academics at the university such as Professor Godfrey Thomson, the pioneer of IQ testing, and Simon Laurie, professor of the theory, history and practice of education. In England, the Girls' Public Day School Company/ Trust (GPDST) had been set up by Maria Grey[5] in Chelsea in 1873. In 1886, St George's Training College for the purposes of training well-educated women to be teachers in secondary or higher schools was established in Edinburgh, an obvious choice because 'it jealously guarded the Scottish institutions of the church, law, education, banking and finance' (Shepley 2008: 4). Furthermore:

(t)he women of the Edinburgh movement belonged to the network of influence and social solidarity which characterised the new town. Their fathers – merchants, bankers, lawyers, landowners, doctors, well-placed clergymen and professors – had the means to provide their daughters with the leisure and connections essential to their success. (Shepley 2008: 4)

In the days when walking to school was the norm, Melville Street was highly convenient for denizens of Edinburgh's New Town. Comments Roberts: 'a suburban railway also helped parents to avoid the local school: that sense of escaping the "rough" children lies deep in the Edinburgh psyche'[6] (Roberts 2007: 16–17). The curriculum at St George's was unashamedly academic, eschewing 'traditional accomplishments' for women (like running a home), and having no truck with quaint notions that women's brains were not suitable for studying maths. Having no endowments to rely on, fees were slightly higher than the norm (roughly nowadays on a par with Edinburgh Academy, and more than £1,000 p.a. above the 'Merchant Company' standard). Nigel Shepley, who taught history at St George's and who wrote the school history, observed:

> It must be said that there was an element of class consciousness in the rejection of the older [Merchant Company] schools, the kind of snobbery which came as naturally to the Victorians as their prudery, cabinet puddings, and empire building. The very term 'Merchant Company' smacked of trade and business. St George's from the beginning attracted the daughters of professional men and the upper classes. Oddly, by our standards, this was the one feature of the school which was least criticised. It was simply taken for granted. (Shepley 2008: 34)

Fees, set at one guinea annually for entrance, and six guineas per term, were higher than those at Merchant Company schools. The whole point of St George's was 'to serve as a model for girls' secondary schooling in liberal subjects, to further the campaign for women's higher education, to facilitate the training of women teachers, and to prove their worth on secondary schools' (Shepley 2008: 35). Classes were smaller; no prizes were awarded; numerical marks were avoided. Education was serious, enlightened and progressive.

The social clientele seems not to have changed a great deal over the century. Shepley, who as school historian had access to these data, comments:

> The school register and census returns show that the pupils of the 1890s came from professional, middle class and prosperous business families. An analysis of the school roll in 2000 showed little change. Unlike some Edinburgh schools, St George's never had any large endowments. Its income has come almost entirely from fees which, for one girl, would take half of the average income of those

in the lower fifty percent of workers in the United Kingdom. The school has therefore been socially homogeneous and largely exclusive throughout its history. (Shepley 2008: 151)

St George's seems to have been the (anonymised) setting for Sara Delamont's ethnographic study in the early 1970s which she called St Luke's, according to Alasdair Roberts (2007: 202), but in truth its distinctive features are not hard for any reader to spot.[7] Delamont identified distinct 'social' categories at St Luke's which she calls debs, dollies and swots and weeds. By and large, 'debs and dollies' came from entrepreneurial homes, whereas 'swots and weeds . . . were preparing to enter the intellectual elite of the country' (Delamont, in Walford 1984: 80). Thus

the "swots and weeds" valued St Luke's for its academic standards and its music. They actively disliked the sports and the religion, but did not mind the uniform or the rules. In contrast, the "debs and dollies" hated the uniform, complained of "petty" rules about behaviour and deportment, but were (mostly) happy with the sporting programme. They saw schooling as about facts, and objected when teachers tried to monitor other aspects of their lives. (Delamont 1984b: 81)

The rapidly changing history of girls' schools in Edinburgh is reflected in Roberts's observation that 'of the 34 independent schools recognised under the 1882 Educational Endowments etc Act, only 13 were left by the 1920s' (Roberts 2007: 202). Nor did it end there. St Denis and Cranley schools amalgamated with each other and then with St Margaret's, which itself had consolidated onto the Newington site, only to close down in 2010, ostensibly under pressure from co-educational schools. The Ministers' Daughters College in Kilgraston Road closed in 1969, as did St Margaret's Convent School in 1986. The move to co-education saw George Watson's Ladies College amalgamate with the boys' school at Colinton Road in 1974. Only St George's, with its distinctive ethos and culture, provides single-sex education for girls, although Mary Erskine's ('single-sex but closely twinned' as its website has it) with a separate site in Ravelston imbues it with distinctive space separate from Stewarts-Melville on Queensferry Road less than two miles distant.

Historically, in educational terms, at independent schools, girls were treated as after-thoughts to boys, so schools were traditionally geared to be extensions of the home, and, indeed, often took place in private houses. On the other hand, in public schools[8] from the sixteenth century, girls were taught alongside boys. Their opportunities beyond what is now called the primary stage were much more limited, but the few who did make it through to mathematics and Latin in the nineteenth century were treated as what Lindy Moore calls 'invisible scholars'; for the time, that was remarkably progressive (Moore 1984).

In private schools, the focus was on 'lady-like' activities while careful not to imply 'housewifery', but to oversee servants until these became a scarce commodity. It is hard to escape the notion that 'training for marriage' was the aim, but stymied by single-sex education unless you could rely on your brothers' friends in the marriage market. St George's was the (fierce) exception, having no truck with notions that maths and sciences were not womanly pursuits. In any case, the more state regulation in terms of teaching standards, curriculum review and building requirements were imposed, the fewer small single-sex schools survived. Girls began to receive a proper education in maths and science, and not simply art and music. As girls went in numbers to university, credentials mattered, and the academic rankings of some schools were not adequate, and in any case, co-educational education solved many of the problems of scale and costs.

Social networking mattered in this bourgeois city. One respondent told Alasdair Roberts:

> The culture of Edinburgh, the way its 'society' was organised, was also a shock because I soon found out that if your parents did not meet certain people, doors did not open easily. Life seemed to revolve around what your father did and what school you attended. (Roberts 2007: 202)

One wonders whether 'the marriage market' still operates that way in Edinburgh, though it is likely that university now provides much greater choice and opportunity for partnering, especially where marriage itself is a less favoured institution.

Attacking Fees: The End of Grant-aid

It would be easy to assume that fee-paying schools in Edinburgh and elsewhere have always been 'independent'. Not so. The Public Schools Commission[9] [sic] reported that in 1969 there were twenty-nine schools receiving grants directly from the

Scottish Education Department. All but two charged fees, and were known as 'grant-aided' schools (Walford 1987). Unlike direct-grant schools in England, the amount of the grant 'was related to the total maintenance expenditure rather than being a fixed per capita sum and was largely used to substantially reduce fees for all fee payers well below what they would otherwise have been' (Walford 1987: 114–15). In 1968, there were over 12,000 pupils in the secondary sector of grant-aided schools, of whom about 1500 had their fees paid in whole or in part by the local education authority. Hence, around 80 per cent of pupils paid full fees. Walford observed that in England only 28 per cent paid full fees in direct-grant schools. He commented:

> (T)he direct grant schools were an essential part of the maintained sector, acting as 'super' grammar schools, while the grant aided schools were an extension of the independent sector selecting not only on academic ability but also on ability and willingness to pay reduced but still substantial school fees. (Walford 1987: 115)

Fee-paying had long been a feature of the Scottish educational tradition, and until the early 1970s there were a small number of selective schools within the 'public' sector which charged fees, the likes of the Royal High School of Edinburgh, and Glasgow High School.

There was a view held, notably by John Highet in his 1969 book with the revealing title *A School of One's Choice: A Sociological Study of the Fee-paying Schools in Scotland*, that virtually anyone could afford school fees. In a splendid expression of his prejudices, he observed that:

> Many working-class people annually spend sums much greater [than Glasgow High's top figure of £234 2s. p.a.] than those at the bottom and middle of that range, and more than £23 on (for example) smoking, drinks, entertainment and, in some cases, bingo and other forms of betting and gambling conventional in their group culture. (Highet 1969: 184)

Thus, 'it is matter of priorities in personal and family values' (Highet 1969: 184). Walford, nonetheless, was critical, citing the fact that the Royal High School of Edinburgh charged £41.42, and all those living outwith the city paid £65 in total. There was also the matter of school uniforms and other extras to be taken into account. He pointed out that in 1966 average weekly earnings were only £20.78 so:

> (a)t the very minimum the fees were half an average week's earnings and four times that amount for the major schools. Such amounts are certainly not 'very small'. Further, those fees were at almost their lowest level ever in 1968 as the range of fees had remained unchanged since 1952. (Walford 1987)

If, in 1951, the average weekly wage was £8.60, even the cheapest fees cost well over an average week's pay.

We will return to Highet's curious but inadvertently interesting study presently, but first we need to consider what happened to grant-aided schools, this seemingly half-way house between public and private educational sectors, in Scotland. Says Walford,

> most of the grant-aided schools were highly academically selective and, in contrast to the direct grant schools, fee paying was not a sign of failure, but of academic success, even if it was success only from within those families able and willing to pay the fees. (Walford 1988: 142)

Unlike England, Scotland did not have a tradition of boarding schools; it was a day pupil market in the cities.

In 1974, Labour returned to power, minded to phase out both grant-aided and direct-grant schools. At the time (1974/5) grant-aided schools received just over £4m annually from the Scottish Education Department. There was planned to be a rapid reduction to less than £1m in the 'assisted places scheme' (APS) by the mid-1980s. Walford observed: 'Where in 1973 the grant-aid has supported more than 40% of expenditure, by 1978/9 this figure was down to less than 10%' (Walford 1988: 145). Opposition was mobilised by the Scottish Council of Independent Schools (SCIS) run from the office of the Merchant Company of Edinburgh, who, of course, had their own schools, and interests, to defend. The reduction in grant-aid saw the closure of John Watson's school in the West End in 1976, which saw no future without the grant, and merged with its George Watson's namesake.

The election of a Conservative government in 1979 saw the creation of the 'assisted places scheme' (APS). The associated grant was designed to cover about 20 per cent of grant-aided schools' running costs, around £3.39m in 1980/1, and there was a sleight-of-hand increase planned by the Scottish Office to bring it to £4.43m by 1986/7. Ultimately, however, the last payments for grant-aid were made in 1984/5. Walford observed: 'the APS is an excellent example of how a general policy decision made in London can be shaped by Scottish pressure groups in such a way that their interests are preserved and enhanced' (Walford 1988: 146). APS in Scotland was presented in terms of 'parental choice' rather than on academic selection, as befitted the ruling political ideas of the Thatcher government (recall Highet's book title, *A School of One's Choice*).

In 1986/7, there were forty-one APS schools in Scotland. Parental choice gave considerable leeway to schools as regards selection, and some gave preference to the children of former pupils or, as in the case of the Merchant Company, the children of its members. It turned out that the schools were using a high proportion of the APS money to help parents who had already opted into the private sector, particularly when death or redundancy might have meant pupils leaving school. It was not geared to helping those *not* already in the fee-paying sector (Walford 1988: 150–1). By the mid-1980s, around one in eight pupils aged eleven years or over were on APS in Scotland. The beneficiaries in particular were the Merchant Company schools who had about 16 per cent of the schools' rolls on APS. Walford calculated that Heriot's had about 200 pupils out of 1400 on APS, while the likes of Loretto, Fettes and St George's had far fewer, respectively, twenty-two out of 400, twenty-six, and a mere thirteen in the case of St George's. The phasing out of APS reinforced the distinction between the 'fee-paying' and 'education authority' schools, such that the day pupil schools (including Heriot's) became firmly 'independent', while the Royal High School (moving to Barnton in west Edinburgh in 1968), and James Gillespie's, whose endowments were non-existent, became co-educational comprehensive schools in 1973. It is perhaps significant that both schools were rebuilt by the local authority, Edinburgh council, in the late 1960s, respectively in 1968[10] and 1966. It would have been beyond these schools to refurbish without state money.

Going Independent

In retrospect, the late 1960s/early 1970s was the cusp of social change in fee-paying schools. Before that, fee-paying, however modest, was not uncommon in some state-sector schools. Once grant-aid was abolished, the likes of the Royal High School and Gillespie's (which had, in 1968, charged fees of, respectively, £41–£44 p.a. and £40 p.a.) became comprehensives in the state sector. Supporters of the grant-aided scheme, such as John Highet, who thought that the working-classes could well afford modest fees, after all, in his view costing as much as going to the bingo or drinking, considered that grant-aided schools

> stand somewhere between the fee-paying public schools and the independent schools, and it could be said that, in several important respects, they have the best of both worlds: a greater measure of freedom than the one group, and less dependence than the other on what ceiling on their fees-scale 'the market' will bear. (Highet 1969: 57–8)

Highet's study was indubitably parti-pris: in his review in *Sociology*, Andrew McPherson, who founded the Centre for Educational Sociology at Edinburgh University, wrote that Highet's book 'gives us little education, less sociology and, surprisingly for one who complains of the lack of argument based on evidence, even less hard, relevant data' (McPherson 1970: 263–4). It is true that Highet's purpose was, in his own words, 'to provide fee-paying parents with a platform from which to speak' (Highet 1969: 5), and he has a chapter entitled 'Is there a case against Scotland's fee-paying public and grant-aided schools?', to which his answer is that it is 'the most arrant romanticism' to think that fees deprive working-class children of the benefits of fee-paying education (Highet 1969: 268).

So why take Highet's study at all seriously? Despite itself, it reveals a lot about the culture of fee-paying just at the point it was undergoing major transformation. Highet captures the moment of change, without explicitly intending to do so. His concern was that

> within the foreseeable future . . . there may no longer be any fee-paying public schools [*sic*] in Scotland – unless those who regard their retention as in the interests of the educational well-being of

the country take effective action while there is still time. (Highet 1969: 23)

His study involved interviews with school representatives, and a sample survey of parents, not particularly helped by his curious view that 'sociological research in many fields of operation is in large measure an exercise in public and personal relations' (Highet 1969: 187), which possibly tells us more about his own approach than research methods as generally practised.

Highet noted that fee-paying schools, notably in Edinburgh, occupied social niches. Thus,

> The Edinburgh Academy . . . is still closely linked to the legal profession. This is true too of George Watson's, though to a lesser extent. Partly because of the school's strength in biology, many Heriot's boys become medical doctors, some of them entering the public health service, and there is a residual medical strain. Melville has an established connection with accountancy. (Highet 1969: 146)

We do not have to accept these statements as 'facts' (presumably, Highet did not survey systematically where school graduates went) but they reflect the accounts and beliefs of the day as regards occupational specialisations in the city. They are operating truths, just as the belief that there was a hierarchy of fee-paying schools was itself a social account. Thus,

> Many former pupils of other [than George Watson's] fee-paying schools expressed to me their opinion that Watsonians at heart resented the fact that their school, as grant-aided and not an independent school, had a social status inferior to that of The Edinburgh Academy. (Highet 1969: 151)

On the other hand, 'Watsonians in particular boast, no doubt with pardonable exaggeration, that wherever a Watson's leaver makes his career, fellow-Watsonians will be there to welcome him' (Highet 1969: 150). The old-school tie worked: 'Even to get started at all, at the stage of applying for your first job, it can help if you are wearing the tie of one of "the right schools". For example,

> in Edinburgh up to a few years ago an applicant for a job in fields such as insurance who was from a non fee-paying school or a not-quite-accept fee-paying school was at a considerable disadvantage

in his competition with applicants wearing the 'OK ties'. (Highet 1969: 151)

We can accept that what Highet was doing was reproducing faithfully what his respondents were telling him; he was, after all, sympathetic to their cause, and had no reason to do otherwise. He is also interesting on the hierarchy of Edinburgh schools in the late 1960s. From Edinburgh middle-class talk, 'and especially mothers' coffee-morning chit-chat', a social status league table emerges (in descending order): Fettes>Edinburgh Academy>Merchiston>Melville>George Watson'>Daniel Stewarts>Heriot's – then the Royal High School. There is even a section entitled 'Mothers' Moods and Relationships', relating to coffee mornings, tenseness over entrance tests (said a respondent: 'One woman didn't speak to me for years because her son didn't get in and mine did' (Highet 1969: 211). Highet's 'ethnography' is revealing. 'You can say that not merely Edinburgh law but pretty well Edinburgh itself is run by Academicals and Watsonians' (an Edinburgh Academy mother). 'The Academy made you look down on the others but up to the boarding schools' (Academical). 'I had it very much in mind that any son of mine should go the Academy, to follow me in the business – I followed my father' (Watsonian lawyer).

Why did parents send their children to fee-paying schools? – 'because you get a better education there' – a revealing cliché. There was also an element of avoiding the 'Qualifying' (11+ in England), and thus having your children 'condemned' to Junior Secondary schools. Furthermore, 'To get anywhere at all in Edinburgh, you must go to a fee-paying school' (Highet 1969: 243), also described as the 'Edinburgh disease' or 'the fee-paying schools rat-race', 'the game you just have to learn to play'.

From fifty-plus years on we get a glimpse into the social and educational world of Edinburgh in the 1960s, a world of social anxiety and social status, reflecting in essence a local bourgeois labour market dependent on who you knew, who could pull strings for your offspring in terms of the local professions. Running through the verbatim comments is this sense of localism and knowing 'the right people', of dinner parties and social occasions usually orchestrated by women/mothers (one doubts that coffee mornings still exist, at least on that scale), exchanging gossip and information. Changes were afoot. Immigration from England 'coupled with other changes in the city's employment pattern has proportionately increased the predominantly B2 [white-collar middle class] character of its independent and grant-aided schools' (Highet 1969: 167). Given that Highet was sympathetic to 'independent' schools, and presumably was keen to represent their 'point of view' ('a platform from which to speak', after all), he would have been viewed as 'one of us' and not a hostile academic. Plainly, this was not a ploy on Highet's part. Andrew McPherson's review of his book concluded:

> (A)lthough Highet interviewed several hundred fee-paying parents explicitly to provide them with a platform from which to speak, he apparently felt that the thesis of working-class fecklessness would be accepted by his audience, along with his other major contentions, without evidence. (McPherson 1970: 264)

As late as 2017, the political row rumbled on. George Foulkes, who had been education convener on the Edinburgh council in the mid-1970s when the grant-aided scheme was under attack, and instrumental in ending fee-paying at the local level, took issue with Cameron Wyllie, then the head teacher of Heriot's, over charitable status for fee-paying schools. In a response, Wyllie said the peer appeared to have 'a particularly angry bee in his rather grand parliamentary bonnet' and described him as a 'form of fierce sea life' circling the 'good ship "Jinglin' Geordie"' (the founder, George Heriot, had been jeweller to the king James VI). Wyllie continued:

> It is just abject nonsense to say that removing business rates relief, or removing Gift Aid, or even insisting on fee-payers paying VAT on school fees would raise more money for state education. The effect of any or all of these things would be to make independent schools more elitist by driving up fees and reducing funds available to provide bursarial aid.[11]

Documenting Schools

In truth, most books about schools are celebratory and rarely analytical. They are, by and large, vehicles for reminiscence among 'old boys and girls'. Two such, on Edinburgh, are by Alasdair Roberts; the first on girls' schools (*Crème de la Crème*, 2007 and 2010 – note the Muriel Spark allusion), and the second, on boys' schools: *Ties that Bind*, 2009). Lindsay Paterson's perceptive review observed:

> Roberts is thus rich and detailed on what he calls 'symbols and impressive occasions' – the annual celebrations, the great sporting matches, the dramatic and musical activities, the moments of significant memory where an inspiring teacher shapes a child's character for life. (Paterson 2012: 177)

Nevertheless, he comments, two crucial aspects are not fully dealt with: there is nothing about former-pupils associations as agents of power (that, at least, Highet had an inkling of); and little on the formal curriculum (less than 10 per cent, in books of more than 220 pages).

Of the two books by Roberts, the one on girls' schools is the more interesting, possibly because so many came and went, and in any case it was re-printed, in 2007 and 2010, suggesting it had greater appeal. As regards the book on boys' schools, it is what is not there that is interesting – the role and influence of such schools in the social order. Does, for example, an expensive education actually pay off? This is possibly too tricky to handle, and Roberts sticks with some anodyne topics: a lot of sport, cadets in khaki, FPs, information derived in the main from school magazines, and designed to amuse rather than enlighten. Those who wish to check out the public fame/notoriety of fee-paying schools – sex, drugs, rock and roll – can easily do so on the web these days. All the schools have websites, more or less informative, and most listing famous alumni, although the Edinburgh Academy makes a virtue of a necessity by listing 'convicted criminals' (one such, Roger Jenkins who once ran for Scotland, but that was not what got him into trouble with the law).

Nigel Shepley's history of St George's is more illuminating, written by a professional historian with access to school records. In any case, he has a more interesting tale to tell about a school which has strong views about women's education. As befits a school which predated the Merchant Company ones, and with a kenspeckle history, Brian Lockhart's *Jinglin' Geordie's Legacy* (2009) is a good example of the genre.[12] Local authority schools, even the Royal High School which dates back to 1128, do not have a formal published history. However, Norah Carlin's *Holy Cross Academy Edinburgh: The Life and Times of a Catholic*

School, 1907–1969 (2009), a school which no longer exists, tells the story of the Catholic community and its education in the city.

WHAT'S THE PAY-OFF?

Running behind much of the writing on fee-paying schools in Edinburgh is the question: does it actually pay to be educated privately, and if so, in what senses? Highet's respondents, interviewed in the late 1960s, obviously thought it did, and went to considerable financial lengths to buy into it. Nowadays, when school fees are at least half of the average manual wage, is it worth sending children to fee-paying schools? Here we confront the question of output measures. Does 'private' education make a material difference to one's lot in life? Is access to university easier? Does it advance social mobility at a time when research suggests that elites are disproportionately privately educated (see Social Mobility Commission: State of the Nation, 2018–19[13]).

We are fortunate in having rigorous and systematic studies which shed light on this issue. Historically, the demand for private education was partly fuelled by educational selection, notably the 'Qualifying'/11+. In other words, it was a safety net for those who failed, and as a result were likely to end up in junior secondary schools. With the introduction of comprehensive education, this function of private schools was removed, or at least alleviated (Sullivan and Heath, in Walford 2003). It is not difficult to show that fee-paying schools have higher achievement levels in terms of exam results, and university access; but they have privileged intakes in terms of parental social class, education, reading behaviours, cognitive skills, and general interest in the child's education. It is quite another matter to pinpoint whether, all these considered, there is 'value-added' from fee-paying schools themselves. Put more crudely, scholastic achievement might simply be the result of extraneous, family, factors, and not the schools themselves. Paying fees might simply be a waste of money, for the best of education authority schools may provide the required outputs in terms of exam qualifications, and access to university. Furthermore, time-scales may be too short to measure lasting social and educational effects.

In a remarkable piece of work, Lindsay Paterson, Alan Gow and Ian Deary (2014) have analysed the Lothian Birth Cohort 1936, first surveyed in 1947, and then re-interviewed in 2004–7.

Respondents completed the same intelligence test as they sat in 1947, seventy years on. Thus, they were able to measure whether the type of secondary school attended had any influence on outcomes across sixty years. They modelled school effects taking into account cognitive ability at age eleven, levels of parental education and father's social class. The research question was

> whether the similar origins and present social purposes of the independent and education-authority old senior secondaries meant they had similar effects on their pupils' life-course in the late 20th century, or whether having become more socially exclusive from the late 19th century onwards had moved the independent schools in a distinctive direction. (Paterson et al. 2013: 3)

Undoubtedly, those attending grant-aided or independent senior secondary schools had higher levels of social class both of fathers (68 per cent in social class I or II; compared with 42 per cent at old senior secondary education authority schools) and in terms of respondents' own achieved social class (81 per cent in I or II; but 86 per cent of those at comparable education authority schools). In terms of 'inflow' into class I, for example, just over a quarter came from the fee-paying sector, while 30 per cent had been at senior secondary former Higher Grade schools.[14] The point is a familiar one to students of social stratification, namely, that social classes I (and II) are diverse in their social origins because of the post-war expansion of the professional and managerial sectors (summarised in McCrone 2017a: 233–4). On the other hand, almost half (46 per cent) of social classes IV and V (and also IIIm) attended junior secondary schools. Unsurprisingly, the oldest schools, public and private, are associated positively with attainment, thus, 'the senior-secondary schools were associated with a class advantage over and above their association with lifelong learning' (Paterson et al. 2013: 12).

Then there is the Edinburgh question. The authors find that junior-secondary schools in the city are associated with much lower class positions relative to elsewhere, whereas the advantage of having been in the old education-authority sector is greater than elsewhere. In other words, 'the difference between the school sectors is more marked for people who attended secondary school in the city than for those who did not receive their schooling in the city' (Paterson et al. 2013: 17). Surprisingly, perhaps, it was the oldest senior-secondary schools in the city which were associated with high lifelong educational attainment (the contrast is with junior-secondary schools) such that the stratified nature of the city's schools mattered, but 'the most differentiating schools were the old schools in public management, rather than those which operated independently of elected control' (Paterson et al. 2013: 19). Put another way, the major fissure in terms of life-long achievement was not between fee-paying schools and those in the education-authority sector, but between 'old' and 'new' schools. The authors concluded:

> (I)t does not have to be the case that schools have a direct effect on their pupils 60 years after they have left. All that is needed is that schools set people on a path which, though not determining their later experiences, places them in a sequence of new situations that continue to stimulate or impede their development. (Paterson et al. 2013: 19)

What is it about such schools that makes the difference? Cristina Iannelli has shown that 'curriculum matters in the acquisition of different social classes of destination but it matters more for children from advantaged social backgrounds than for children from lower classes of origin' (Iannelli 2013: 907). These data are drawn from the National Child Development Study (NCDS) across the UK, a continuing longitudinal study of all those born in one week in 1958, and at secondary schools between 1969 and 1976. The fact that high-status subjects such as languages, sciences, English and maths are commonly studied at fee-paying schools, even controlling for individual and family characteristics, seems to be what makes the difference. Not only do fee-paying schools provide a safety-net against the possibility of ending up in lower social classes, curriculum 'explains the effect of selective schools that could not be explained by the social class and ability of their pupils' (Iannelli 2013: 924). In other words, she concludes, the content of education – studying core subjects like languages, English, maths and sciences – 'counts more in the reproduction of social inequalities than the structure of the school system' (Iannelli 2013: 925), which would help to explain the finding by Paterson et al. that 'old' senior-secondary schools and fee-paying schools had much in common as regards achievements of pupils compared to their younger counterparts.

It is fair to say, perhaps, that the pay-off of fee-paying schools derives from the curriculum taught, all other things being equal, and in that regard they have much in common with 'older' state secondary schools in Edinburgh. If there is a difference, it is in the fact that they achieve social mobility sooner than their state-educated counterparts. The highly stratified character of Edinburgh's schools seems to lie much more in the historic senior/junior secondary distinction, than in the private/public one. In that regard, going to a fee-paying school is, in terms of social mobility, more of a sufficient than a necessary condition for improving one's lot in life.

AN EDINBURGH RULING CASTE?

Let us return to the popular notion that Edinburgh is a city 'swarming with castes' (Heiton 1861), and that these castes are created and amplified by the school system in the city. Michael Dale, who was Festival Fringe Administrator from 1981 to 1986, and complaining about the lack of support for Festival and Fringe, blamed 'the Edinburgh establishment – monolithic, entrenched, anonymous, secretive and powerful as nowhere else' (Dale 1988: 18). That is as may be, easy to state but difficult to prove; but a fairly widespread conspiracy theory.

Highet's book *A School of One's Choice*, published in 1969, was on to something, even if he did not recognise it. Edinburgh, and its schooling system, was on the cusp of change. Recall his respondents' comments: 'Sending to a fee-paying school is the done thing in Edinburgh', and another, 'To get anywhere at all in Edinburgh you must go to a fee-paying school'. 'Getting anywhere' would have meant going to university, or following in father's footsteps into professions or business. Localism invariably ruled. Lindsay Paterson has shown that for 1870, 1910 and 1952, almost 90 per cent of university entrants in Lothian went to the local university (Paterson 1993). Other regions in Scotland had similar retention rates. By the 1950s, about 5 per cent of secondary pupils in Scotland were in fee-paying schools, but they represented about four times that (20 per cent) of higher education entrants since the 1960s. Such schools 'were firmly rooted in local bourgeois culture, and tied to the local university' (Paterson 1993: 237).

Post-1960s, there has been a precipitate fall in 'localism' as regards universities, dropping across Scotland from above 60 per cent down to 40 per cent in 1990. This sharp decline in regionalism, however, is not accompanied by a trend to leave Scotland for university education.[15] The proportion staying within Scotland remained at around 90 per cent throughout the thirty years. The falling percentage going to local universities was especially noticeable in Lothians and the Borders where it fell from 76 per cent to 27 per cent between 1960 and 1990. 'Regionalism' for the ancient universities as a whole fell from 57 per cent in 1970 to 39 per cent in 1990, and by 1990 only 38 per cent of Lothian 'school products' went to the local university. Within Scotland, only Glasgow and the south-west remained high (around 75 per cent). Nor were fee-paying schools very different. Paterson (1993: 246) observes:

> In both Edinburgh and Glasgow . . . 81% of independent-school leavers in 1963 entered the local universities; the corresponding figure for public schools[16] as a whole were 73% and 81%. This intense localism of the independent schools is even more surprising when we consider that their pupils were generally more middle-class than pupils in the public schools.

Thus, 'regionalism' was the dominant practice of middle-class pupils in urban fee-paying schools. Furthermore, he observes:

> (E)ven from Edinburgh independent schools in 1990, 70% of university students entered a Scottish university; from Glasgow independent schools, the figure was over 95%. Thus, we have a decline in Scottish regionalism amongst this elite, but no evidence of a decline in the Scottishness of their education. (Paterson 1993: 248)

So what has occurred is a 'general nationalisation' of the Scottish middle classes as regards university education, 'a development that might have long-lasting effects on the political and cultural consciousness of the new Scottish middle class' (Paterson 1993: 252).

We can now see that what Highet was describing in the late 1960s (prior to the introduction of the comprehensive system) was a localised system of power within which fee-paying schools played a key role. The 'nationalisation' of higher education broke that link such that a larger proportion of pupils went elsewhere (but still within Scotland) for higher education. Those who did not go to university (and the best estimate for the late 1960s is that around 11 per cent of the age cohort would have been in any kind of higher education (and 8 per cent in university)[17]) would have entered the labour market aged eighteen, possibly in professional and managerial jobs[18]; hence, the significance of Highet's 'old school tie'. The 'nationalisation' of higher education broke that link with two effects: local pupils could go elsewhere within Scotland, and usually did; incomers taking up positions both at university and in the professions such that the tightness of fit between schools, university and occupations no longer operated the way that it had.

CONCLUSION

To describe the Edinburgh elite as 'monolithic, entrenched, anonymous, secretive and powerful' might make for good journalistic copy, but poor sociology. It is always difficult to disprove conspiracy theories especially if they contain a grain of truth, and we run the risk of the 'false negative'. At the core of such accusations has lain the (fee-paying) school system – hence the question in the title. There is always the point that if something is believed to be the case, it is true in its consequences because people act as if it were so (classically, W. I. Thomas's 'definition of the situation', 1923). It may be a fair guide to their actions, even if objectively misguided.

The undoubted significance of the fee-paying sector in Edinburgh has helped, historically, to give the city much of its social and political colour. Can we be sure, however, that 'what school did you go to?' carries the same import it once did? After all, fee-paying schools fed into local higher education at a time when less than 10 per cent of the age cohort went to university. Today, that figure is virtually 50 per cent, half of the age cohort. Furthermore, a much higher proportion of university entrants from Lothian schools go elsewhere (in Scotland), and a concomitant higher proportion flow into the city's higher education establishments than ever before.

Edinburgh is also a city with a much higher proportion of residents born outwith Scotland; as many as 30 per cent, with half that number born in the rest of the UK or in Ireland, and a further 6 per cent in the rest of the European Union (2011 census figures). By way of contrast, twenty years previously, only 10 per cent were born furth of Scotland (1991 census). Edinburgh's own figures, based on Department of Work and Pensions National Insurance number registrations for overseas workers, reveal that the largest numbers of overseas migrants living in the city[19] are from Spain, Poland and Italy. Undoubtedly, the most cosmopolitan of the Scottish cities – only Aberdeen comes close – Edinburgh's relative economic success has brought about a transformation in its social composition. 'You'll have had your tea' still makes for one of the standard Edinburgh jokes, but something of a cultural residue than a current descriptor. Asking the question 'what school did you go to?' stands a fair chance at the end of the second decade of the twenty-first century of being a question simply about education, and far less about social status and power in this most bourgeois of cities.

NOTES

1. Fees given here are taken from schools' websites.
2. To save the reader puzzling it out, ESMS stands for Erskine Stewart's Melville Schools; not the most memorable of acronyms.
3. Merchiston Castle takes the view that 'boys learn differently than girls'. For example, that 'boys tend to attribute successes to their own efforts and failures to external factors, while girls show the reverse; the perception of failure may inhibit subsequent performance' (https://www.merchiston.co.uk/about-us/boys-learn-differently-from-girls/). St George's is concerned with 'empowering girls to believe in themselves' (boys are accepted into the pre-school nursery).
4. Two examples of such buildings are the Salvation Army hostel on the corner of the Cowgate and St Mary's Street, and the old school in Davie Street also on the Southside, now converted into a block of flats.
5. Muriel Spark's classic *The Prime of Miss Jean Brodie* (1961) credits the curriculum at the fictional Marcia Blaine School for Girls (a thinly disguised James Gillespie's), arguably too close to 'Maria Grey' to be a coincidence. Muriel Spark was not averse to airbrushing history if it suited her novelistic purposes. Nigel Shepley in his fine history of St George's observes that she 'omits to tell us where this most renowned of Edinburgh teachers was trained'. The head teacher at Gillespie's was trained at St George's – naturally.
6. Consider Muriel Spark's description of fear and excitement when Miss Brodie's 'girls' ventured into the Old Town. 'The Canongate,

The Grassmarket, The Lawnmarket, were names which betokened a misty region of crime and desperation: "Lawnmarket Man Jailed" (Muriel Spark 1965: 32).

7. Delamont herself comments: 'In talks great stress was laid on the research being conducted in all the fee-paying girls' schools in Edinburgh, to confuse those who knew the city. When challenged by anyone who had guessed the real identity of St Luke's, I have always refused to make any comment, and pointed out that it could have been X, Y, Z or W school instead' (Delamont 1984a: 31). Delamont's masking of school identity is commendable, but, fifty years on, loses much of its social impact, for those erstwhile pupils are now over retirement age.

8. In the Scottish sense of 'public'.

9. John Newsom chaired the first report published in 1968. David Donnison chaired the second, in 1970. The Public Schools Commission was set up by the Labour government.

10. The Royal High School had a further major refurbishment in the early 2000s, costing around £10m (using PFI). Gillespie's underwent similar about a decade later. Both were rebuilt on existing sites.

11. <https://www.scotsman.com/education/edinburgh-private-school-head-accuses-george-foulkes-of-vendetta-1-4631000>.

12. Brian Lockhart was educated at Heriot's, and became head teacher of Robert Gordon's school in Aberdeen from 1996 to 2004.

13. <https://assets.publishing.service.gov.uk/government/uploads/system/uploads/attachment_data/file/798404/SMC_State_of_the_Nation_Report_2018-19.pdf>.

14. These were senior secondary schools with origins in Higher Grade schools, 1903–23 – 35 per cent of all schools, which is the largest category. 'Old' senior secondaries had their origins pre-twentieth century, and were managed by the education authority (but only accounted for 9 per cent of all schools).

15. All data are taken from Lindsay Paterson's article 'Regionalism among entrants to higher education from Scottish schools', *Oxford Review of Education*, 19(2), 1993.

16. What I have chosen to call 'education-authority' schools.

17. I am grateful to Lindsay Paterson for these estimates.

18. Recall that in the 1960s direct entry into civil service and banking/accounting jobs was much more common, with the possibility, especially in the latter cases, of taking 'professional exams' in terms of career advancement. It is a moot point as to their significance today.

19. There are 4,780 Spanish nationals, 4,610 Poles, and 3,290 Italians (figures for 2015–17, with Edinburgh registrations providing the

largest percentage for Spain (55 per cent of the Scottish total), Italy (44 per cent), India, France, Greece, and China (around 40 per cent each) (source: Edinburgh by Numbers 2018). The data provide a useful proxy for the nationality of recent migrant inflows to the city.

7

Enlightened City:
Cultural Power and University Life[1]

Edinburgh is unique among Scotland's 'ancient' universities in
having a university founded by the city, and not by the medieval
church. Created in 1583, its purpose was never clear. Historian
Michael Lynch expressed this ambivalence nicely:

> Was it intended to be a college devoted to the liberal arts or a
> Protestant seminary, designed to produce much-needed recruit for
> the parish ministry? Was it to be a new-style college or old-style uni-
> versity? Was it to be a college for the town, or an institution meant
> to attract students from afar? The irony is that the scheme was, at
> one time or another in its pre-history, all of these things. (Lynch, in
> Anderson et al. 2003: 6)

In this chapter I will explore the centrality of the University of
Edinburgh to cultural and social life in the city. Readers might
cavil at that, on the grounds that it is, these days, not the only
university in the city; that there is much more to 'enlightenment' than the university in question, particularly in the shape
of cultural and professional institutes; and that, arguably, the
University of Edinburgh[2] has played a less than fulsome part
in the cultural and intellectual life of the city, certainly for one
considering itself the Tounis College.

UNDERSTANDING THE TOUNIS COLLEGE

The university, through Edinburgh University Press, published
an 'illustrated history' in 2003, written by three of its most prominent historians: Michael Lynch, who dealt with the creation of

the college; Nick Phillipson, who wrote about the making of an enlightened university; and Robert Anderson, the construction of the modern university. The book is short – just over 200 pages including pictures and illustrations – and published 20 years after its tercentenary, for reasons not given in the book, but possibly because in 1983, the university was going through one of its periodic financial crises, and thought that it could not commit to spending money on something as 'impractical' as a history. The late Michael Moss, University of Glasgow historian, in a review in the *English Historical Review*, observed that:

> The book is a good read, but it is deeply frustrating. Every page leaves questions unanswered. This is not the fault of the talented troika but of the constraints of space. At a time when higher education is daily in the news and is widely perceived as a motor for economic development and social progress, university histories can no longer be dismissed as simple boosterism, although this undoubtedly was part of what lies behind this publication – all too evident from the principal's anodyne foreword. Edinburgh is far too important in western culture to be served by such a short study. Scholars needed a bigger canvas against which to set their studies of subjects as disparate as the impact of Edinburgh medicine on the English-speaking world and the powerful ideas of the Scottish enlightenment. (Moss 2004: 811–12)

Moss's point is well-made. Other Scottish universities have been much better served in their histories than Edinburgh, most notably Glasgow (by Moss himself, and by Rick Trainor), Strathclyde (by Callum Brown) and above all Aberdeen, whose history ran to half-a-dozen volumes. Somehow, Edinburgh's seemed classically too little and too late, and fitted the accusation that it was something of a cheapskate in a city where 'having had your tea' touched a familiar nerve. It would have been preferable to have each of the three prominent historians write a volume each, and for specialised histories, for example, to be written possibly on law, medicine, religion, education and science. The fact that Edinburgh still has a university press, when only one other Scottish university has one,[3] and few exist in England other than Oxford, Cambridge and in modern times, Manchester, belies the fact that Edinburgh University Press (EUP) is required to stand alone in financial terms, and receives little or no subsidy from the university which carries its name.

This chapter, then, centres 'the university' at its heart of cultural discussion, even although there are three other such institutions in the city: in order of foundation, Heriot Watt, founded as a Mechanics' Institute in 1824, raised to a college in 1885, sharing engineering courses with Edinburgh by 1900, and becoming a free-standing 'university' in the 1960s. Queen Margaret University began as Edinburgh's domestic science college, best known simply as 'Atholl Crescent', moved out to the western suburbs, before becoming a university on the eastern fringes of the city bypass in 2007.[4] The fourth university, Edinburgh Napier, was founded in 1964 as a local authority technical college, became a university in 1992, and renamed as Edinburgh Napier University in 2009, presumably because no one really knew where it was, and in any case, 'Edinburgh' had something of a cachet, but arguably too often confused with 'Edinburgh University' which presumably was the point of its renaming.

The Making of a University

Edinburgh University took a long time to get going. By 1587, it had forty-seven graduates; the teaching force was half a dozen in the early seventeenth century; and a hugely adverse staff–student ratio of 1:80, a *magna multitudo* of students. The library was very small, dependent on charitable donations, and indeed it was not even called a 'university' (but a college) until 1685. It had a strained relationship with 'professional' organisations such as the church, the Faculty of Advocates, the Colleges of Physicians and of Surgeons, which were in many ways rival centres of learning. Michael Lynch sums up its early history as follows:

> The story of the first century of the town's college ends as it began. A purge [of religious factions on the town council] brought it into being in the form it took in October 1583 – a liberal arts college rather than a Presbyterian seminary. Another purge, in 1690, formed the prelude for a further attempt to transform its role – this time from 'King James's University' into a strict Presbyterian college. (Lynch, in Anderson et al. 2003: 49)

Nick Phillipson picks up on these tensions in his account of the eighteenth century. The college was placed in an impossible position; neither 'illustrious school' nor productive Presbyterian seminary. It took two prominent principals, William Carstares in the early eighteenth century and William Robertson in the later part, to establish the university. Carstares remodelled it on Leiden University, and founded the medical faculty (known as the Dutch strategy). Robertson, 'by far the most formidable Principal the college had ever had' (Phillipson, in Anderson et al. 2003: 79) set about building the university in the Old Quad. Robertson, who was principal from 1762 until his death in 1773, was particularly astute about the university's relations with the people of the town. A. J. (Sandy) Youngson, twentieth-century professor of political economy and author of *The Making of Classical Edinburgh* (1966), observed that Robertson considered it necessary for students to live with the townsfolk.

> This method [is] more advantageous to youth than keeping them shut up in colleges, as at Oxford and Cambridge. He [Robertson] says that when young men are not kept from intercourse with society, besides that they do not acquire that rude and savage air which retired study gives, the continual examples which they meet with in the world, of honour and riches acquired by learning and merit, stimulate them more strongly to the attainment of these; and that they acquire, besides, easy and insinuating manners, which render them better fitted in the sequels for public employment. (Robertson, quoted in J. Grant *Old and New Edinburgh*, 1882[5])

This advice stood the college in good stead in its relations with the city, even though it was not without tensions and conflicts. In Phillipson's summing-up:

> It was the unique interplay between city and college, between a sense of the practical and the philosophical, between learning and public life in a city preoccupied with its own future that shaped the educational culture of the college in the 'long Eighteenth Century'. It was that which made it possible for the Tounis College to develop as an enlightened university. (Phillipson, in Anderson et al. 2003: 101)

Why the interest in the early foundations of the university when we are asking who runs Edinburgh in the twenty-first century? Because, to use the metaphor, it is the university's and the city's respective DNAs, in the sense that dubiety and contradiction, in terms of what learning and education are for, which have shaped both institutions over the next two centuries.

Robert Anderson provides an account of the modern university which takes up the second half of the book. In truth, all
universities faced similar problems, but Edinburgh's was com-
pounded by its relations with the city. The Universities Act 1858
took formal control of the university out of the hands of the town
council, and reinforced the point that Scottish universities were
indisputably public institutions. The 1858 Act also required the
four universities to coordinate their curricula and assessment,
a stipulation that did not end until 1966. A residual sop at
Edinburgh was the quaintly named Curators of Patronage with
joint university-city membership which continues to nominate
principals to this day.[6] Power, however, passed to the University
Court and, on academic matters, to the Senate. Nevertheless,
comments Anderson, 'If control of its own membership is a
mark of university autonomy, Edinburgh University still showed
significant accountability to outside interests' (Anderson, in
Anderson et al. 2003: 120). By the late nineteenth century, in
terms of social class, 'an open, urban university like Edinburgh
had a very different profile from Oxford and Cambridge', reinforced by the fact that 'Edinburgh was always the most cosmopolitan of the Scottish universities' (Anderson, in Anderson et al.
2003: 132). Between the 1870s and 1914, around two-thirds
of *students* were born in Scotland, notably Edinburgh and east
Scotland. However, by 1933, a survey of Edinburgh's *graduates*
indicated that just over half were still living in Scotland (and half
of these lived in Edinburgh and the Lothians), with 28 per cent
in the rest of the UK, and 17 per cent overseas, reflecting the
export of skills, notably in medicine.

The student body was overwhelmingly male, and there was
resistance to the entry of women as students until 1892, despite
the Universities Act of 1884. By 1911, only one in five students
were female, and it was not until 1966 that Edinburgh appointed
a woman professor (in physiology). The ethos of the student
body was thoroughly male, and the Student Union, financed
largely by student fundraising, was modelled on a gentlemen's
club (membership by subscription helped to keep the numbers
down). Nevertheless, 'in an urban university like Edinburgh, the
invention of tradition and the separation of the student community had natural limits and persistent attempts to introduce the
wearing of gowns were never successful' (Anderson, in Anderson
et al. 2003: 143).

True to William Robertson's strictures, Edinburgh remained an essentially non-residential university, and students came to rely on 'digs' with redoubtable landladies especially across the Meadows in Marchmont. This was a natural extension, in any case, to the taking-in of paying lodgers, which was common in Edinburgh as elsewhere. On the other hand, many students in the first half of the twentieth century lived 'at home', for around 40 per cent of Edinburgh students had been educated wholly or partly in the city. Most male students had attended the Edinburgh fee-paying schools, while as many as half of (the small number of) women students had attended the two Merchant Company 'Ladies Colleges'. Anderson observes:

> these backgrounds encouraged cliquishness. But those who came to Edinburgh from outside were also struck by the university's integration into the urban milieu. It was physically situated in a crowded and dingy part of the town [the Southside] with its own attractions and dangers. (Anderson, in Anderson et al. 2003: 145)

The balance of local identity and cosmopolitanism, democratic opportunity and social privilege, changed only very slowly, until well into the twentieth century (Anderson et al. 2003: 157).

As we saw in the previous chapter, many school leavers went directly into local businesses where the old school tie still prevailed, at least by repute (Highet 1969). The Merchant Company, after all, had funded chairs in accounting (1919), and in the organisation of business and commerce (1925). Anderson points out that the most prestigious careers were in the civil service, and the 222 successful Edinburgh candidates between 1896 and 1944 were drawn from classics or history, and as many as one-third had attended George Watson's. Far more graduates became teachers. Anderson observes that Edinburgh was less well placed to tap into corporate wealth: 'The city lacked the sort of industries which created big fortunes, and if local magnates made contributions, they often preferred to finance projects of personal interest and prestige unrelated to their businesses' (Anderson, in Anderson et al. 2003: 166).

The numbers of staff had grown since the luckless 'regents' had to manage almost a hundred students on their own through to graduation. By the First World War, the staff–student ratio had fallen to one in fourteen, with forty-three professors, eighty-seven lecturers, and more than a hundred assistants. By the end of the nineteenth century, the professoriate (earning between £800 and £1,200 p.a.) had begun 'to occupy handsome flats in the West End, or villas in Newington and The Grange and to count among the bourgeois elite of the city' (Anderson, in Anderson et al. 2003: 171).

The university had around 4,000 students in the 1930s, rising to more than 5,500 in the post-war period, and just under 10,000 by the early 1970s, although this 'drifted upwards' only slowly until the 1990s. By the new century, numbers stood at around 20,000, especially with the incorporation of Moray House College of Education in 1998, and more than a decade later, of the Edinburgh College of Art (2011).

Moray House had an interesting and somewhat strained relationship with Edinburgh University. Supported by the local Kirk Sessions, it had offered teacher training since 1835, but almost immediately was affected by the Disruption of the Auld Kirk in 1843, when virtually all staff and students joined the Free Kirk and had to leave the premises. Land and buildings were purchased between the Canongate and Holyrood Road, its present site. The college embedded itself in the local community, reflected in their habitats at the behest of the Free Kirk: 'The Church opposed a "monastic" hall of residence for men, who stayed with relatives or in lodgings; young women who could not travel home duly lived in boarding houses' (Bain 1985: 2). Pupil teachers came, in the 1860s, mostly from labouring or artisan families, while young women were mainly of shop-keeping stock. Roughly split between men and women, they numbered 115:

> Moray House students . . . worked directly for the community of Edinburgh. A Children's Church brought 100 to the practicing (demonstration) school, where students sat as monitors, 'perhaps the most educative factor in their College life'. They also took cloth-ing and other gifts to poor families. (Bain 1985: 4)

After the Second World War, the college grew as a major research institution with Godfrey Thomson establishing its international reputation in testing. By 1948, Moray House (IQ) Tests were being administered to two out of every three British pupils. Thomson was both college principal and chief researcher. However, 'While the Principal continued his meticulous attempts to measure ability in [this] research, he delegated much of the college administration to his colleagues' (Bain 1985: 7). Those days, by the 1970s, were coming to an end, and the college was persuaded, reluctantly, into a merger with the Dunfermline College of Physical Education, located, despite its name, in west Edinburgh having moved there from Aberdeen.[7] More enthusiastically, the principal, Gordon Kirk, at any rate, was more enthusiastic about linking up with Heriot Watt to become its Institute of Education in the early 1990s (Kirk 1995: 13–14). Behind this lay the college's relationship with Edinburgh University. Edinburgh was on the doorstep, barely half a mile away; it had had a joint undergraduate degree, the Bachelor of Education (BEd), broken off when the college linked up with Heriot Watt, which by this point had moved to the fringes of the city, to Riccarton. Ultimately, however, the college was amalgamated into Edinburgh as the Faculty of Education (1998), reflecting the fact that, in the welter of amalgamations, it was too small to survive on its own, as indeed were the colleges of education around Scotland. Size mattered.

This expansion in student numbers was largely at the behest of the state, which by the early 1950s was funding around three-quarters of the university's income through the University Grants Committee (UGC, subsequently, the University Funding Council), compared with the pre-war situation whereby roughly one-third of income came from the state, one-third from student fees, and 17 per cent from university endowments. This, of course, made universities 'dangerously dependent on the goodwill of politicians' (Anderson, in Anderson et al. 2003: 191). State funding derived from the Anderson Committee Report's 1960 recommendation[8] that all students with a university place – those whose higher qualifications awarded an Attestation of Fitness[9] – should have their fees paid by the state and get a maintenance grant based on family circumstances; which benefited students from working class families who were often the first to go to university.

Partly as a result, comments Anderson (no relation to the report's author),

> Slowly but surely – more slowly in Scotland than elsewhere, but more rapidly at Edinburgh than Glasgow or Aberdeen – the universities became detached from their regional roots, and pupils in

Edinburgh schools began to think of going anywhere but to their local university. (Anderson, in Anderson et al. 2003: 195)

Thus, as we saw in the previous chapter, by the turn of the century, around equal proportions of students at Edinburgh (40 per cent plus) were domiciled in Scotland and in the rest of the UK, and one in ten from overseas. This latter proportion increased substantially in the next twenty years as universities found their state grants cut, and were forced to attract 'full fee' students from abroad, notably to short postgraduate Master's courses.

THE UNIVERSITY VERSUS THE CITY

The expansion of the university had its own impact on relations with the city. In 1962, the university proposed a massive comprehensive development area with the aim of creating a 'cultural precinct'. This was not a new battle but the latest in an old war dating back to the university's 1949 development plan which proposed demolishing, among others, many of the eighteenth-century Georgian buildings in George Square, provoking opposition from the Cockburn Association, the Saltire Society, the National Trust for Scotland, and the-then Scottish Georgian Society. The Abercrombie Plan, also of 1949, had views about George Square. It supported the idea of creating a 'cultural precinct' around the square, and condemned its south side (where the university library now stands) with the judgement: 'The architecture of the buildings in George Square . . . by no means deserve pride of place in Edinburgh's heritage. Why then allow them to stand in the way of a great project?' (Abercrombie 1949: 72, plate XLIV). Showing a drawing indicating the inadequacy in scale of the existing buildings to form a 'town square', it argued that 'larger buildings are required to improve the composition of the garden square with town buildings. This can be done in the University scheme' (Abercrombie 1949: 72). Exactly why a 'town square' in a university precinct was necessary is not at all clear.

Abercrombie's Plan, however, was grist to the university's mill as well as serving its own designs for the grandiose 'bridges relief road' which would circumvent the precinct. In any event, a compromise plan emerged to preserve the west side of the square, and half of its east side, with the university library (designed by Basil Spence in modernist style) and what became the Adam Ferguson Building replacing the buildings on the south side. The university also built two tower blocks, named the David Hume Tower, and Appleton Tower, on the square's east side, but whether these 'larger buildings' were what Abercrombie had in mind is doubtful. In any event, the integrity of George Square was destroyed, and this continued to rankle for decades after the 1960s/70s when they were finally built. Putting the words 'university' and 'George Square' into the same sentence is guaranteed to continue to raise the hackles of Edinburgh citizenry to this day.

It was not simply George Square which was at issue but the university's location in, to quote again Robert Anderson, a 'crowded and dingy part of the town [the Southside] with its own attractions and dangers'. In 1962 the university embarked on its own Comprehensive Development Area (CDA) which would involve the city clearing swathes of what it deemed sub-standard housing in Bristo Street/Charles Street/Crichton Street – known as Parker's Triangle after the department store at its apex – in preparation for a dental school that never got built.[10]

Inventing a Precinct: Edinburgh and its Environs

The university's Professor of Urban and Regional Planning was Percy Johnson-Marshall who acted as planning consultant for the project. Percy, as he was generally known, 'regarded himself as a reverent follower of Patrick Geddes' (Johnson and Rosenburg 2010: 216), who believed that the Southside suffered from 'obsolete development and bad layout' (Johnson and Rosenburg 2010: 216), but it was impossible to reconcile these contradictory views.[11]

Student unrest in Edinburgh post-1968 was as much about what the university was doing to the local community, aided and abetted by the city planners who had schemes of their own, as it was about wider cultural/political matters. Much of this was distilled in *The Student* newspaper where Jonathan Wills (a geography student and a gifted cartoonist) invented the student character Gaston Le Jobbe, and what Anderson calls 'amusing but vicious caricatures' (Anderson, in Anderson et al. 2003: 203). He reproduces one of the cartoon genre in which

Percy ('Pursey Jumbleston-Mumblehall') has his arm round a bowler-hatted council officer, and saying: 'You council chaps must come over to Adam House and see my exhibition – Michael [Swann, the principal] and I have great fun with all those little building blocks – it's jolly nice playing with those super squares and things – you get nice rectangles y'know. One must be modern, what?' The bowler-hatted council chap simply mutters: '*och*' (Anderson, in Anderson et al. 2003: 203). Robert Anderson comments that Michael Swann, who left the university to become chairman of the governors of the BBC, was 'a man of conservative cast' who had contributed to the Black Papers on education.[12] Swan was principal from 1965 to 1974, and served by University Secretary Charles Stewart who was in post from 1948 to 1978. Both principal and secretary were more used to 'gentlemanly' times (Swann had been at Edinburgh as Professor of natural history, nowadays usually called zoology, since 1952), and found the challenge from student politicians, notably Gordon Brown who was elected as student rector to succeed cartoonist Wills in 1973, hard to bear. Brown cut his teeth in student politics before going on to other political things.

The 1960s student revolt came late to Edinburgh, in the early 1970s, and focused mainly on internal matters: the right of students to elect the rector (who had no real power other than chairing the university court), following the 1966 election of journalist and commentator Malcolm Muggeridge (christened St Mugg by the satirical magazine *Private Eye*) described by Anderson as 'a stern Christian moralist' who resigned two years later over the installation of a condom machine in the Student Union.

The other issue agitating students in the 1970s related to what the university's planning proposals were doing to the local community. In a university where many students lived in communal flats around the Southside, this was fertile ground for agitation, especially where the local community and architectural conservationists made common cause with the students. Anderson sums the period up as follows:

> The university also sponsored a Comprehensive Development Area, which would have destroyed almost all the surrounding residential and commercial buildings. Fortunately, these plans were not carried out, but during this complex saga the university often seemed

insensitive and arrogant, and suffered from growing public feeling against the destruction of inner-city communities, and over the conservation of older buildings, even where these were not of outstanding architectural merit. (Anderson, in Anderson et al. 2003: 197)

The university, in fact, was not entirely to blame, because the CDA was a joint plan between the city, the university and Murrayfield Real Estate Company, who later 'developed' the much-maligned St James Centre (see Chapter 8). The plan was to demolish the area south of the Royal Mile (roughly speaking, bounded by the Cowgate, Nicolson Street, Rankeillor Street and the Pleasance), and build a six-lane motorway as an inner ring road in its place (Abercrombie's Bridges Relief Road revisited). The result was extensive planning blight lasting more than ten years, and a protracted series of planning enquiries. It took five years before the council could give formal approval to the CDA by which time the oil price hike in 1973 delivered the *coup de grâce* to the scheme, aided and abetted by the formidable array of conservation bodies and agitating students. (Glasgow's inner ring road also began in 1965, running out of traction by 1972, by which time economic, political and architectural forces were arrayed against such schemes). Jim Johnson and Lou Rosenburg in their book *Renewing Old Edinburgh: The Enduring Legacy of Patrick Geddes* (2010) summed it up as follows:

> very much against the odds, the central spine of the inner South Side of the city, from South Bridge to Clerk Street, managed to survive largely intact and it was possible to preserve and upgrade many of the Georgian buildings in the locality. (Johnson and Rosenburg 2010: 219)

Which led ultimately to a process of regeneration in the Old Town which was, more or less, in keeping with Patrick Geddes's notion of 'conservative surgery'. (As we shall see in Chapter 8, another controversy, Caltongate, arose in 2014, rebadged as 'New Waverley'.)

In many ways, the university found itself carrying the can for the city over the Southside schemes, for it had no responsibility for a six-lane motorway running through the city centre. What it could be accused of was complacency tinged with arrogance. Principal Edward Appleton (after whom one of the towers was subsequently named) had described the 1960s CDA scheme as 'the university in the city, and the city in the university' (George Rosie, 'Edinburgh University as Property Developer', in Peacock n.d.). The writer Michael Fry in his history of Edinburgh (2009) attacked Appleton thus: 'he brushed aside all proposals other than his own as "wholly unacceptable to anyone who understands the workings of a modern university" (a category evidently confined to himself)' (Fry 2009: 360).

The other George Square tower, the David Hume Tower (commonly known as the DHT), was not short of controversy. The poet Robert Garioch, in his poem *A Wee Local Scandal*, wrote

> The University has got a wee
> Skyscraper at the corner of George Square
> Fowerteen stories, the day I wes there;
> It's maybe sunk; I've no been back to see.
> The Hume Tower – it hits ye in the ee,
> Yon muckle black triangle in the air,
> a grand sicht frae the Meedies, man; it fair
> obliterates Arthur's Seat; nae word of a lee.
>   (Robert Garioch, *Collected Poems*, Polygon, 2004: 100)

Writing in 1994, the writer Allan Massie wondered how 'they had the nerve to name it after David Hume, who had been denied a professorship by the same university on account of his religious views?' (Massie 1994: 246). In 2020, Massie got his wish, but not in a manner he would ever have approved of; the university demoted David Hume Tower to, simply, '40 George Square', because a campaigner for Black Lives Matter claimed to find a footnote[13] in his work condemning him as 'an out-and-out racist' who wrote racist epithets (https://www.bbc.co.uk/news/uk-scotland-edinburgh-east-fife-54138247). That it took so long for anyone to notice the incriminating footnote was itself remarkable, given that it had been commented on by numerous authors over many years.[14]

The 1970s controversies over the university's plans stimulated a number of publications by the Edinburgh University Student Publications Board (better known as EUSPB) who published *The Student* weekly newspaper (with Wills's cartoons on the activities of Gaston Le Jobbe a feature). EUSPB also published the iconic *Red Paper on Scotland*, edited by Gordon Brown, student politician *nonpareil*, which played a key intellectual role in the campaign for a Scottish Assembly/Parliament (for an account, see Miller et al. 2010). Students, journalists, politicians (Brown, but also Robin Cook, as MP for Central Edinburgh) cooperated in publications such as *The Unmaking of Edinburgh* (Peacock n.d.); and *Forgotten Southside* (1974), also edited by Peacock, a post-graduate architecture student at the time.

Furthermore, academics in social science and architecture banded together to revive derelict property on the Southside, as an early housing association, calling it *Edinvar*. The university had a large portfolio of tenemented flats which it was only too glad to sell off. Thus, Edinvar bought a block in Buccleuch Place for £1700 (the university had bought it between 1958 and 1962 paying £1190 piecemeal for the flats), in expectation of its CDA (Rosie, in Peacock 1974: 29). Edinvar, formed in 1973, was also associated with the Lister Housing Cooperative (1976) which had been formed to oppose the university's plans to knock down the Georgian flats in Lauriston, further west, and build a postgraduate medicine building adjacent to what was then the Royal Infirmary. This opposition succeeded, and the flats were refurbished and restored for social use. Ultimately, Edinvar became part of Castle Rock Edinvar Housing Association, and the association with the university was retained in its name only.

Robert Anderson concludes his fine history of the university (2003) with these words:

> Ever since its foundation, the university has balanced its obliga-
> tions to the city, the nation, the Empire, the international academic
> community. But when fewer than half of its students come from
> Scotland, and the once close links with local schools have all but
> dissolved, the community base is perhaps part of the balance most
> in need of attention. (Anderson in Anderson et al., 2003: 209)

Prophetic words, for the university was never far from controversy, and another arose precisely over those 'community' links.

WHOSE UNIVERSITY IS IT ANYWAY?

In the late 1980s, Edinburgh University was caught unawares by a controversy about 'Englishing'. Put most starkly, the claim was that Edinburgh had become, to all intents and purposes, an 'English' university, especially in terms of its intake. It was by no means the first to encounter such claims, for St Andrews

in the 1970s had been embroiled in controversy about the high
failure rates among first-year Scottish students, or rather, those
who came with Highers. Such, it was argued, was the density of
non-Scots at St Andrews (over 50 per cent) that undergraduate
courses were being taught to a post A-level standard, thereby
disadvantaging Scots with Highers, or so it was claimed.

The Edinburgh controversy focused on student intake, that
non-Scots, but to all intents and purposes the English-domiciled,[15]
were being preferred by university admissions officers. Scottish
Education Department (SED) Statistical Bulletins since 1980
were showing that Scots-domiciled entrants to Scottish universities had decreased in net terms by 11 per cent, while students
from elsewhere in the UK had increased by 25 per cent. In 1980,
three-quarters of full-time undergraduates at Scottish universities
were domiciled in Scotland; and by the end of the decade, it had
fallen to two-thirds. Furthermore, there was a marked variation
between universities, with St Andrews and Edinburgh having
far more non-Scottish students than Glasgow and Strathclyde.
Much depended on which year to benchmark, but Edinburgh
had seen the steepest increase in non-Scots, rising from around
20 per cent in the 1970s, to 40 per cent by 1985. What could
be more plausible than that university selectors were biased in
admitting 'people like themselves': white, middle-class, privately
educated and male? Arguments based on plausibility are frequently attractive, but rarely based on systematic evidence.

The Englishing of Scotland?

What gave the controversy added impetus was that arguments
about 'Englishing' had much wider currency in the 1980s. It
was not simply universities which were being targeted, but other
Scottish institutions, notably the Arts, and land-ownership.[16]
Scottish Television (STV) ran an hour-long programme in the
autumn of 1988 spelling out the process of the *Englishing* of
Scotland. Mrs Thatcher had been elected in 1979, but without
a mandate in Scotland, even though there were 22 Conservative
MPs (out of 71) elected on 31 per cent of the Scottish vote,[17]
a remarkably high proportion given what was to happen to
the Tories in the 1990s. Later in 1988, the teacher's union, the
Educational Institute of Scotland (EIS), ran a campaign against
government policy under the banner of defending Scotland's

heritage against 'Englishing'. These anti-government campaigns were mobilising a sense of national grievance, which Labour, not ostensibly a nationalist party, was happy to capitalise on.

The claim that Scotland's universities were being threatened fitted the general expectations in a country which had voted for devolution in 1979 by 52 per cent to 48 per cent, but in insufficient numbers to make it happen.[18] There was also a cultural underpinning to political claims. Edinburgh academic and philosopher George Davie had published an influential book called *The Democratic Intellect* in 1961 which argued that a distinctively Scottish general curriculum grounded in philosophy had been squeezed out over the previous century by 'English' practices, notably the specialised honours degree. His 'anglicisation' thesis was largely taken as read, even though it had been subject to criticism (see Anderson, *Education and Opportunity in Victorian Scotland*, 1983). Lindsay Paterson (in private correspondence) has made the point that Davie confuses the intellectual and sociological meanings of anglicisation. While the intellectual case is based on an analysis of the university curriculum and teaching methods, it is cogent and accurate, reflected, for instance, in the dominance of specialist degrees. The sociological case, that there was pressure to bring Scottish education into line with England, cannot be sustained. He pays no attention to the gradual democratisation of secondary schooling led by the Scotch/Scottish Education Department, his arch-villain, nor to Scotland's early introduction of formal school-leaving exams in 1888. If school examinations are a 'British' invention, then that is because Scotland led the rest of Britain. In that regard, he distorts Scottish cultural history.

The Davie thesis provided a ready-made cultural context for the controversy about non-Scots entrants to Scottish universities. It caught the zeitgeist of the 1970s and 1980s just at the point at which political and cultural change in Scotland was in the air. No amount of careful scholarly refutation of the Davie thesis was likely to change that. What gave it particular piquancy was the view that Scottish universities were encouraging the trend by being 'biased' in favour of A-levels, which had wider cultural, and political, ramifications. The problem was that those opposed to 'Englishing' needed little convincing that it was happening, while those in favour of it, or seeing it as inevitable given the relative sizes of the Scottish and English 'markets' for higher education, did not feel the need to examine the evidence either. As a result, the thesis became a piece of cultural orthodoxy.

Edinburgh University found itself on the back foot, just as it had over the Southside planning controversy, both reflecting its tendency to contemplate its navel. It was ill-placed to argue against the conspiracy thesis, that its admissions officers pre-ferred 'English' students. For one thing, the thesis presumed that universities 'select' their intakes, when there is a compli-cated process of self-selection based upon students holding a number of conditional and unconditional offers of places at different institutions (see McCrone 1990). It was a strange argument that just at the moment where universities were being seriously eroded of their autonomy by central government cuts, that they had greater power to make major shifts in the student intake. In any case, Robert Anderson has shown that historically Glasgow and Aberdeen admitted far more 'lower class' students (respectively from working-class (Glasgow) and agricultural (Aberdeen) backgrounds) than Edinburgh and St Andrews; and reflecting that Glasgow and Aberdeen took longer to enter UCCA (University Central Council on Admissions[19]) than Edinburgh and St Andrews. UCCA also had the effect of spreading students further afield than their 'local' universities by encouraging them to apply elsewhere.

It is possible, nevertheless, that significant historical differ-ences have built up an ethos for different universities which is reproduced over time. There is something of a self-fulfilling prophecy about such 'reputations', in that when students come to apply to universities they operate to channel choices in terms of whether they take 'people like me', or not. There is, further-more, an extreme form of the 'meritocratic' argument that as long as Scottish-domiciled students were treated fairly at non-Scottish universities, why shouldn't non-Scots come here? This is to ignore pedagogical and curriculum differences between the Scottish education system and the rest, which were at their peak in the late 1980s when anti-Thatcher nationalism was on the rise. The 'meritocratic' argument also fails to recognise that, allegedly, to dilute the Scottishness of universities like Edinburgh is the failure to recognise difference of history, culture and even 'soul'. With hindsight, we can now see, more than thirty years on, that Edinburgh University was caught flat-footed by its fail-ure to read the cultural and political runes in the 1980s when nationalism in its various forms was becoming the dominant prism through which social and educational changes were being transmitted. The repatriation of the Scottish universities[20] has meant that they are required to operate at least at both Scottish and British levels, and in many ways have found it difficult so to do because they have poorly understood the contexts in which they operate.[21] Arguably, Edinburgh University had been caught up once more in political and cultural processes it poorly comprehends.

CITY OF ENLIGHTENMENT

Just because Edinburgh had an (ancient) university does not make it so different from other cities. What did make the difference was that the university was at the centre of an intellectual hub of knowledge. There was, for example, the Royal Society of Edinburgh (RSE), founded in 1783 largely at the behest of the Tounis College; and William Robertson, its principal, had laid the foundations before his death in 1773. The historians of the RSE, Campbell and Smellie (1983), asserted that Edinburgh became the only city in Britain which had both an active scientific society and a university, a judgement pertaining to the late eighteenth century, and one ignoring European experiences such as Bologna, and provincial English cities and universities from the early nineteenth century (Birmingham and Manchester being obvious examples). The likes of Thomas Jefferson averred that, as far as science was concerned, 'no place in the world can pretend to be in competition with Edinburgh' (Campbell and Smellie 1983: 7); another instance of Edinburgh (city and university) living off past moments.

The RSE, founded in 1783, had forerunners and competitors: the Rankenian Club (1716–74) for literary social meetings, the Society for the Improvement of Medical Knowledge (1731), and the Philosophical Society, RSE's immediate precursor. Its main competitor was the Society of Antiquaries which also sought a Royal Charter, and the university was fearful that its mooted lectures on natural history might rival its own.[22] 'Heated exchanges' occurred, not uncommon in such circles, and the university raced to have its Royal Charter granted in 1783 'for the advancement of learning and useful knowledge'. Campbell and Smellie comment that 'The Royal Society of Edinburgh was thus founded as the outcome of great activity catalysed by intense controversy behind the scenes rather than by the impetus of cultural requirement' (Campbell and Smellie 1983: 4–5). In other words, it was a matter of 'politics' rather than 'culture'. The RSE's first meeting was held in the college library, with the Duke of Buccleuch as president and John Robison, Professor of natural history, as general secretary. Invitations were sent out to 'a select number of other gentlemen' (Campbell and Smellie 1983: 5) including the Lords of Council and Session, Barons of Exchequer, and professors of each of the Scottish universities, but very much on Edinburgh's terms and premises. Steve Shapin[23] underlined 'the deep involvement of a scientific enterprise [RSE] in local cultural politics' (Shapin 1974: 2), and commented that 'the founding of the RSE was the result . . . of the particular position that scientific culture came to occupy in the local context' (Shapin 1974: 2). There were tensions between the sciences and the humanities:

> Although it was originally founded to cater for intellectual activity across the entire spectrum, with equal 'Physical' and 'Literary' classes, the RSE, by the early years of the nineteenth century, had developed into an almost exclusively scientific organization – one of the most distinguished of its kind in Britain. (Shapin 1974: 37)

Shapin's assertion that '(E)ighteenth century Edinburgh was a city preponderant and given over to the production of culture and services rather than to the production of things' (Shapin 1974: 3) is a familiar if erroneous judgement, which readers of this book will recognise as a convenient falsehood (see the work of Richard Rodger). Shapin judges that the RSE was the result of

> (R)ealignments among traditional cultural institutions, established to safeguard traditional interests. In view of the circumstances of its founding, it is hardly surprising that it came under attack from those whose conception of the organization of science was heavily influenced by a liberal scientistic model of society. (Shapin 1974: 40)

Above all, the growing influence of natural scientists was their desire to establish the epistemological and methodological autonomy of science. Tensions there were, between the physical (scientists) and literary (humanities) classes – almost equal numbers in the early years, but dominated by the former in later ones; between landed power and liberal conceptions of society;

between the RSE and the Society of Antiquaries, who were eventually reconciled, moving into the same building in George Street. Not everyone was content. Robert Knox (1791–1862), anatomist and in cahoots with Burke and Hare in the pursuit of researchable cadavers, despite being acquitted of wrongdoing by the society in 1829, asked rhetorically, 'why should you throw away your money upon a Society rapidly hastening to the guidance of bankers' clerks, fifth-rate medical practitioners and the like. You gain nothing of Science, and as little honour' (Campbell and Smellie 1983: 71–2). Those who would defend the society argued that 'it is generally acknowledged that the most important function of the Society is to afford a unique opportunity in Scotland for scientists and scholars of all disciplines and persuasions to meet' (Campbell and Smellie 1983: 11). Not, however, if you were female, for, as Campbell and Smellie pointed out, 'the Laws of the Society indicated but did not specifically state that Fellowship be confined to the male sex' (Campbell and Smellie 1983: footnote 10, 56). Eventually, this was changed but there was a longstanding grievance that RSE was a society dominated by old white males.[24]

The point remains that while RSE has members beyond Edinburgh, and indeed, Scotland, if nothing else, its title and location, and its historic links with Edinburgh University confer a powerful nexus between city, RSE and university. The RSE does not belong to the University of Edinburgh; but it often seems that way.

Professional Edinburgh

Edinburgh is a 'professional' city. In Chapter 3, we saw that the city has significantly more people employed in professions (34 per cent) than in Scotland and Britain as a whole (in each case, 23 per cent). If we include those described as 'associate professionals and technical', over half (52 per cent) of people employed in the city are in, or ancillary to, professional occupations.[25] Thus, Edinburgh has more people in professional employment by a factor of 150 per cent[26] compared with the national averages.

The critic might argue that 'professional' jobs are simply better paid with added status and restricted practices. Not so. Being a member of a professional association is usually required if one wants to practise as, say, a lawyer, doctor, architect, accountant and so on. If nothing else, 'professional indemnity' is well worth having, as it defends the practitioner from lawsuits. You can, for example, sue your plumber for negligence, but suing your doctor or lawyer is quite another matter. You will be confronted with the full might of professional services. This is not simply about protecting self-interests, but guaranteeing a level of services and training by those so registered.

The threat, for the professional, is being 'struck off', unable to practise within the law. Your plumber or electrician or builder might simply reinvent themselves in another guise and carry on as before. Nothing of this is to imply that said trades are more venal and self-serving than doctors or lawyers, for example; merely that 'professions' carry duties and responsibilities, and are subject to serious sanctions if not carried out according to professional codes of conduct. Being 'struck off' is tantamount to professional and employment death. In the words of Paisey and Paisey, who reviewed education and training in four professions:

> A major factor in the professionalization of each profession was the establishment at an early stage of educational requirements which sought both to restrict entry, thereby preserving competitive advantage, and acted as evidence of the professional competence of the practitioner, therefore, providing public confidence. (Paisey and Paisey 2000: 108)

If Edinburgh is a city where professional employment matters far more than elsewhere, then rules and codes of conduct are policed by professional associations; and many of these are headquartered in the city reflecting its position as a national capital. Why, however, discuss professions in the context of 'enlightenment'? Simply put, professionalisation involves education rather than simply training on the job. David Walker, who was an eminent Regius Professor of law at Glasgow University put it well: 'it is not the function of the university to give purely professional training or expressly prepare a student for professional examinations or for the practice of any profession . . . its proper function is to study and teach law' (quoted in Paisey and Paisey 2000: 78). In other words, there is a close nexus between professions and university education. Thus, professions are embedded in 'enlightenment'.

The Paiseys' study (2000) is interesting, because it provides a comparison of the professional education for accountancy (the authors were asked to carry it out by the Institute of Chartered Accountants of Scotland (ICAS), and it was published under their auspices) along with medicine, law and architecture for comparative purposes. In Scotland at any rate, all four professions now insist on a university degree followed by professional training, with the exception of medicine a relatively recent change, because 'the academic arm confers status as well as subject authority' (Paisey and Paisey 2000: vii). The professional criteria of all four fields were established in the nineteenth century reflecting the historical growth of the professional bodies. While medicine is often regarded as the epitome of professions among its members, and law is an established and respected profession, architecture is usually seen as a more youthful profession, whereas the Royal Institute of Architects in Scotland was (re) formed in 1916, younger than the better-known RIBA (founded in 1834).

Accountancy in Scotland, on the other hand, and its professional body, ICAS, is the oldest in the world, founded in 1853 in Edinburgh and in Glasgow, and 1866 Aberdeen, with Royal Charters quickly following a year or two later. (In England and Wales, the equivalent body, ICAEW, only got its Royal Charter in 1880.) The local accountancy bodies in the three Scottish cities were merged in 1951.

It was not the case that the Scottish organisation, ICAS, is somehow subordinated to its English/British counterpart for it provides affiliations and validation for many similar organisations elsewhere in the world should they wish to do so. Indeed, members of ICAS voted to reject a merger with the English/British body in the late 1980s (Paterson 1994: 171). In each of the four professions studied, a university education was deemed to be essential for practising the relevant profession, dated back to the nineteenth century, and reinforced and consolidated in modern times. Lest it be thought otherwise, the authors of the comparative study conclude that: 'the accountancy profession enjoys a relationship with its professional bodies that is arguably stronger than that which exists in Medicine, Law and Architecture' (Paisey and Paisey 2000: xi). And the relevance to Edinburgh? All four professional bodies are headquartered in the city. We might note too that medicine in Edinburgh has separate Royal Colleges for surgeons and for physicians, while in Glasgow they operate as one.

There is an important sociological point to be made. If professional practice is about education, and not simply training, then the relevant professional bodies are rooted in the educational and scholarly institutions of the city. The nature of 'enlightenment' in Edinburgh, then, is not simply about having an 'ancient' (if younger) university than other Scottish cities, but that it is connected into bodies such as the Royal Society of Edinburgh which draws its Fellows not simply from academia, but professional and business life. The spread and density of professional bodies in the city reinforces this commitment to 'enlightenment' and the pursuit of knowledge rather than narrow 'technical' specialty.

And as if to confirm the interconnectedness of knowledge and professional status, Edinburgh's New Club has a significant number of 'professional' members as evinced by the 2008 membership list[27]: while lawyers outnumber others (with over 120 members either with law degrees or in professional practice), doctors, as one would expect, are also well-represented, but on a par, so are accountants and chartered surveyors,[28] all with around fifty members. It is this density of professional associations and related activities which contributes to an enlightened city, and related status, positive and negative. If Edinburgh gives off an aura of exclusivity, that is related to its interconnected spheres of education, professions and the ferment of ideas.

CONCLUSION

It is impossible to work out who runs Edinburgh without proper consideration of the Tounis College, its oldest university, which is not only a major employer in the city, but has had its own, often unfortunate, impact on the fabric of the city. The university is also embedded in the pursuit of 'enlightenment', not always successfully, but crucially connected into learned societies like the RSE, as well as the professional institutes in the city.

Edinburgh, in its various manifestations, has benefitted from the commodification of 'enlightenment'; the view that in the title of one book: *How Scots Invented the Modern World* (Arthur Herman,[29] published in 2001). Here is an obvious tourist trail to add to the plethora. Some are more 'educational' than others, such as *Curious Edinburgh* which was established by members of the university's Science Studies Unit (http://curiousedinburgh. org/scottish-enlightenment-tour/), while others are more 'commercial' as on Trip Advisor (one reviewer begins: 'Hugo hauls ass through passageways in the New Town'). In short, you can take your pick from tours with greater or lesser intellectual content, turning the city into a vast tourist trail, as residents weave their way through groups standing windily on pavements while guides sell their various wares. All help to commodify enlightenment, education and Edinburgh as a seamless web as if it had never been other.

All told give off an aura of culture and learning, at least in principle, even though on the ground, as it were, its practices and policies are not always in the public interest. The city, though, is a place subject to radical physical change, and in the next chapter we will consider these: they are 'Pies in the Sky', and 'Holes in the Ground'.

NOTES

1. I am grateful to Lindsay Paterson for his generous advice in writing this chapter.
2. To avoid tedious repetition, I will refer to the University of Edinburgh as 'the university' or even 'Edinburgh' where that meaning is clear and unambiguous. A few years ago, in one of its many PR makeovers, it stipulated that its 'proper' title was '*The* University of Edinburgh', and not 'Edinburgh University' (definite article was *de rigueur*) and insisted that all letterheads and communications be adjusted accordingly. It is unlikely that the university has ever been able to enforce its use.
3. After a tempestuous period when it was taken over by media mogul Robert Maxwell and his Pergamon Press, Aberdeen University Press went into liquidation in 1996. It was re-formed in 2014. For a brief account, see <https://en.wikipedia.org/wiki/Aberdeen_University_Press>.
4. Its website says it was founded in 1875 in Musselburgh, which is taking liberties with history. What was founded in 1875 was the School of Cookery in central Edinburgh. As Queen Margaret College/University it moved from Clermiston in west Edinburgh in 1970, and to Musselburgh in 2007. For a history, see Tom Begg's *The Excellent Women* (1997).
5. Cited in A. J. Youngson (1966) in footnote 26 on page 305.

6. The university's website gives this account: 'The 1858 Act also makes provision for the Curators of Patronage, whose powers are now very largely formal. By that Act, the patronage of seventeen Chairs, previously in the gift of the Town Council, was transferred to seven Curators of Patronage. In accordance with Edinburgh Ordinance No 173, four of the Curators of Patronage shall be nominated by the University Court and three by The City of Edinburgh Council. The Curators also have the right of nomination to the office of Principal and now have the patronage of sixteen Chairs and a share in the patronage of the Chairs of Agriculture and Rural Economy, Civil Law, Constitutional Law, Humanity, Scots Law, and the George Watson and Daniel Stewart's Chair of Political Economy.' <https://www.ed.ac.uk/governance-strategic-planning/governance/university-governance/curators-of-patronage>.

7. 'The Dunf', as it was known, had been founded in 1905 by the Andrew Carnegie Trust in Dunfermline as a physical education training college for women. It was moved to Aberdeen during the Second World War, and permanently there in 1950. In 1966, the College moved to custom-built accommodation at Cramond in Edinburgh. On merging with Moray House in 1998, it sold the Cramond site and moved to Holyrood in 2001.

8. <https://discovery.nationalarchives.gov.uk/details/r/C4386398>.

9. For an excellent account of how Scottish universities developed, see Donald Withrington's 'The Scottish Universities: Living Traditions? Old Problems Renewed?' (Scottish Government Yearbook 1992: 131–41).

10. In 1989, the-then Secretary of State for Scotland, Malcolm Rifkind, declined to fund Edinburgh's Dental School.

11. I was a postgraduate student in Percy's Department of Urban Design and Regional Planning between 1969 and 1971. He was undoubtedly a modernist, having learned his trade in the postwar London County Council, with a liking for the grand sweeping gestures which would usher in the New Jerusalem. He often alluded to Geddes in his lectures, but arguably as rhetorical window-dressing.

12. The Black Papers on education of the 1970s had as their main recurrent topics the student unrest of the 1960s and 1970s and the problems facing comprehensive schools. See <https://en.wikipedia.org/wiki/Black_Papers>.

13. The remarkable thing to many, including the author, was that students had taken the trouble to do such a detailed reading of the footnotes in David Hume's work; or possibly not.

14. James Beattie had taken Hume to task as early as 1770: <https://en.wikipedia.org/wiki/An_Essay_on_the_Nature_and_Immutability_of_Truth>. I am grateful to Lindsay Paterson for drawing my attention to Beattie's work.
15. 'Domicile' refers to students' home addresses at the time of university application.
16. The agit-prop theatre company 7:84 (7 per cent owned 84 per cent of land) had been founded in 1971 by playwright John McGrath, their most famous play being *The Cheviot, the Stag and the Black, Black Oil.*
17. Labour had double the number of seats (forty-four), and 41 per cent of the vote; the SNP two seats, and 17 per cent.
18. Opponents of Scottish devolution had forced what was known as the 40 per cent rule, such that this proportion of those on the electoral register had to vote in favour. Not everyone voted, and this included dead people, thus deemed to be No voters by default. It was, in retrospect, a gerrymander which worked.
19. UCCA began in 1961, and was the central clearing house for university admissions. It was succeeded by UCAS (Universities and Colleges Admissions Service) in 1993 when the admissions systems for universities and polytechnics were amalgamated.
20. The 1992 Further and Higher Education Act repatriated control of Scottish universities and colleges, first to the Scottish Education Department (by then known as the Scottish Office Education Department, a change largely forgotten subsequently), and post-devolution in 1999, to Scottish Government.
21. The writer Peter Scott, who edited the *Times Higher Education Supplement* (THES) for many years, before becoming Professor of higher education studies at University College London, has written perceptively, as befits someone from Berwick-upon-Tweed, about Scottish universities. See his article, 'Scottish Higher Education Regained: Accident or Design?', *Scottish Affairs*, May 1994, vol. 7 (First Series), no. 1, pp. 68–85; and his blog of July 2021: <https://www.hepi.ac.uk/2021/07/21/scottish-universities-are-a-casualty-of-the-independence-debate/>.
22. The RSE's Charter explicitly forbids that to this day.
23. Steve Shapin was a member of Edinburgh University's science studies unit from 1972 until 1989. See <https://en.wikipedia.org/wiki/Steven_Shapin>.
24. The term 'old (or angry) white men' became a term of abuse which emerged in USA in the early 1990s in response to affirmative action (of gender and 'race'). It then entered wider cultural and political discourses. See, for example, 'Royal Society of

Edinburgh president dethroned after fellows' revolt', *The Times*, 19 February 2021. Dame Ann Glover, President, had wanted to extend her term of office, along with other elected officials, for what *The Times* called 'unexplained special reasons'. The former dean of the Edinburgh Law School said that in his judgement, the extension was in breach of the society's laws and would make her continuation in office illegal.

25. For details, see <https://www.nomisweb.co.uk/reports/lmp/la/1946157416/subreports/empocc_time_series/report.aspx?>.

26. In comparison, Glasgow has 29 per cent directly employed in professions, Dundee 25 per cent and Aberdeen 22 per cent.

27. To remind the reader, 2008 is the latest year for which we have data in the public sphere, but, arguably, it is indicative of the modern membership all the same.

28. We have not explicitly dealt with surveyors and their professional body, the Royal Institute of Chartered Surveyors. Suffice it to say that they present themselves on their website as follows: 'RICS in Scotland works closely with Scottish Government on matters relating to land, property and construction': <https://www.rics.org/uk/about-rics/where-we-are/uk-and-ireland/rics-in-scotland/>.

29. The author Arthur Herman is described as a coordinator of the Western Civilisation Program at the Smithsonian Institute in Washington DC. He had a brief stay in Edinburgh as a teenager.

8

Developing Edinburgh:
Pies in the Sky, Holes in the Ground

In this chapter I will explore planning developments in Edinburgh; in the subsequent one, the case of the Edinburgh trams, the 'big ticket' development which, though up and running after a fashion since 2014, has been the most controversial development of them all, and still not complete seven years later. Why examine planning developments anyway? It is because systems of power are, by and large, opaque; and often it is difficult to see where power lies. Developments, however, are actions which illuminate power; they shine light on how decisions are made, and who benefits (and loses). In other words, we stand a better chance of seeing more clearly who runs things.

Edinburgh is no stranger to planning controversies, arguably more than most cities, in part because of its historical and architectural features – the council issues a Building Heights and Roofscapes Planning Guidance[1] – but mainly because of pressures to develop in a bounded city with, at least historically, a tight green belt policy. The Abercrombie Plan of 1949 reflected those pressures, which have amplified in the subsequent half-century. We take as our marker the building of the city bypass around the city in the 1980s, which in hindsight has encouraged building up to the city limits, and beyond (see Figure 8.1, page 198).

CITY AS GROWTH MACHINE

Edinburgh is a city with many holes in the ground, none more famous than the opera-house-that-never-was in Castle Terrace until it was filled in by an office block/ theatre (The Traverse) in the 1990s.[2] In previous chapters we have seen how planning and development have driven much of the city's politics, dominated so long by local building and property trades, shaping what the American sociologist Harvey Molotch called, memorably, the 'growth machine' (Molotch 1976). The political economy of place seems an apt way of understanding the social, economic and political processes which have shaped the social ecology of the city, underpinning its ecology of power relations. Not that this was unique to Edinburgh; rather, it provides a good example of a place where power and property are intimately connected.

By 'growth machine', Molotch meant that

> a city and, more generally, any locality, is conceived as the areal expression of the interests of some land-based elite. Such an elite is seen to profit through the increasing intensification of the land use of the area in which its members hold a common interest. (Molotch 1976: 309)

Furthermore,

> We need to see each geographical map-whether of a small group of land parcels, a whole city, a region, or a nation not merely as a demarcation of legal, political, or topographical features, but as a mosaic of competing land interests capable of strategic coalition and action. (Molotch 1976: 11)

The point is not that Edinburgh is unique, but that the dominance of local property interests through the political process lasted much longer than in comparable cities. In short, local capital was historically dominant. This was recognisable to Molotch in the context of American cities: that because the city is a growth machine, 'it draws a special type of person into politics, businessmen, and among businessmen, the most parochial sort' (Molotch 1976: 317). The reason seemed obvious, that 'people often become "involved" in government, especially in the local party structure and fund raising, for reasons of land business and related processes of resource distribution' (Molotch 1976: 317). There is a rider: that 'when growth ceases to be an issue, some of the investments made in the political system to influence and enhance growth will no longer make sense' (Molotch 1976: 329).

Molotch was writing about US cities in the 1970s. To what extent does his analysis apply to Edinburgh fifty years later? We saw in Chapters 2 and 3 that local capital no longer dominates local politics; that, quite literally, the (Progressive) party was over. And yet, the politics of land development has never been so significant. What, we might ask, does that tell us about the connection between property and power today? To what extent has it changed, and why? And, crucially, who benefits?

Out on the Edge

Our first task is to document the key developments in the past twenty or thirty years, since the creation of the city bypass in the 1980s. The city bypass road system was created in sections: first, the Colinton section opened in 1981, then Dreghorn in 1985, Sighthill in 1986, Burdiehouse and Sheriffhall in 1988, and finally, the Gilmerton section in 1989; creating a semi-circular road around the city, like a belt from coast to coast. Quickly, the development attractions became obvious: the earliest was The Gyle on the west side. This swathe of development lay between the Edinburgh bypass (officially designated as the A720), and the city, thus taking advantage of being on the 'right' side of the green belt, which did not, in any case, stop the Royal Bank of Scotland (RBS) building on the old Gogarburn mental hospital site, nor inhibit the expansion of Edinburgh airport. There was the suspicion that greenbelt rules could be overturned if the price was right. There was a public inquiry for The Gyle in 1987, and unsurprisingly, approval was given by the Secretary of State for Scotland (this was pre-devolution) a couple of years later. The shopping centre, scaled down to 100,000 square feet so as not to compete with nearby shopping sites, was opened in 1993. Originally a joint venture between Edinburgh council, Marks and Spencer and Asda (Asda was replaced by Safeway then Morrison's), The Gyle was bought outright by M&S who sold it on to pension fund USS (Universities Superannuation Scheme) in March 2000.

Alongside the 'district shopping centre', as it was designated, was Edinburgh Park, opened in 1995, with a new 'urban quarter' planned for Edinburgh Park in 2017. The council, and particularly Labour's council leader, Donald Anderson, later to figure in the trams story, and George Kerevan,[3] at the time the Labour convener of the economic development committee, took the credit for the development, and arguably encouraged Anderson in particular to promote city economic development more actively.

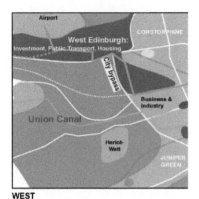

WEST

Figure 8.1 City of Edinburgh
Council Development Plan –
Spatial Strategy

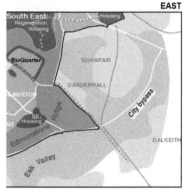

Edinburgh Park

The appeal of Edinburgh Park derived from its position near road, rail and air links, but above all, as the review of Edinburgh's office stock for 2010 commented:

> it appealed particularly to organisations with large numbers of 'backroom' staff, who needed good working conditions and proximity to facilities, for example, the Gyle shopping centre and who didn't necessarily require a 'prestige' address or the high density networking and personal contacts associated with the city centre.

It was, in other words, classic 'back-office' space on relatively cheap land, although the assumption that back-office staff needed access to shopping, whereas, revealingly, downtown 'contacts' in places like the New Club were considered to be for higher executives, is an interesting division of cultural and economic labour. Certainly, it did not prevent RBS seizing upon the Gogarburn site, allegedly to the detriment of Napier University who were spread thinly over many sites, and who had made a bid for Gogarburn, losing out to a then-rampant RBS and Fred Goodwin as company headquarters.[4] This was designated, hubristically, as a 'world headquarters' by Goodwin, a 'campus', thereby fudging knowledge and commerce, on a site opened by the queen in 2005. That RBS, as well as Edinburgh Airport close by, had breached the Green Belt spectacularly on the westward side of the bypass, drew little comment; it was, after all, in the interests of economic 'development'.[5]

The BioQuarter

Close to the east end of the bypass another grand scheme was proposed: the BioQuarter, designated by Scottish Government in 2012 as an Enterprise Area, stressing its strategic economic importance including 'green growth'; it was, after all, a green-field development, but one in which planning guidance set a target for greenhouse gas (GHG) emissions 50 per cent tighter than baseline building standards. The anchor was to be the relocated Royal Infirmary of Edinburgh (RIE), a cluster of two hospitals (RIE and the Hospital for Sick Children), university research facilities (the Edinburgh University medical faculty), and start-up facilities for life science businesses. The new hospital(s) was to be the critical anchor load for the whole development. This was high ambition for exemplary sustainable development, but was largely unfulfilled. Local decision-making was governed by complex interlocking public procurement, different development timetables, sector specific funding, and private finance initiative (PFI) rules. The decision by NHS Lothian not to proceed radically reduced likely carbon savings. In particular, the loss of the Royal Hospital for Sick Children as a heat buyer (serious delays were incurred by building design faults in the cooling system) meant that modelled carbon savings fell dramatically. Organisations, synergetic on paper, were governed by their own sectoral rules (such as those of health boards), all seeking in terms of their own logics the 'best value' for their organisation; and so the collective actor/free-ride problem remained unresolved.

Shawfair

Just over the hill lay the Millerhill Energy-from-Waste plant on a brownfield site of the former Monktonhall colliery,[6] and technically in the county of Midlothian. In 2003, the local council had the vision of a model development combining former coal mining areas with greenfield land, and commissioned a study to assess the feasibility of developing 'Shawfair' mine water district heating scheme using the former coal mine as heat source.[7] In 2005, a joint venture was established between Midlothian Council and a private developer, based on a mine water geo-thermal heat network. By 2009, the developer had withdrawn due to the financial crisis and banks crash, and the heat source was abandoned. Five years later a much more conventional 'private new town' named Shawfair, borrowing the name of a nearby farm,[8] was formed as a joint venture between the landowner (Buccleuch Estates) and a house builder (Mactaggart and Mickel). By 2016, a recycling and energy recovery (RERC) scheme at Millerhill had been designed around a waste treatment plant run jointly between Midlothian and City of Edinburgh councils around waste collected by each council which would otherwise go to landfill. It had been almost a decade since the district energy proposal for the Bio-Quarter, just a mile or two as the crow flies, over the hill, had referenced the Millerhill RERC as an area-wide heat source for its own scheme. Grand plans at either site had come to little that was new and sustainable.

It may seem odd to focus on development in Edinburgh on its west and east peripheries, but it reflects the fact that infrastructural developments like building a bypass carry their own logic. A city which had struggled to hold the line against developments in the Green Belt found it so much harder to do so when a road belt invited its further erosion by building up to and over the bypass. That, furthermore, there was a complex interchange of public and private capital indicated the way things were going, the former aiding and abetting the latter.

Downtown Developments: There Shall be a Scottish Parliament

The most obvious, and controversial, development in central Edinburgh was the building of the Scottish parliament, opened on its permanent site in 2004. When the devolution referendum was passed in 1997 by a large majority, the task was to find a site. It had been assumed that the former Royal High School building on Calton Hill would be chosen – it had, after all, been designated as such in 1979 before the scheme was scuppered by the rigged referendum,[9] but it quickly became obvious that it was inappropriately small. In any case, it was asserted that Calton Hill had acquired 'shibboleth' status in the eyes of the incoming Labour/Liberal Democrat administration.[10]

At the time, Holyrood – there were brewery offices on the site – was nowhere in the race; the front runners were a new-build at Victoria Quay adjacent to the new Scottish Office block in Leith; and similar on a former railway goods yard at Haymarket. Both came in at modest, ostensible, prices of £40m; even though the £40m price was highly notional and waved in the air by the then First Minister Donald Dewar, who possibly knew better than to give an exact figure. It was then claimed by the opposition parties that the ultimate price was ten times that. Forty million pounds would have bought very little; possibly a modest office block extension in Leith, which many feared and some hoped in that it would diminish the status of a 'parliament' which they did not want in any case: kill home rule by limiting its vision, diminishing its purpose.[11] The Scottish Executive/government set up a public inquiry chaired by former Conservative politician and lawyer, Peter Fraser, Lord Fraser of Carmyllie QC, which reported in 2004, and had the effect of deflating public and political indignation. What Scotland got, on the site of the former brewery next to Holyroodhouse was not a mock Gothic edifice, but a construction, in the words of its architect, Enric Miralles, 'that is not monumental in the classic sense'. As I wrote at the time, 'the models we have to hand do not fit our needs: Scotland is not ruled by a patrician class, nor by a burgher class, nor by a godly class. Maybe we need a parliament *sans class*; classy, to be sure, but the property of the people, the common weal: a parliament for a new century' (McCrone 2004: 10).

What's in a Name? From St James Centre to Edinburgh St James

Never think that the present has little to do with the past. The east end of Edinburgh is now dominated by a Quarter, no less[12];

calling itself Edinburgh St James, but better known to locals as the St James Centre. At least that is what it used to be when, post-1960s, it was a combination of Scottish Office block (New St Andrews House, to distinguish it from its older and more illustrious art deco St Andrews House, round the corner in Regent Terrace), and adjacent shopping centre. It has always been an interesting site, and Abercrombie had designs on it in his 1949 Plan:

> The St James Square area was selected because it offers a natural compact area . . . with magnificent views from its steep slopes to Leith Walk, the Firth of Forth and the Fifeshire mountains [*sic*[13]]. Here it is suggested that Edinburgh might find the most appropriate site for a Civic Theatre and Concert Hall with music practice rooms and lecture rooms in the upper storeys . . . The huge building would be approached from St James Square . . . (Abercrombie 1949: 57)

The problem was that a property free-for-all had degraded the site into a slum over the past century or so, with in-building between the tenement blocks. A tale well told by the journalist George Rosie (https://sceptical.scot/2019/08/the-tangled-history-of-edinburgh-st-james/), Moultrie's Hill[14] became home to a piece of New Brutalist architecture described by the *Architects' Journal* as 'a monstrous aesthetic and social blot'. Rosie described it as 'that notorious array of dark, concrete-clad buildings that became the most roundly disliked modern architecture in Scotland', a contentious judgement only in the sense that there is no shortage of competing candidates.[15] The Royal Bank of Scotland had thought about siting its headquarters there, close by its St Andrews Square office, but George Mathewson who took to the idea lost out to incoming Fred Goodwin who got his way by acquiring as his 'World HQ' the site at Gogarburn on the western fringe as described above. St James Centre had been anchored by John Lewis department store, which continued business throughout the demolition and rebirth of 'Edinburgh St James', designated a 'Quarter' no less, in the words of the developers' hype[16]:

> The scheme has been designed to create an intuitive and accessible circuit around the city. Anchored by places and experiences, it will draw people from one place to the next, becoming a key component of the map of Edinburgh. Inspired by the great gallerias of the world, including Galleria Vittorio Emanuele in Milan, to BCE

Place in Toronto, the integrated approach to the planning, design and management of the project will create a unique, inspiring place to live in and visit.

Anyone who knows Milan might consider that a very tall order, and requiring a population like the *Milanese*, who are steeped in shopping. Glasgow may be miles better, but even it is not up to a Milan standard of shopping. There is uncritical support for the project from different levels of government, local and central. CEC planning convener, Neil Gardiner[17]: 'Despite pressures from online shopping nationally, Edinburgh has a buoyant retail industry evidenced by the £1bn investment in the Edinburgh St James development due to open in 2020.' Edinburgh's economy convener, Gavin Barrie, said:

> The new St James will transform the east end of Edinburgh's Princes Street, providing much needed premium retail space and leisure facilities, new homes and a world class five-star hotel in the heart of the city – creating thousands of jobs in the process and adding millions to the Scottish economy each year. (See note 16)

Behind all this lay the hand of Scottish government. Economy secretary Keith Brown said[18]:

> The Scottish government warmly welcomes this major investment in Edinburgh and Scotland, which will have significant positive impact on construction activity, jobs and the economy. I am particularly pleased that the Scottish government has been able to help unlock the investment by working in partnership with the Scottish Futures Trust and Edinburgh City Council on the *Growth Accelerator Model* through which we will be contributing significant sums and assisting the council to manage risk. This is a major signal of investor confidence in Scotland, and provides further demonstration that Scotland is open for business.

We will find the Growth Accelerator model playing a major part in this tale of Edinburgh's developments.

Who are the actors? Given the obvious fact that most players are not local, anchoring the development is vital. The architects Allan Murray, who operate from a small office in a fairly insalubrious part of Edinburgh (off Harrison Road in Shandon/ Gorgie), were described as the 'concept architect' for the development (it was London-based Jestico + Whiles who were responsible for what became known to locals as the 'golden turd' hotel).

Allan Murray Architects (AMA) were also involved in the other city development scheme, Caltongate (q.v.). AMA have been described by a competitor as a 'developer's architect'. The main contractors were Laing O'Rourke who were the largest privately owned construction company based in the UK, with ARUP the structural engineer and TÜV SÜD, a German company based in Munich, providing services engineering including a CHP energy centre for the development.

Who owns it? That is not an easy question to answer, given the convolutions of development politics and economics. It seems, however, to be Nuveen Real Estate who are a subsidiary of TIAA, Teachers Insurance and Annuity Association of America-College Retirement Equities Fund. This is a Fortune 100 financial services organisation based in New York with assets of 1 trillion USD, and founded – ironically – by Andrew Carnegie. In 2017, TIAA was largest global investor in agriculture, and the third largest commercial real estate manager in the world. Nuveen is the investment manager of TIAA, and TH Real Estate, the developers of SJC, is described as an 'affiliate' of Nuveen. It was formed out of the 2014 merger of Henderson Global Investors' real estate business and TIAA-CREF. In 2016 TH Real Estate sold a 75 per cent stake in SJC to the Dutch pension asset manager APG, which is the asset manager for the Netherlands' biggest pension fund, ABP. TH Real Estate continue to hold 25 per cent of SJC.

The new Quarter achieved instant notoriety associated with the design of the hotel, known variously as the Golden Turd, or, in politer circles, the Walnut Whip[19]; in the words of the developer[20]: 'designed by [London] architectural practice Jestico + Whiles, has also been carefully designed to evoke the spirit of the Capital'. The winding bronze-coloured steel 'ribbon' facade has been likened to 'spirals of paper, a reference to the many printing presses which uses to pepper the surrounding area in past times'. That is a strange reading of history, for there is little evidence that the top of the Walk was ever a centre of printing.[21] George Rosie's list of erstwhile residents of Moultrie's Hill makes no mention of printers and printing. The development squeezed through the planning committee by a vote of seven to five, despite the opposition of the city's planning department. It did so on the dubious distinction that 'at least it's better than [what was there before]', a response which framed the whole development and helped to mute criticism. Nevertheless, it does not take much to imagine the 'golden turd/walnut whip' becoming a subject of local derision, and it is unlikely to weather well in the Edinburgh climate. It has the potential to become a notable successor to the erstwhile 'monument to a drunken scaffolder' (officially 'The Kinetic Sculpture' (1973–83) which used to decorate the centre of the Leith Walk/Picardy Place roundabout close by; designed to light up, it rarely did).

Luring shops away from Princes Street (more than a dozen niche chain stores) may well be behind CEC's proposal to relax restrictions on food and drink shops on Princes Street. The developers Nuveen claim that the development 'will help move Edinburgh further up the UK retail rankings, from thirteenth to eighth and will support the city's tourist industry'.[22] The fact that there is a general crisis in the retail shopping model, and reactions against massive tourist influx, does not seem to impinge much on this development. The unforeseen impact of Covid-19 makes its future even more unpredictable. The physical/environmental aspects of this development left much to be desired, notably, the 'cliff' elevation as viewed from Picardy Place; the use of limestone over sandstone as cladding; the loss of active frontage on Leith Street; future adaptability and durability – the previous scheme lasted only thirty-five years. Office development was dropped from the original planning application, and in any case, there is too much dependence on retail, in the context of declining high streets. The Cockburn Society's director at the time observed[23]:

> Much of the story of Edinburgh is to do with under-statement and economy of means, attitudes which gave rise to a remarkable urban fabric of continuity and homogeneity. Unlike any other development project in the city St James is about a whole quarter and trying to repair the urban grain; it is not the place for 'standing out', but for 'fitting in'.

The strong implication is that the scheme failed to do that. Despite claims from the developers that 'we have a special focus on sustainability', the development plans basement parking for 1500 cars, three times the number of spaces as previously. This, together with car dominance in Picardy Place, indicates that statements about sustainable transport are not serious. Nor do statements from the developer that 'we have built key relationships with city institutions such as Edinburgh Airport' strike one as a commitment to sustainability; and surely Edinburgh airport is a private profit-seeking company, not a 'city institution' in any meaningful sense of the term, and in any case, one with its own problems as regards climate change. 'Edinburgh St James is also committed to setting positive green benchmarks' sounds meaningless, as does 'rather than making a profit and return, it is about being part of a wider city for a long period of time'.[24] In a nice example of the biter bit, the developers formally objected to the plans for the Dunard Concert Hall close by on the grounds of its height. The concert hall is being funded by the Dunard Fund and the Royal Bank of Scotland, with contributions from Scottish and UK governments, and City of Edinburgh Council.[25]

Behind Edinburgh St James lies the hand of Scottish government and its Growth Accelerator model (GAM). The road design around the Quarter has been criticised by one local councillor as locking 'the city centre into very high volumes of private vehicle use'. Furthermore, the GAM agreement allowed for up to £61.4m to be invested in public spaces surrounding the site, and suggestions that it allows the developers not to pay £1.4m in public spaces. Sustrans criticised the 'gyratory' Picardy Place design for not meeting national standards on street design guidance from Scottish government. The campaign group Living Streets Edinburgh commented on an 'evident lack of transparency about the relationship between the council and the developer, with big decisions on traffic and parking being taken behind closed doors before local people and citizens as a whole can have their say'.[26]

What, then, does the St James Centre/Edinburgh St James/ Quarter, however badged, tell us about who runs Edinburgh? The professional planners employed by the council were against it; the councillors narrowly in favour, mainly on the grounds that it was an improvement on what had gone before. Scottish government was in favour, and had a historic claim by way of its New St Andrews House office-block, but badged the development as a chance to use its new device, the Growth Accelerator model. And private capital? Certainly not local: a US teachers superannuation fund, then a Dutch pension fund, with interest in capital appreciation. Assets are considered as financial numbers, not physical entities; what Arnaboldi and Lapsley (2010) have called 'the calculable city'. Appreciating financial assets is what matters, the rest is dressing-up. Recall Harvey Molotch's notion of the city as a 'growth machine', but in which local actors are bit-players faced with global and highly mobile capital. There are local actors, local facilitators, notably AMA (Allan Murray Architects), who have finessed a range of services and are described as the 'concept architect' with eyes and ears to the local ground. We will see AMA's local hand behind other schemes in the city, none more so than in our next example, Caltongate.

Caltongate (No More)

It is unusual to have a site with a gross floor area (GFA) of between 50,000 and 100,000 square metres in the centre of a historic city, but that is what constituted an area in Edinburgh's Old Town east of Waverley station, and bounded by the High Street, the Canongate and Holyroodhouse. Historically, this was an industrial zone, containing gas works and breweries, and latterly a bus depot and garage. This development resulted largely from the demolition in 2005 of the New Street bus depot (owned by Eastern Scottish/SMT) as indicated on the city's masterplan. Subsequently, the new CEC offices were built on the western part of the site next to Waverley station, and Caltongate, as it was initially designated, was located largely on the eastern side of New Street. Formerly, this site (known as North Back of Canongate[27] and later as Back Calton Road), contained gas works and related premises running along a road connecting Holyrood and Leith Street, occupying the low land between the High Street ridge and Calton Hill and running in a gloomy gully between them. The land between the Canongate and Calton Road comprised, historically, the 'lands' of medieval houses on the Canongate. In modern times, there were few people living there, which made mobilising the local population to oppose the scheme almost impossible, for most, in any case, were clustered in affected properties at the bottom of the Royal Mile.

The initial proposal by developer Mountgrange, who allegedly bought the site for £20m in 2004 (*Sunday Times*, 29 March 2009), was for a £300m development project (on a 220,000 sq ft site) with a 200-bed five-star hotel and conference centre, and arts quarter [*sic*], a new public square, offices and 200 new houses, a quarter of these designated as 'affordable'. It would have involved demolishing a 1930s block of tenements designed by legendary city architect Ebenezer MacRae. Local architect, Allan Murray Architects (AMA: q.v.) won the contract to design the development. In any event, Mountgrange collapsed in 2009; its sole funder for this project having been HBoS (Halifax/Bank of Scotland) who withdrew their support for the project in the context of the wider banking crisis. The Caltongate scheme had drawn the ire of Historic Scotland and the Edinburgh World Heritage Trust, and UNESCO queried the city's World Heritage status. Deloitte, Mountgrange's administrator, tried to sell on the development, and various companies expressed an interest including Prism Developments, a Canadian company. Said one property insider:

> We checked with contacts in Canada and they said that these guys are basically frontmen with a number of secondary developments in Canada. It is a small operation that goes out and looks for investors. That does not make them bad people but it means they have no real experience. For a scheme of this size, it is unusual that the bank would look to move it forward with someone who has no real track record. But as long as they get their money in, they won't care. (Cited in *Caltongate Development News*,[28] 16 December 2011)

Nothing came of that.

The city, meanwhile, was keen for some sort of development to go ahead, given that the bus depot site had been cleared. Councillor Tom Buchanan, the city's economic development leader at the time, said:

> Obviously we would like somebody to take the Caltongate site forward. We will not get into detailed discussions until we know what they have agreed with Deloitte. But if someone takes on the former Mountgrange land we will look to enter into discussions on the way for forward. (*Caltongate Development News*, 16 December 2011)

By 2010, the site had been sold, in a closed deal, to South African developer Artisan Real Estate Investors, registered in the Isle of Man, which was convenient for tax purposes. By 2013, the city council's development sub-committee voted eleven to two to grant Artisan a three-year extension to the original planning consents. The company was thereby legally entitled to demolish the two listed buildings, the Sailors' Ark, and Canongate Venture, but gave an undertaking not to do so. Marion Williams, director

of Edinburgh's Cockburn Association, said the planning committee's decision was one of the worst she had ever seen:

> Our major concern is the developer is receiving permissions to
> demolish two buildings where there has been work done to prove
> there are viable alternatives. And the material conditions behind
> the original planning consent have changed because the economic
> climate in 2008 was completely different to where we are now in
> 2013. (*Caltongate Planning Consent News*, 21 March 2013)

The crunch came in January 2014 when a revised scheme was
approved by councillors, the development management sub-
committee voting it through narrowly, eight to six. In the revised
scheme, the two listed buildings were not to be demolished, but
turned into hotels: Sailors' Ark into a so-called aparthotel (only
the façade on the Royal Mile was retained), and Canongate
Venture into a five-star hotel. The scheme as a whole was criticised for over-providing hotels, offices, pubs/clubs and retail
outlets. Housing space had been cut, with only 185 apartments,
around 40 per cent fewer than originally planned. The architect,
however, remained the same, Allan Murray Architects. The local
Green party councillor, Nigel Bagshaw, described the development as 'alien' to the character of the Old Town and not 'out of
place on the surface of the moon'.[29] One councillor who voted
the scheme through declared it 'not hideous enough to oppose'.
A band of Scottish authors,[30] albeit not many of whom lived
in the city, described it thus: 'a massive stale, sterile modernist
confection of concrete by a South African speculative developer
which is completely at odds with its surroundings, is to be built
in the heart of the Old Town, just a few hundred yards from the
historic Canongate Kirk and Holyrood Palace'.

The council itself had pre-empted things by decanting to a
new-build called 'Waverley Court' in 2007 on the western
site of New Street. In the words of a local architect (personal
communication):

> It's a large lumpy building spread over the old goods yard, which
> broke several of CEC's own planning guidelines about restricting
> heights to maintain clear views down the valley. Fatally, it fronts
> onto East Market St. without any attempt to provide interest or
> inducement to passers-by – its only public face is the entrance on
> the SW corner, marked by the ridiculous 'man on scaffold'. It's not

surprising that there is no footfall along E Market St., and the new 'Square' is devoid of life.

Furthermore, there was an ill-judged proposal for a new road linking Waverley Station and the Scottish parliament, to be named 'Parliament Way'. This was to run along East Market Street then curve south to link up with Canongate more or less where the new pend has been created linking the New Waverley 'square' to Canongate. Anyone who knows the city would cut up Jeffrey Street or Cranston Street from Waverley to get onto the Canongate rather than face the dreary East Market Street. 'Parliament Way' never made it past the drawing-board.

Nevertheless, rebranded as 'New Waverley',[31] the *soi-disant* 'urban district' (not, in this case, a Quarter) was to have a public square, three hotels (two, at the time of writing, have been built – they are (down-market) Premier Inns, one of which described as a 'hub', 'features micro-rooms like those found in Japan' (as if Premier Inn rooms were not small enough). The Sailors' Ark has become an 'aparthotel' (Adagio) facing on to the Royal Mile.

By mid-2019, the square and hotels had been built. The area is curiously dead. In mid-August 2019 (pre-Covid), on a sunny early afternoon around 2 p.m., with the Edinburgh Festival in full swing and tourists streaming down the Royal Mile a few yards away, there was little foot traffic in 'New Waverley' (or 'Caltongate' if you prefer). The public square was empty apart from a couple of skateboarders; not surprisingly, given the permanent building shadow, and winds blowing in this windy city along the Waverley valley. There was no through traffic, especially on foot, and tourists head west, not east, towards the centre of town. There is a desultory attempt to 'locate' the place by setting up stone benches inscribed to Robert Sibbald who had a 'physic garden at several sites in this area'. In a cold and windy city, few are likely to sit for long on these cold marble benches. Billboards advertised coming features, including a 'food and flea' market, but anything less welcoming, or indeed, likely, is hard to imagine. At best, it might attract touring strollers, much as the farmers' market on Castle Terrace does of a Saturday, but not for local shoppers: for there aren't any. They were written out of the script some time ago.

A further feature of the scheme is the renovation of C-listed Victorian railway arches, largely derelict or used as lock-ups hitherto. These were to be converted into 'new retail and leisure' facilities including bars, restaurants and retailers. Said project director, Clive Wilding[32]:

> The arches will bring an interesting and vibrant new dimension to our New Waverley development, which is now progressing on all fronts. We are now speaking to a wide range of potential occupiers but want to see them converted into bars, cafes, restaurants and independent niche retailers – as well as providing distinctive venues for arts events and food markets. This will bring tremendous energy to the area, linking closely to both the Royal Mile and the new public square which lies at the heart of the development.

The asking rental of these arched premises was purported to be £18,000 p.a.: '15 of the 19 arches are tall enough for public use', the largest over three floors, topped by a rooftop terrace, and evidently aimed at the bar/bistro trade. It remains to be seen whether there will many takers, especially post-Covid.

One of the curious and common features of both Caltongate/'New Waverley' and St James, is that we come across a familiar architect: AMA, Allan Murray Architects. We might wonder why a small practice based in a modest building in a modest part of Edinburgh should be so prominent. Presumably they were engaged by global property developers precisely because they *were* local, and thus adjudged better able to read the political/cultural signs. A social anthropologist who did research on Caltongate for her PhD thesis drew this comment from a rival architect about Allan Murray (personal communication):

> Edinburgh's a small place. Allan and I have sat next to each other, working for other people. Allan – on one level you can't argue with success, and Allan has worked out how to do it. Unfortunately, we have a culture that asks not for architecture but for boxes to be ticked. And Allan knows how to do that. He knows how to tick the urbanist box, just enough – to tick them just enough – tradition, just enough; modernity, just enough; consultation, just enough; urbanism, just enough; sustainability, where you can nail a bit of wood to the side of your windows and that means the building's sustainable – and all that. So Allan knows how to do that . . .

Caltongate is past tense; rebranded now as New Waverley, presumably because of a history of failure and controversy associated with the old name.[33] The site was always going to be a cost

as well as an opportunity. It was a (post)industrial site dominated by a large bus storage depot, and gas works. Back-Calton
Road was, for much of its history, on the road from nowhere
to nowhere, a back passage from old town to east-end of the
new. Salubrious it was not. It is a substantial site – 122,000
sq ft – adjacent to the iconic Royal Mile and on the route to
Holyrood – parliament and palace, but off the beaten track,
which presumably is why the first developer, Mountgrange,
wanted to knock down Ebenezer MacCrae's tenement to open
up the new development and incorporate it into the new, and
so imbue the new with something of the old. This failed, and
the successor had to make do with an archway cut into the
tenement, matching the archway across the High Street into
Moray House. It is not a route one would want to take late
at night. If you wanted to go from the top of the Walk to East
Market Street, better to cut through Waverley station as the
locals do.

Furthermore, there are few people living there. True, there
were not many to begin with – when this development was
mooted, though plenty in eras past before slums were knocked
down – and protesters were hobbled by this lack of population
mass. Canongate had been cleared of its people long ago. Hence,
Caltongate/Canongate/Old Town residents associations never
quite fitted together well enough. Nevertheless, in the 1980s
renovations and conversions in Calton Road proved that there
was demand for housing in the area. In 1985, the property company Kantel converted the Old Balmoral brewery for housing,
and on the opposite side of the road, Stenhuis did similar for
the Craigwell brewery building. In their book *Renewing Old
Edinburgh*, Jim Johnson and Lou Rosenburg (2010: 231–3)
commented: 'these pioneering ventures opened up other opportunities for incremental renewal in this neglected part of the Old
Town, and led to the building of Buchanan Court, and new block
of flats and offices further west along Calton Road' (233). Some
years later, the house builder Barratt built larger housing developments. There was, then, scope for repopulating the area, but
it is hard, by 2019, to see 'public' housing being built by a council so beholden to the tourist industry and cultural capital. On
the other side of Holyrood Road/High Street the Dumbiedykes
development of the 1970s was the last major public housing
development. It would not happen today. Indeed, the two areas,

Dumbiedykes and Canongate, had much in common – sites of industry and homes of working-class people (after all, once they were twinned as, respectively, 'Back-South and Back-North of the Canongate'). Times have changed. 'Residents' there may be in 'New Waverley' but it lends itself to pieds-à-terre, 'Airbnb'-land/holiday lets and empty people spaces, much like what Quartermile (the old Royal Infirmary of Edinburgh at Lauriston) has become on the southside, a nowhere place, an investment opportunity rather than a vibrant social space. Dead spaces have costs. As it stands, Caltongate/New Waverley, call it what you will, is a nowhere place. And even if people were to live there, how could one really tell?

The *Edinburgh Guide*[34] makes an interesting juxtaposition:

> As might be expected, a project of this size has polarised public opinion between those who have welcomed the *jobs and the economic benefits* of revitalising a large, unused part of the city, while critics have said the project has been rushed through and pays scant regard for the *heritage values* of the area.

Note what is being juxtaposed there: 'jobs and economic benefits' in a 'large, unused [*sic*] part of the city', versus 'heritage values': no mention there that people have been socially cleansed from the area, and no mention of the possibility of their return.

Back to the Periphery: The Waterfront

Along the north coast of Edinburgh is an area designated as The Waterfront, a brownfield polluted site of 350 hectares of former industrial land running from Leith to Granton, and described by the council as a 'waterfront of international stature', including 18 km of coastline from Cramond to Musselburgh. The area especially to the west around Granton sits on stepped topography with three distinct levels from the shore such that developers see the advantage of the views to the north-east and the north-west, albeit it is a windy site. It is also a seriously polluted one, with fragmented ownership. At one point in the early 2000s, there were as many as six masterplans for Granton, each one pursued by different owners, and in addition to an earlier (mid-1990s) council masterplan designed to take a wider strategic view covering Granton harbour, and the National Grid assets in the west, notably around the Granton Gasworks, historically the largest in Scotland.[35] The two major owners, the National Grid, and Forth Ports Authority, privatised in 1992, had their own designs on/for the area, and the council's masterplan came to nothing.

Forth Ports, which had been established in 1967 and which provided pilotage on the Forth from the late 1980s, set about acquiring the ports of Dundee and Tilbury on the Thames, and subsequently owned six ports in Scotland including Grangemouth and Rosyth. In 2007 it bought the Nordic Group which managed terminal operations at Chatham, also on the Thames. In 2011, Forth Ports agreed a £760m takeover by the Arcus European Infrastructure Fund, a former European unit of the collapsed Australian investment firm, Babcock and Brown. Subsequently, in 2018, Arcus sold its shares in Forth Ports to PSP Investments, a Canadian Crown Corporation, one of the largest pension fund managers with more than Can$168m in 2019. PSP Investments, based in Ottawa, Ontario, invests funds for the pension plans of the Canadian Public Service, the Canadian Armed Forces, the Royal Canadian Mounted Police and the Armed Reserved Force. It has a diversified global portfolio composed of investments in public financial markets, private equity, real estate, infrastructure, natural resources and private debt. The affairs of Leith/Granton Waterfront would, on the face of it, seem of little direct interest to such a pension fund colossus, except in terms of the site's appreciation in value.

It matters to the City of Edinburgh Council (CEC) who sought to manage the Waterfront development as a part-private/part-public 'hybrid', using an arm's length company, Waterfront Edinburgh Ltd (WEL), in a joint venture with Scottish Enterprise. Indeed, the stimulus for the Edinburgh trams project, discussed in the next chapter, aimed to drive the trams to Newhaven/Granton as an economic booster for north Edinburgh. The bank/financial crisis of the late 2000s put that project on hold, and instead the trams went in the other direction, west, to the airport, before being revived as a north Edinburgh project in 2019. As we shall see in the next chapter, the special purpose vehicle (SPV) for the earlier project was also an arm's length company, TiE – Transport initiatives Edinburgh. Both SPVs, WEL and TiE, failed and were consigned to history, and the council took back direct control. In order to make the Waterfront project happen, CEC acquired the former Granton gasworks from National Grid

Property, so that it controls forty hectares-plus of development land at Granton Waterfront.

With hindsight, The Waterfront suffered from fragmented ownership, multiple changes of landowners and developers, as well as free-rider, collective action problems. The 2020 Waterfront is envisaged as a leading exemplar of low-carbon development, aiming for 3,500 net zero carbon homes with low energy bills and running costs, thereby making £12m estimated savings in household energy bills over thirty years. CEC is aiming to turn The Waterfront into a cultural hub housing the National Museums Collection Centre, the Performing Arts Studio Scotland (PASS), leisure, hotel and recreation developments including a marina, private housing developments, and coastal parks running from Lauriston Castle and Cramond in the west, to Granton in the east. The council leader commented:

> Granton is a hugely important area for the Council and the City. It is not only a Strategic Development Area in the Edinburgh Local Development Plan, but also one of seven strategic sites prioritised in the Edinburgh and South-East Scotland City Region Deal.

(Note that The Waterfront and Shawfair both figure in this City Region Deal.)

Truth to tell, The Waterfront is a complex, messy, development. It stretches for three miles from the Port of Leith in the east, to Granton harbour in the west. It is, by default, a hybrid development, part speculative and part council-led, with the latter a 'joint vehicle' with Scottish Enterprise. Ownership is fragmented – central Granton alone at one point had around 200 land owners – and National Grid who owned the gasworks, eventually sold out to the city council in 2018. Forth Ports had been promoting Western Harbour and Leith Docks in the east when imports of coal for Cockenzie power station in East Lothian came to an end. The complexity of the whole can be gauged by the 'Introduction to The Waterfront' by the 'Major Waterfront Team Manager' in 2015 (https://studylib.net/doc/5393522/an-introduction-to-edinburgh-waterfront). Not only is much of the land 'brownfield' and polluted, the council has perforce stepped in to build the central road, 'Waterfront Avenue', and construct a 45 ha public park having bought over National Grid's 'ForthQuarter' development (another Quarter, note) in 2018, and dispensed with the services of its special

vehicle Waterfront Edinburgh Ltd (WEL). Urban geographer
Hamish Kallin described the Granton end of the development
in 2015 as a 'landscape of waiting', 'a desolate and windswept
former harbour, pockmarked with piles of architectural detritus'
(Kallin 2015: 253).

Despite a more proactive approach by the city council, there
still exist tensions between public and private interests, and little
evidence of sharing risk and reward between them. By default,
the council has had to pick up the pieces, in the light of state
commitment (Scottish as well as British) to laissez-faire and 'let-
ting the market decide', which it is highly unlikely to do in any
case, left to its own devices, in contrast to most European state
developments. Deciding to go ahead with further tram developments in 2019, despite no delivery of Lord Hardie's report which
finished taking evidence around that time, reflects the council's
aim to use trams as the key booster device. Furthermore, the
council envisages The Waterfront as a leading exemplar for low
carbon, helping it to achieve local and national targets; aiming
for 3,500 net zero carbon homes with low energy bills and running costs, estimating £12m savings in household energy bills
over thirty years – a tall order, given the council's low level of
ownership, and hence direct control.

WHAT'S IN IT, AND FOR WHOM?

This chapter has sketched out some of the key planning developments since the opening of the city bypass which changed the
geography and the geometry of city development. Our focus
here has been on the major land developments rather than those
focusing simply on housing, for example, on the grounds that
these matter more in shaping Edinburgh, and in any case, housing is simply a bit-part of the whole development, another box
to be ticked by the developer ('sustainable' housing is always
good). We will explore this further in the next chapter when we
examine the trams project, complete, and yet incomplete. The
city itself is a considerable motor for change, especially in its
central status in the wider city region. It has hitched its wagon
to a net-zero development strategy, directly and indirectly, with
the capacity for multiplier benefits in the shape of improved rail
links (Shawfair being a major beneficiary, but also further afield,

Tweedbank at the other end of the Scottish Borders railway back into Edinburgh).

There is the risk that ambitious local sustainability and low carbon developments result merely in limited carbon reductions, for these are caught up in a complex overarching framework of rules geared to short-term economic growth and gross value added (GVA) metrics and sectoral performance indicators. Repeated technical–economic feasibility studies, coupled with the fact that carbon reduction is marginal to performance requirements and contracts, means that local plans are necessarily opportunistic due to periodic public funding which are commonly governed by financial years and electoral cycles. Government capital planning and sectoral investment rules are geared to short-term price such that there are no regulatory or governance routes to solving the collective actor/free rider problems at a local scale. And as we saw in The Waterfront in particular, short-term sectoral interests and performance rules militate against local coordination and collaboration for long-term benefits.

What of the view that Scottish politics and governance are 'different'; that party-political interests north of the border are of a different flavour than south of it? We have seen that Scottish government, whose political ideology might be best described as 'social market centrism', has its own financial devices, such as the Scottish Futures Trust, but we would be hard pushed to claim that it differs significantly from its predecessors, the private finance initiative (PFI) or public–private partnership (PPP). One key device has figured in our story: the Growth Accelerator model (GAM), a funding mechanism for the effective identification and delivery of public sector enabling infrastructure which stimulates private sector investment and the wider economy.

We might take the view that what national governments, Scottish or British, do is one thing; that local government is quite another. Closer to home, research by academic Andy Inch shows that this is too sanguine a view (Inch 2018). Research carried out by Inch for the Royal Institute of Chartered Surveyors (RICS) in 2015, and used in a later 2018 article, shows that the culture of land-use planning in Scotland, and Edinburgh in particular, has been targeted as an object of modernising reform, 'exploring how "culture change" initiatives played a prominent role in stabilising a new settlement around "open for business" planning between 2006 and 2012' (Inch 2018: 1076). Inch comments:

> The last 40 years have undoubtedly seen a series of distinctive shifts in urban governance that have affected states and cities globally, albeit in highly differentiated ways: commitment to market mechanisms, the fostering of entrepreneurial values and inter-urban competition have become familiar planks of a new common-sense that has been widely if unevenly installed across diverse settings and sectors. (Inch 2018: 1077)

Two key discourses have mattered in this process: 'modernisation' and 'culture change'; 'strongly disciplined by neoliberal and managerial logics, producing a particular narrow definition of "open for business" planning whose dominance was reinforced rather than undermined by the effects of crisis and austerity' (Inch 2018: 1078). 'Modernisation' and 'culture change' have no fixed real-world referents, and are purely performative terms, taken to mean what they are chosen to mean in particular contexts. The Scottish government mantra of being 'open for business' is passed down to local authorities on the basis that 'he who pays the piper calls the tune', reflecting that fact that 85 per cent of local government spending comes from the centre,[36] and is not raised locally. 'Open for business' planning has become the new common-sense. Inch expresses this nicely in the following comments from CEC planning team leaders whom he interviewed:

> I suppose it's about identifying who stakeholders are, so it's all linked to customer servers providing a more transparent, efficient planning function really and providing resources where it's needed . . . everybody is your customer, so it could be that you're a customer, someone in transport is a customer, the public is a customer, the council is . . . so I suppose everybody is really a customer, and I suppose it's about working with everybody to get the best . . . the best outcome. (ECS09, team leader, quoted in Inch 2013: 44)

And another:

> I think we benchmark the other Scottish cities and we are the best performing overall of the four cities, in some cases by quite a margin, you know and we have no embarrassment about performance of the authority and planning that we deliver, but . . . the resource is

not there to do something even better. (ECS02, team leader, in Inch 2013: 43)

Note the language of markets and 'customers' (as many as six mentions in the first short comment). The first team leader reinforces the point:

> I think the perception that, you know 'Edinburgh's not open for business', that's one that we're always fighting and . . . I think it's wrong. The perception that planning is slow, that we can't make decisions or we're too . . . I suppose it's not transparent I suppose . . . we would really like to change that but that's a real uphill struggle. (ECS09, team leader, in Inch 2013: 49)

From the inside, those who did not buy into the new ideology were dismissed as 'dinosaurs' who had not really grasped that new ways of working were required. From the outside, one critic of this view put it as follows:

> (P)lanning remains wedded to the idea of a presumption in favour of economic development, wedded to a politics where politicians worship at the shrine of GDP and jobs as the only things that matter, while we have culturally a primacy of economics over politics, society and the environment, the planning system is simply an economic tool. So we needed to set what we were saying inside a cultural basis that said, no, actually there's a huge picture here that we've got to change, we have to achieve sustainable development, and sustainable development is not the same as sustainable economic growth. (NL05, environmental NGO, in Inch 2013: 29)

It becomes clear in Inch's report that requiring such 'culture change' has become widespread in government at different levels, and that 'modernisation' has the believed capacity to make planning systems 'fit for purpose' (to encounter another iconic phrase). And, of course, 'culture change' is a key part of the discourse of new public management (NPM), a concept we will return to in our next chapter on Edinburgh's trams. Inch concludes that a reshaping of 'the public interest' as a justification for planning encompasses a more explicit understanding of 'the role of planners as market actors in their own right, involved in shaping land and property markets to ensure that the wider benefits of sustainable economic growth are achieved' (Inch 2013: 54–5).

CONCLUSION: WHOSE CITY IS IT ANYWAY?

What runs through these accounts, but is rarely mentioned explicitly, are issues of ownership. Public agencies perform an enabling function, and contribute considerable sums of public money, but site ownership of assets is not local, nor even national, and increasingly global. St James Centre, Caltongate/New Waverley were developed and owned by overseas investors, pension funds and hedge funds. The Waterfront has disproportionate public ownership largely by default, because of the failure of private developers to take on responsibility for the whole site. In one sense, who owns these sites does not matter much, because their interests are served by slicing and dicing assets in the 'calculative city'. The aim is to invest, raise the value, and sell it on for profit. It is unlikely, for example, that the American College Retirement Equities Fund (St James), or the Pension Fund of the Royal Canadian Mounted Police (Waterfront), or even the UK Universities Superannuation Scheme (USS) (Gyle) know of, or care much for, their investments in the Edinburgh sites.[37] The aim is to have appreciating assets in their property portfolios.

That is the world we now live in, a contrast with local ownership and control practised by those who ran the city not many years ago (see Chapter 3). Public agencies are now engaged in leveraging private equity into development schemes. Local architects become adept at translating planning requirements for the benefit of global developers (recall the comment about local architects AMA doing 'just enough' as regards the boxes to tick: tradition, modernity, urbanism, sustainability). The skill lies in knowing what planning authorities require 'on the ground', literally and metaphorically; it is often a question of what one might get away with. Much of these processes are opaque, and rarely are they subject to the public gaze, except when they have to be defended and voted upon in council. Every now and again, the whole process goes spectacularly wrong, and much is intriguingly, and inadvertently, revealed as a result: which takes us the' Saga of the Edinburgh Trams' in the next chapter.

NOTES

1. <https://www.edinburgh.gov.uk/downloads/file/27602/edinburgh-design-guidance-january-2020>.

2. <https://canmore.org.uk/site/133343/edinburgh-the-exchange-castle-terrace-saltire-court>.
3. Kerevan ultimately jumped political ship and joined the SNP, becoming an MP for East Lothian in 2015, losing his seat two years later.
4. <https://www.independent.co.uk/news/business/news/rbs-former-ceo-fred-goodwin-kisses-goodbye-his-executive-suite-it-opens-house-innovative-start-ups-10517211.html>.
5. Journalist Ian Fraser demolished the pretensions of Goodwin and RBS in his book *Shredded: Inside RBS: the bank that broke Britain*, 2014, updated in 2019.
6. The Monktonhall mine opened as a 'superpit' in 1967, and closed thirty years later.
7. To get a flavour of what this post-industrial site now looks like, read Paul Gorman's 'Into the Gyre: King Coal's Graveyard': <king-coals-graveyard-a-walk-in-midlothian-mining-country.pdf>.
8. The fact that the developers felt the need to invent a new name, Shawfair, to counteract 'the blemish of place', reflected the desire to escape the coal mining and heavy industrial associations with existing communities such as Danderhall, Woolmet and Millerhill. The coal legacy was to be buried, not celebrated.
9. Subject to the 40 per cent rule whereby that percentage of those on the electoral roll had to vote in favour for it to pass. The 52/48 per cent vote in favour (ironically, the same UK result as in the 2016 Brexit referendum) was judged to be insufficient.
10. Called in those days an 'Executive', lest the populace think a 'Parliament' too grand a term and one which might give people ideas above their station. The first act of the SNP government elected in 2007 was to change the name accordingly. The building itself has since been designated to include a new home for St Mary's Music School: <https://www.bbc.co.uk/news/uk-scotland-edinburgh-east-fife-58847225>.
11. I wrote an essay, 'Devolving Scotland', in a book by architect Alan Balfour called *Creating a Scottish Parliament* (2004), to celebrate the opening in 2004 of the custom-built parliament by Catalan architect Enric Miralles.
12. The current developers' fad is to call sites 'Quarters'; we will encounter more of these sorts of thing later in the chapter.
13. Few have heard tell of the Lomond Hills as 'mountains', which, presumably, Abercrombie was referring to.
14. Moultrie's Hill, according to the Edinburgh Post Office directory in 1851–2 housed: 'a painter, an architect, a surgeon, a builder, a cabinet maker, an upholsterer, a commercial agent, a glazier, a chaplain, an enameller, a saddler, a water officer, an accountant,

a coal merchant, another three messengers-at-arms and Carl Pein, 'professor of the oboe'. Moultrie's Hill has had a makeover in recent years as 'Multrees Walk', a windy collection of upmarket shops notably lacking customers.

15. There used to be a reverse prize for 'The Plook on the Plinth award', last seemingly awarded to Aberdeen in 2015 for its neglect of Union Street. The lack of such awards since does not imply that there are no likely candidates.

16. <https://www.edinburghnews.scotsman.com/news/inspiration-behind-edinburgh-st-james-centre-unvelied-1-4941613> (5 June 2019).

17. <https://www.edinburghnews.scotsman.com/news/politics/restaurants-and-bars-to-be-allowed-on-edinburgh-s-princes-street-under-planning-shake-up-proposals-1-4978943> (7 August 2019).

18. <https://www.bbc.co.uk/news/uk-scotland-scotland-business-37691842> (18 October 2016).

19. Presumably, the BBC felt unable to use the more common descriptor in its article of 13 March 2021, 'How has Edinburgh's landscape changed in a year?': <https://www.bbc.co.uk/news/uk-scotland-edinburgh-east-fife-56351231>.

20. <https://www.edinburghnews.scotsman.com/news/inspiration-behind-edinburgh-st-james-centre-unvelied-1-4941613> (published 5 June 2019).

21. The Southside has a much better claim to the accolade, with Nelson, Bartholomew's, Chambers, and many more.

22. <https://www.nuveen.com/global/strategies/real-estate/properties/united-kingdom/edinburgh-st-james>.

23. <http://www.cockburnassociation.org.uk/blog/22/41/St-James-Quarter/> (posted 27 January 2015).

24. <https://www.rli.uk.com/edinburgh-st-james/> (last accessed 29 November 2021).

25. <https://www.bbc.co.uk/news/uk-scotland-edinburgh-east-fife-59416522>.

26. <https://theferret.scot/st-james-quarter-edinburgh-regeneration/> (last accessed 29 November 2021).

27. What is now Holyrood Road was South Back of Canongate.

28. <https://www.edinburgharchitecture.co.uk/calton-gate> (last accessed 29 November 2021).

29. <https://www.architectsjournal.co.uk/news/murrays-controversial-caltongate-scheme-scrapes-through-planning> (last accessed 29 November 2021).

30. <https://www.scotsman.com/arts-and-culture/caltongate-will-tear-apart-fabric-edinburgh-1542744> (last accessed 29 November

2021). Those signing the petition were: Hugh Andrew (of local publisher Birlinn Books), William Boyd, Hugh Buchanan, John Byrne, Artemis Cooper, William Dalrymple, Lucy Ellmann, Janice Galloway, Ian Jack, Jackie Kay, A. L. Kennedy, Alexander McCall Smith, Amanda Mackenzie Stuart, Todd McEwen, Candia McWilliam, Andrew O'Hagan, Don Paterson, Robin Robertson, James Simpson, Alexander Stoddart, Lachie Stewart and Irvine Welsh.

31. With hindsight, anything with the suffix '-gate' has problems, evoking the most notorious 'gate' of them all: Washington DC's Watergate. Ironically, Edinburgh has an even older historic Watergate, located at the very bottom of the Royal Mile.

32. <http://newwaverley.com/new-waverley-to-flourish-underneath-the-arches/> (last accessed 29 November 2021).

33. 'New Waverley' runs the risk of people thinking it has something to do with Waverley station further along Market Street to the west. And 'Waverley Court' is the address of City of Edinburgh Council on the other side of New Street. So this is not 'Canongate', and 'Caltongate' is no more. This renaming runs the thread through from Waverley Bridge along Calton Road to Holyrood. No wonder the original developer wanted to knock down a MacCrae tenement to connect the development to the Royal Mile. Instead, they got an(other) archway.

34. <https://www.edinburghguide.com/caltongate> (last accessed 29 November 2021).

35. See James Gracie's *Stranger on the Shore: A Short History of Granton* (Benderloch: Argyll Publishing, 2003).

36. <https://www.gov.scot/policies/local-government/local-government-revenue/>.

37. As a recipient of a USS academic pension, it comes as a surprise that somehow I have a share in the Gyle, but may not tomorrow if the Trustees decide to place their funds elsewhere to get a better return.

9

Lost in Leith:
Accounting for Edinburgh's Trams

Why write about Edinburgh's trams in a book about who runs Edinburgh? Studies of local power often run aground on the rock of assumptions; that non-decisions are as interesting as actual decisions. The Edinburgh trams issue, and the ensuing inquiry, gives us a glimpse of structures of power and influence. Who matters, and who doesn't? Who pulls strings, and why? Which constellations of power are drawn in to bring things about, or in negative form, to prevent an outcome? And are there institutions and organisations which matter more than most; vestiges of power and influence? Thus, we are likely to learn more from controversies when struggles are more explicit than when things are as they appear. These are broad questions, providing a context for the study of Edinburgh's trams.

Simply put, the saga of the Edinburgh trams, and the ensuing public inquiry, sheds light on systems of power and influence in the city. Drawing mainly upon inquiry evidence, we can piece together why the project was over-budget, curtailed in length, and failed to meet the original timetable.[1] We can see how blame was apportioned by key actors. 'The trams' as it's come to be known as shorthand, is a 'megaproject', to be understood in the context of outsourcing the state, both national and local. More generally, it treats Edinburgh as an example of the 'calculable city', in which assets are treated as future forms of revenue rather than as public resources.

The trams saga, at the time of writing, more than two and a half years after the inquiry ended, is not yet complete, as Lord Hardie who chairs it still has to publish his report on 'what went wrong'; the inquiry itself has cost at least £10m. However, the collection of evidence to the public inquiry – some 7 million words – came to an end over two years previously. It provides both a statement and transcript evidence from key players, and is the basis for the account here.

The chapter has three sections: first, the story of the Edinburgh trams project; second, 'the blame game', in which accusations flew about hither and thither; and thirdly, my analysis of why 'the trams' went horribly wrong. Finally, and briefly, we will return to the question of power in Edinburgh.

TRAMS: ANCIENT AND MODERN

It is useful to start with a short history of the trams project. Edinburgh, like many towns and cities, once *had* trams, but they were made redundant in the 1950s (the last tram operated in November 1956) because they were deemed passé, street-clogging, tram-lined, and well past their sell-by date. The economist John Kay, a native of the city, wrote in *The Financial Times* (28 March 2005):

> When I was a small boy, my father took me to see Edinburgh's last tram. The city's mayor, grandly titled the Lord Provost, waved graciously as a decorated tram rolled along Princes Street into history. The following day, workmen began ripping up the tracks. But today Edinburgh is planning a new tramway. Trams used to be seen as noisy, expensive, dangerous andinflexible: relics of a past age, doomed by the efficient modern bus. What has changed?

Nothing at all, Kay concluded.

Reinventing Trams

Nevertheless, at the turn of the new millennium, the leader of the (Labour) council, Donald Anderson, asserted, without presenting evidence, that Edinburgh's bourgeoisie were far more likely to travel by tram than by bus. Trams, after all, badged cities as go-ahead and modern. The wheels, evidently, had come full-circle. *Buses* were now deemed passé. Life for the new trams began at the turn of the twenty-first century when they took centre-stage in the City of Edinburgh Council (CEC) Transport Strategy. The first steps were tried out in the CERT (City of Edinburgh Rapid Transit) scheme in the west of the city, a hybrid rail/road scheme known as a guided busway, a private–public partnership (PPP) which was abandoned in 2001. The trams plan was grandiose. In the original plan, line 1 ran for almost ten miles from the city centre, down Leith Walk to Newhaven, and back up via Crewe Toll to Haymarket running on the old Caledonian railway line. Line 1 would thus connect the new housing developments on the Granton shoreline with the rest of the city. Line 2 (eleven miles) was to run from the city centre to the airport. A final route, the more speculative line 3, was to run from the city centre to the new Royal Infirmary of Edinburgh (RIE) and thence to Newcraighall. CEC was not deterred by the scale of the proposed project, and in any case, the designated road/railway for CERT, the city thought, could be used for the trams thereby reducing the costs, or so it seemed at the time. The problem was how to pay for them. CEC designed a congestion charge with two points of charging, inner and outer city. This, they hoped, would pay for the RIE route. The rest was up to government, the former Scottish Executive, with a Labour/LibDem coalition in power at Holyrood between 1999 and 2007. The Scottish Executive, and Wendy Alexander as minister for enterprise, were keen on PFI schemes and insisted that Edinburgh trams be developed by a special purpose vehicle (SPV), an arm's length council company, which became TiE (Transport initiatives Edinburgh), which was created in 2002. The Blair government at Westminster promoted public–private partnerships, and set up the Office of Government Commerce as part of the Treasury in 2000 to facilitate such; it was closed by the Conservative/Lib Dem coalition government in 2011.

The Scottish Executive duly came up with £375m (over 90 per cent of the estimated cost), and ARUP, a multinational engineering consultancy, was contracted to pronounce on the feasibility of the scheme. ARUP thought that 'the overall modelling framework appears sound', but doubted how much passenger demand would result from the Granton development. ARUP had done a calculation of the financial case in terms of net present value (NPV) which showed that a full PFI option was 52 per cent higher than for the up-front grant option which was the one pursued. ARUP warned, presciently, that

> it may be argued that a benefit/cost ratio of this level [1:1.21[2]] does not represent a particularly strong case in terms of economic value

of the scheme. The economic case could become marginal as a result of relatively small changes in costs or revenues. (ARUP 2004: 4)

The income stream for the line to the new Royal Infirmary at Little France was to be the congestion charge. CEC was committed to a city referendum on the issue, but the congestion charge with two charge points in the city was so overly complex that it was defeated in 2005 by a margin of three to one.[3] Nevertheless, a combination of central government funding and council prudential borrowing made the scheme seem feasible, but one stripped down to the airport-city centre-Newhaven route. In south-east Edinburgh, a line was to run out Dalkeith Road to RIE at Little France and beyond. The main rationale, though, was the regeneration of north Edinburgh, down to Leith and over to Pilton by way of Newhaven, serving new housing on a brownfield site where the gasworks used to be. The department of economic development in CEC took the lead. CERT failed because, allegedly, Lothian Buses (LB) crowded it out, and its rival FirstBus withdrew. In his evidence to the inquiry, former chief executive of LB, Neil Renilson, said: 'Lothian [Buses] was merely reacting in such a fashion to try and protect its market' (Inquiry evidence, 22 November 2017: 192).

In 2005, the international conglomerate Parsons Brinckerhoff (signature project: Boston's Big Dig, which proved to be well over budget and timetable[4]) were contracted by TiE to do the design (as SDS), and McAlpine contracted to do the utilities diversions. Just to complicate things, McAlpine were bought over by Carillion the following year; Carillion were to go bust in 2018. In 2007, TiE appointed the Spanish company CAF (Construcciones y Auxiliar de FerroCarriles) to provide the actual trams, and a consortium of Bilfinger Berger, and Siemens (both German) as the main contractor.

'Not our Project': Governing Trams

Scottish government was by this time called a 'government' not an 'executive' after the SNP took power at Holyrood in 2007, albeit with a single seat advantage over Labour. The incoming (minority) SNP government wanted to cancel the scheme on the grounds that the funds could be better spent. However, it was defeated in the Scottish parliament, when other parties

(Labour, Tory and Liberal Democrat) all voted in favour of the trams. The SNP government set a maximum budget at £500m (index-linking the original £375m) – 'not a penny more' in John Swinney's phrase – and took the line that CEC was the promotor of the scheme, not the Scottish government. Seemingly given a clean bill of health by both ARUP (2004), and Audit Scotland (2007), TiE proceeded with the scheme. The die was cast for TiE when the moment came to dig up the roads, notably in Leith Walk, Haymarket, and on Princes Street in 2009. No obvious work was being done because of contractual difficulties with the consortium (Bilfinger Berger, Siemens and CAF).

TiE was later to be described by Labour council leader Donald Anderson as a 'delinquent vehicle for delivering trams'. Anderson left politics in 2007, and became an employee of PR company Newgate who happened to have BBS as a client. Delays came about because Parsons Brinckerhoff (SDS) did not deliver the design in time. The utilities diversion, the multi-utilities diversion framework agreement (MUDFA), exemplified the confusion. TiE appointed Alfred McAlpine Infrastructure Services as contractor. Carillion bought over McAlpine in December 2007, and assumed contractual responsibility. When Carillion completed its work package in late November 2009 (but at which point diversions were not complete), TiE appointed Clancy Docwra and Farrans to complete utilities diversion works.

Edinburgh was never going to be an easy dig. In George Rosie's words[5]:

> In digging up the street the workforce came across, inter alia, 100-year-old water pipes, cables from the previous tramway, the remains of a Carmelite priory and a leper hospital, a Victorian water culvert running under Princes Street and more than 300 long-dead corpses lying under Constitution Street in Leith, some of which had lain there since the end of the fifteenth century.

Estimates of contract costs versus final costs (calculated by Turner and Townsend, the agents appointed by CEC post TiE's demise) showed that Infraco ('infrastructure company') costs from Newhaven to Haymarket had almost tripled (£38m to £112m), airport to Gogar by a mere 40 per cent, and the Haymarket corridor by 60 per cent. Siemens, who did the overhead wires, connectivity to grid and the controls, doubled their budget, and no one quite knows where the money really went.

In all likelihood it provided 'mobilisation' to completion, and got the trams on track. The sum of £776m is what it took to finish it (the so-called Phoenix option) thereby adding 42 per cent to the original estimate.

It was obvious quite early on, and certainly by mid-decade, that TiE was not working out; it went through a rapid sequence of senior staff. The overall problem was that TiE had no specific expertise on building/managing light rail systems, and were overly heavy on 'finance' rather than civil engineering. Much has been made, subsequently, of the fact that TiE chief executives did not have the necessary expertise. It did not look that way on paper. The first CEO, Michael Howell, had a degree in engineering and economics, had worked for Cummins Engines and GE Transportation Systems (locomotives), and for RailTrack. He lasted four years at TiE (2002–6), his contract not renewed by the council. His successor, Willie Gallagher, had worked as an industrial electrician for ScottishPower. He lasted two years. He was succeeded by David Mackay who had been a chief executive with John Menzies. He also lasted two years. Finally, Richard Jeffrey, who was the last TiE CEO (2009–11), had worked for Babcock Brown and had been managing director of Edinburgh Airport from 2001 to 2007. True, these TiE CEOs were light on light rail, but they were not short on skills relevant to establishing Edinburgh's trams.

The Council and Trams

There was also serious, and serial, turnover among council officials: retirements by the council's chief executive, its director of economic development, the director of finance, the director of legal services (who joined the trams board in 2007), the director of corporate services (until 2011), as well as councillors: an outgoing Labour administration in the council elections of 2007. Donald Anderson went off to work for PPS/Newgate, a lobbying firm – and ending up lobbying on behalf of BBS.

It is interesting, in retrospect, how detached senior council officials were from the trams project. They had, of course, their day jobs to look after. They had appointed what was called the B-team of more junior council officials to pay attention to detail, and to their credit the B-team seemed to have had a much better grasp of the problems. The principal finance manager, Rebecca

Andrew, observed to the inquiry that 'the wider tram project did not work well together, particularly as it was spread over organisational boundaries and there was distrust between the different organisations involved' (evidence to inquiry, 12 June 2017, para. 88). Her bosses relied more on informal meetings, often chats on a Friday afternoon, to keep in touch. B-team warnings largely fell by the wayside.

It took a new CEO for CEC, Sue Bruce, to bring it to conclusion, breaking through the old boys network. On appointment, she was given, in her words to the inquiry, a 'really patronising document'. 'I was being dismissed and spoken down to, and thus, 'very annoyed', despite the project representing a 'substantial risk to the city' (evidence to the inquiry, 15 March 2018). She brought in her own fixer, Colin Smith, as SRO (senior responsible officer on CEC). Bruce worked with incoming TiE chair Vic Emery ('we worked like two halves of a pair of gloves' – TRI00000084_004, para. 51[6]). Emery, who had previously built destroyers on the Clyde for BAE, saw to it that previous TiE executives were thrown overboard. On her appointment, Bruce instigated the Mar Hall mediation[7] (March 2011) which brought together the key players in the trams project in an attempt to resolve the dispute.

By 2011, virtually all the previous chief officers at key points in the trams project had retired. There were also political changes on the council as Labour control gave way to LibDem/ SNP when proportional representation for local elections was introduced in 2007, and then to a Labour/SNP administration in 2012. This meant that there was little or no continuity, and diminishing institutional memory. Because it was an arm's length arrangement with TiE as a special purpose vehicle, the 'commercial confidentiality' clause was frequently invoked, thus keeping city councillors in the dark. TiE was closed down in August/September 2011. CEC brought in professional project management expertise (Turner and Townsend) to finish off the trams. So TiE: RIP, 2002–11.

The trams were curtailed to York Place – at one point, terminating at Haymarket was even mooted, until Scottish Government let it be known that it would ask for its money back if it did so. What, in essence, had been conceived of as a scheme for regenerating north Edinburgh (which the municipal Tories supported) had become an expensive alternative route west to the airport alongside the flagship number 100 express bus from Waverley Bridge. So how was the final price arrived at? Horse-trading, in effect, finding the tipping-point which brought the contractors back on side. Said Vic Emery: 'it's called a pig deal' (evidence to inquiry, 13 March 2018, p. 52), or to change the animal metaphor, a 'horse trade'. CEC was over the proverbial barrel. It had to come up with more money. It was settle, or else no trams.

The Scottish government under Alex Salmond instructed a public inquiry chaired by Lord Hardie, who had been Lord Advocate for Scotland in the 1997 Labour government. The inquiry began in 2015 and was still running three years later, still collecting evidence, and estimated to be costing upwards of £7.2m. By October 2021, estimates had risen to at least £10m; Hardie still had not reported.

THE BLAME GAME

What went wrong, and why? The 'common-sense' explanation is that it is the fault of incompetent individuals, and there is no shortage of fall guys (all guys, of course). On the other hand, inept individuals are end-of-pipe constructions. The personnel might be thought of as players on the stage; hence, *mise-en-scène*. TiE executives came and went regularly, a standard period of office of two years. The key council officials of CEC had been there for some time, and were a small coterie of internal promotions and appointments led by the chief executive, Tom Aitchison, an inner magic circle. The trams project was the idea of the Labour administration led by Donald Anderson from 1999, and his transport colleague Andrew Burns; both had dreamt up the congestion charge, which was soundly defeated in the 2005 referendum. Both became council leaders, and both left council politics, Anderson in 2007, Burns in 2017.

The project was rolling along the tracks, even if the trams were not. Councillors as a whole were kept at arm's length, for this was an arm's length company within the meaning of the act. They were judged not to be competent or trusted, for they would clype[8] to the press, notably *The Scotsman/Evening News* who vacillated from being champions to critics of the trams as the mood, and circulation, took them.

Contractors were also in the blame game, notably Bilfinger Berger (BB) who had 'previous', as is said in legal circles, at pricing low and hiking the price accordingly. BB had a contract to build two tunnels in Vancouver which were terminated by Metro Vancouver in 2008.[9] It seemed that they had bid $100m, half the next highest bid. This knowledge was used by critics of BB, including Edinburgh's director of corporate services,[10] to the effect that BB had under-priced the job to get the contract and then jacked up the price at an opportune moment (such as when Princes Street works were about to begin, bringing the city centre to a halt). Thus, one gets 'held to ransom' accusations which basically involve accusing contractors of ulterior motives. Whatever the rights and wrongs of the Canadian case, it became a useful weapon in the hands of opponents of BB – in TiE in particular – when they tried to hold BB to contract. Their British director (BB had set out to break into the British market for light rail) was thus described by his German superior 'as a personality he is somebody who is a bit overwhelming in his speeches'.

Aggravation got personal. TiE was accused of making disparaging remarks about 'Germans'. David Mackay, to whom the remark was attributed, said in his evidence to the inquiry that

> In an interview with *The Scotsman*, I described BB as a 'delinquent contractor' who scented a victim, who probably greatly under bid and who would use the contract to make life extremely difficult for the city and they had done exactly that. (TRI00000113_0100, para. 366)

This led to a High Court injunction (on the inference of 'delinquent', deemed to be a criminal act in German law) which was later withdrawn. Dr Keysberg, who was chair of the Bilfinger Civil Board from 2010 to 2012, on being accused by Richard Jeffrey of TiE of describing value engineering as a 'scam', replied: 'I did not know the meaning of the word "scam" and had to look it up in the dictionary in order to answer this question' (evidence to Trams Inquiry, TRI00000050_C _0008).

The final chair of TiE, Vic Emery, was brought in to sort out the mess. Emery had been CEO of BAE Systems building type-32 destroyers on the Clyde and knew a thing or two about contracts. He gave his assessment:

> The project was not set up properly from the beginning. The contract was biased towards Infraco, the engineering was incomplete and the project structure was flawed. The allocation of risk was

inappropriate, probably due to a lack of pre-contract surveying and TIE/CEC were too hasty to conclude a contract without efficient competition. The physical delays were mainly caused by utilities diversions, disputes over changes/additions and delays caused by late engineering. (TRI000000635_0042)

That seems, on reflection, a fair summing-up. The Scottish government, notably its finance minister, John Swinney, was considered by some to be in the blame frame ('it's not my project') but had taken the precaution of insisting that it was Edinburgh's project, not Scottish government's, and ring-fencing its substantial contribution. Swinney, who gave a robust defence of the Scottish government's position, and who, in his evidence to the inquiry described the trams affair as a *bourach*,[11] relied upon Transport Scotland to be the government's eyes and ears, but insisted that CEC was the lead contractor, a position insisted upon by Edinburgh council. In its 2011 report, Audit Scotland observed:

> Transport Scotland does not consider that it has the same oversight role for the trams project as it has for other Scottish Government transport projects [such as the Queensferry Crossing] because it is neither the promoter of the project nor has a contractual relationship with any of the private sector bodies engaged in the project's construction and delivery. (Quoted in Audit Scotland 2011: 5)

There is, however, something unsatisfactory about looking for the failures among the large cast of villains in this tale. One could, without difficulty, imagine a far more competent bunch of actors, but one needs to dig deeper than accusing inadequate individuals.

Trams and Agencement

Sociologists Ian Hardie and Donald Mackenzie (2007), invoking Michel Callon, have made the point: 'Actors do not have inherent properties or a fixed ontology. Their characteristics are constituted by the *agencements* of which they are made up.' *Agencement* denotes both 'assemblage' and 'agency': 'Depending on the nature of the arrangements, of the framing and attribution devices, we can consider agencies reduced to adaptive behaviours, reflexive agencies, calculative or non-calculative agencies, or disinterested or selfish ones, that may be either collective or individual' (Callon and Caliskan 2005, quoted by Hardie and MacKenzie 2007: 58). In other words, we need to dig deeper than simply casting around for individuals to blame.

So what is the *agencement* for the trams? First of all, there is how the city of Edinburgh was, and is, conceived by those in charge of it. Above all, cities are caught up willy-nilly in 'place marketing'. Places are projects, subject to vanity, of which none are more salient than having your own set of trams to play with. Trams can be seen as 'political' economic projects to enhance the city for developers and tourists. They are a far cry from the rattling old things which clanked along Edinburgh's mid-twentieth century streets.

Trams as Megaproject

The most obvious frame for understanding the trams project is in the context of what Bent Flyvbjerg called 'megaprojects'. His book *Megaprojects and Risk: An Anatomy of Ambition* (2003) became a benchmark for understanding cost overruns in public projects; and he was invited to give evidence to the trams inquiry in March 2018 as the expert on megaprojects. In his 2003 book he pointed to the paradox that 'as many more and much larger infrastructure projects are being proposed and built around the world, it is becoming clear that many such projects have strikingly poor performance records in terms of economy, environment and public support' (2003: 3). He continued:

> Megaproject development today is not a field of what has been called 'honest numbers'. It is a field where you will see one group of professionals calling the work of another not only 'biased' and 'seriously flawed' but a 'grave embarrassment' to the profession. And that is when things have not yet turned unfriendly . . . Whether we like it or not megaproject development is currently a field where little can be trusted, not even – some would say especially not – numbers produced by analysts.

So what is Flyvbjerg's answer? Since moving to the Said Business School at Oxford, Flyvbjerg has engaged more with policy than analysis. He gravitated to the work of psychologist Daniel Kahneman who won the Nobel prize – for behavioural economics[12] – in 2002. Kahneman coined the term 'reference class forecasting' which is an 'outside' view (conventional fore-casting taking an 'inside' view) and based on knowledge about actual performance in a reference class of comparable objects.

Flyvbjerg argued that psychological and political explanations are better at accounting for inaccurate forecasts. The latter focus on 'optimism bias', a cognitive predisposition to judge future events in a better light (hope, as it were, triumphing over experience).

Flyvbjerg's evidence to the trams inquiry (22 March 2018) was revealing. What we had all failed to grasp is that 'Optimism bias is pervasive. It's something which is hardwired into our brains' (TRI000005265, p. 8). Patently, there were too many Tiggers involved in the trams project, and insufficient Eeyores.[13] So what could have been done? You needed to carry out quantified risk analysis for which 'basically you get a panel of experts filling out a questionnaire, or better still several questionnaires about likely risks in the project'. In any case, said Flyvbjerg, the Edinburgh trams project was not, in terms of megaprojects, a statistical outlier – in his terms a 'black swan', a project with a very large cost overrun (Taleb 2007). The Edinburgh trams overspend is much lower than the threshold 143 per cent cost overrun criterion. Flyvbjerg put it at a mere 52 per cent[14] over budget.

But the trouble, said Flyvbjerg, is 'that everybody, including experts, are born with biases or develop biases throughout their life, and one basic bias is optimism' (transcript of 22 March 2018, p. 6). Well, then, we could use something called Monte Carlo simulation (*faites vos jeux*) which sounds rather grand, but whose inputs turn out to be 'assessments of experts in QRA'. Nevertheless, said Flyvbjerg, 'it's a very widespread methodology that is used in a lot of places' (8), and has the blessing of 'a Nobel Prize winner called Daniel Kahneman. So it's very solid research'. One suspects that the whole thesis relies on circular argument and self-validation.

What is common to both sets of 'explanations', Flyvbjerg's and Kahneman's, is that they are premised on individualistic rationalism whereby economics and psychology come together to 'explain' the behaviour of (individual) decision-makers. Possibly, for a suitable fee, psychologists could come up with scales of optimism and pessimism to exclude Tiggers and encourage Eeyores. There is no context for socio-political accounts such that certain projects (and classes of projects, notably infrastructural ones) are promoted for the notional 'common good', however flawed. The political-economic context, for example, for regeneration does not figure. The title of his later paper, 'Survival of the Unfittest: why the worst infrastructure gets built – and what we can do about it', says it all, or at least most of it (Flyvbjerg 2009). Strictly speaking, and in analytical terms, it would be necessary to survey all 'successful' as well as 'unsuccessful' projects because the syllogism implies that if 'the worst get built', the 'best' do not. If nothing else, it behoves the author to examine those which come in under budget – and explain why. Somehow relying on self-deception ('optimism bias') or downright lying ('strategic misrepresentation') on the part of individual decision-makers seems to fall well short of the mark as explanation.

State Outsourcing

A more fruitful starting-point would be to take the approach of Ivor Crewe and Anthony King in their book *The Blunders of Our Governments* (2013) which properly placed such things in the context of political-economic vanities, driven not by personality failings, but by the demands of political projects. If there is, in Flyvbjerg's words 'rampant pork-barrel, fast-tracking, bid-rigging' (2009: 362) involved in both central and local government projects, then the explanation lies in politics, or more precisely, in political economy. Furthermore, Flyvbjerg (2009: 365) asserts that: 'the projects that are artificially made to look best in business cases are the projects that generate the highest cost overruns and benefit shortfalls in reality, resulting in a significant trend for "survival of the unfittest" for infrastructural projects'. This surely requires far more systematic analysis (and examination of the counter-factuals) than is given in his work. Flyvbjerg's work owes more to the contemporary zeitgeist of neo-liberalism than to social scientific analysis.

Trams are creatures of our political-economic times. In particular, such projects lie closer to the literature on 'outsourcing the state'. In local authorities in particular there is little or no capacity to carry out infrastructural work directly. A key part of this armoury is the 'arm's length company' (ALCo), able to offer higher salaries to staff (outwith local authority pay scales), and deemed 'competitive' and 'near-market'. Julie Froud and her colleagues argue that contracts are ineffectual tools and 'uncontrolled weapons': 'neither government nor outsourcing company has a clear view from the bridge, and the contract is a contested and uncontrolled object rather than a device with a clear field of action' (Froud et al. 2017: 85).

In local authorities, councillors are at double arm's length: from officials (many of whom move sideways on to ALCos where pay and incentives are greater), as well as from major funders (often central government). Even the formidable audit culture fails to spot blunders until too late (think of Audit Scotland reports on trams in 2007 and 2011). In any case, the whole procedure is premised on there being competitors in the marketplace, but this is unrealistic, given the need for major capital and knowledge – prone to cartels and rigging the market. Too often, bidders have to be cajoled into taking part, and there is no capacity for 'more competition', the mantra from the likes of NAO, the National Audit Office.

We have already seen that the trams contract between TiE/ CEC and BBS was 'biased towards Infraco'. Emery, the last chair of TiE commented:

> My understanding was that the contract was signed when actually it shouldn't have been signed. Normally you wouldn't sign a contract with some of the clauses in it that were in it, which allowed almost the contractor to be able to increase the price. (Evidence to the inquiry, 13 March 2018, p. 32)

Legal contracts, nevertheless, have 'facticity'; namely, the truth status of 'facts', legally watertight, formal 'givens' around which economic relations are structured. They are, however, systematically structured and technically mediated social processes through which 'facts' are converted into realities on the ground. One of the features of contracts is their focus on economic devices for handling risk and reward, central to which 'the notion of the contract . . . is imbued with all kinds of optimism about the ability to control the future through a process of contingent specification' (Froud et al. 2017: 81). Here is that word 'optimism' again. We might ask whether optimism bias is another instance of elevating structural behaviour into a personal and psychological attribute; out, as it were, of 'neuro-psychology/economics'.

Why not, instead, treat optimism as a structural outcome of organisational behaviour? Over-promising is not the unfortunate outcome of flawed personality, but a deliberate claim by bidders to win contracts. Furthermore, 'contracts are typically private, hard to observe and often commercially sensitive' (Froud et al. 2017: 82). External supervision is much harder because of 'commercially sensitive' information, or at least the claim that it is – a way of cloaking and obfuscating price and (lack of) progress.

At the heart of new public management (NPM) is the notion of contract, such as outsourcing, as if law will set an adequate frame on its own. Contracts are actually incomplete because of the inability to compel the other to take responsibility for outcomes which might prove costly; and the inability to anticipate future states and their financial implications. 'Legal' contracts only 'work' when social relations allow them to. We speak of 'breakdown of trust' and invoke law to deal with them, even though recourse to law does not rebuild trust relations, but is in key respects a sign that they have broken down.

Thus, cooperation and trust make contracts work, not the other way around. Outsourcing contracts rest on the fundamental failure to draw the distinction between statistically calculable risk and fundamental uncertainty. Handling the latter is manifestly the domain of the state. There is a 'fantasy of controllability' over future costs which appear to shield the state from risk, while leaving it vulnerable to future uncertainty (like Carillion). This leads to blame-shifting when things go wrong. The-then Prime Minister Theresa May's argument (16 January 2018) that 'the government is just another customer of Carillion' like many others fails to acknowledge the prime role of the state as the political vehicle for handling uncertainty. The 'contract' is defined as a discrete thing, objectified and argued over.

The state has the theoretical power to punish delinquent contractors, including exclusion from future bidding, but, by and large, these powers are not used (Froud et al. 2017: 87). Companies (Stagecoach/Virgin) who encounter 'unexpected difficulties' can simply walk away (as in the case of East Coast trains) whose slate is wiped clean and they are able to bid for future contracts should they wish to. In short, the contract is a weapon for extracting profit which are aggregated into a large portfolio of such contracts, and cannot be checked for accuracy (in any case, deemed to be 'commercially confidential'). It is not simply that so many contracts are 'outsourced' but we have no way of knowing what they cost, unless and until they go wrong, and usually not even then. By implication, 'contracts' act as powerful weapons which suspend ordinary principles of market capitalism where rewards are tied to risks, and there are none-such here. So 'the contract' is a hugely effective device for the outsourcing company because it can deliver high profits from mundane activities, and little investment or revenue risk (Froud et al. 2017: 93).

There is 'corporate reset' if things go wrong; no one is barred for bidding for new contracts, possibly because they are con-glomerates with separate spheres of interest. Thus, BB managed the M74 contract with Scottish government, and 'another arm' of BB did the trams, before it was wound up as a failed experi-ment. Perhaps, on that basis, we might not have ruled out BB(S) re-emerging in Trams2 at least on the grounds of the devil-you-know, and with TiE safely removed from the scene, but that was not to be (see below).

Simply put, the trams project illuminated power, and its oper-ations even when it is a matter of preventing others from wield-ing it. First of all, local politicians have very little say in any of this, unless they happen to be on the board of arm's length com-panies, and even then, become subject to commercial confidenti-ality clauses. The days are long gone when local councils could take on building tramways themselves, if only because they no longer have the financial and technical means to do so. They are stripped down, and stripped out. It is interesting, as George Rosie said in his 2010 article 'The route to nowhere',[15] this trams project is built by foreigners: 'we're travelling on Spanish-built (CAF) trams running on rails forged by Austrians (Voestalpine of Vienna) and on a tramway designed by Americans (Parsons Brinckerhoff) and built for us by Germans (Bilfinger Berger Siemens).'

He has a point, and it is painfully obvious that a clash of cultures ensued between TiE and BBS. There is a sense of quite different business cultures in operation, crudely, that BBS put much store in engineering, technique, doing the job systemat-ically according to the plan, and the Brits doing it by the seat of their pants, fairly fly-by-night, gentlemen's agreements, and reneging on promises: above all, grandstanding like crazy with the aid of friends in the press (especially the *Edinburgh Evening*

News). Sloppy work, much invective, heat not light, umbrage taken, offence given.

One might, however, quibble that the trams bourach was simply the result of foreigners not understanding funny British ways – the Queensferry Crossing contract, for example, came in on time and on budget, and is a 'foreign' bridge to its last nut and bolt (Rosie 2018: 342–60). This seems to have more to do with the dogs of war which deregulation and outsourcing the state have unleashed. In any case, 'misunderstandings' set against 'contractual relations' makes the point that contracts are in essence social constructions. They set the frame, but solve nothing in themselves. It was not brought about by social actors not having the 'correct' psychology, and instead, a surfeit of optimism. The odd fusion of psychology and economics in this regard tells us more about cultural explanations in neo-liberal vogue than properly conducted analytical social science. Furthermore, cities and places are hollowed by politics and money, and replaced by marketing and slogans.

The 'Calculable City'

Let us return to the bigger question: who runs Edinburgh, and what might the trams project tell us about the distributions of power? Irving Lapsley and his colleagues observed that 'The world of cities has increasingly become one of calculating and quantifying, as they compete in an increasingly explicit way with each other for population, economic resources and influence' (Lapsley et al. 2010: 308). We think of cities as a collection of physical assets, buildings and infrastructure, but they are in essence financial numbers (Arnaboldi and Lapsley 2010: 403), the 'calculable city', in which assets are sliced and diced, and fitted with numerical values. They make the point that: 'the accountants' major preoccupation is to provide reliable financial statements. In doing this they have little contact with operational managers but they retain a close relation with accountants in their operational departments. Accountants talk to accountants' (Arnaboldi and Lapsley 2010: 403).

There may be separate administrative departments in the council, but all are governed by financial assumptions, hence, the power of numbers and calculations, hence accountants.

So how come calculations on the Edinburgh trams turned out to be so inaccurate that they were out by 42 per cent? And, in the grand scheme of megaprojects, Edinburgh got off seemingly lightly in that 'black swans', statistical outliers, notionally only begin at three times that overspend. Nevertheless, why the error? In key respects, numbers are a sideshow.

As Lapsley et al. argue, 'Cities have come to mimic large corporations as they engage in various kinds of exercises aimed at projecting and visualizing the city as it should become, and how it should transform itself to get there' (2010: 307). In truth, cities were 'incorporated' much earlier under the Victorian Municipal Reform Acts, and city corporations were essentially similar to business corporations.[16] Edinburgh was known as the 'Corporation of the City of Edinburgh' until 1973 ('Edinburgh Corporation' for short, or 'the Corporation', or, simply, 'the Corpie'). The loss of municipal autonomy (and power to raise its finances) removed this independent status since the 1970s. At the same time, cities sought to reinvent themselves. Lapsley et al. again: 'The targeted audience of visions and strategies can be developers, businesses or residents. The reputation of a city, its image, is perhaps the most visible sign of these visualising efforts' (2010: 307).

In 2004, under the Labour regime when Donald Anderson was the council leader, CEC appointed Sir Terry Farrell, international architect and urban designer, as its first-ever City Design Champion ('design guru'). Farrell had designed the Edinburgh International Conference Centre (EICC) in 1995, for which he won awards. His 'twelve challenges' to the city included the trams as a large transport engineering project, or, in his words, a 'placemaker regenerator' (Lapsley et al. 2010: 313). Farrell argued that 'the city was being held back by a "pervading inertia" within the local authority'; it was 'in desperate need of visionary figures to provide strong leadership', and politicians who needed 'to become more assertive and demanding of their senior officers or things would not change' (Lapsley et al. 2010: 318).

It is interesting to examine Farrell's comments. First, there is no suggestion there that 'pervading inertia' might have anything to do with the fact that municipal budgets have been slashed by central government for a decade or more (and a council tax freeze imposed), and that a hand-to-mouth existence derives from that. Second, the need for 'visionary leadership' and 'strong leadership' anent the trams project (and the congestion charge to pay for some of it) might just have got Edinburgh into financial trouble in the first place; and third, councillors were precisely excluded from influence by the device of arm's length companies and the 'commercial confidentiality' clause. The fashion for single-party 'Executives' to run local councils as Edinburgh witnessed between 1999 and 2007 might have something to do with the relative powerlessness of elected members not included in the 'executive' structures of New Labour and new public management ('new' being the obvious vogue word).

Farrell's report did not figure much in the Edinburgh Tram Inquiry, even though its assumptions and values permeate the *raison d'être* for trams, as a key symbol of 'progress'. Having trams derives from image boosterism, even though regenerating north Edinburgh was jettisoned in favour of trams to the airport, arguably a more relevant 'image-conscious' route to take for tourists and businesses. Ironically, Donald Anderson's comment that trams are designed in the main for the middle classes runs up against the considerable irony that Edinburgh's trams run through the working class districts of Sighthill, Broomhouse, Saughton and Balgreen.

But what of the argument that risk management had been baked into all public programmes? True, TiE had its surfeit of 'risk management consultants', but in the words of Michael Power, this is about the culture of the 'risk management of everything' (Power 2004). How can one make sense of risk assessment and its failures in the trams project? Power's key point is that risk management was above all a defensive strategy for organisations to cover their backs. He called it the management equivalent of political spin, a defensive reaction vis-à-vis reputation in an increasingly demanding environment. In short, 'reputation risk reflects a new sense of vulnerability, a dread factor for senior managers as well as politicians, and had created new demands to make reputation "manageable"' (Power 2004: 61). Going through the appropriate motions of organisational risk assessment has little to do with assessing real, primary, risks and far more with protecting and advancing reputations of secondary risk.

INFRASTRUCTURAL REDEMPTION: ON TO NEWHAVEN

Despite (or perhaps cynically, because of) the fact that the Hardie Inquiry had not reported, the City of Edinburgh voted in 2017 to extend the tram lines down Leith Walk, along Ocean Terminal, to Newhaven, at a putative cost of £207m. Said the Scottish correspondent of the *Financial Times*: 'For Edinburgh, the £207m extension of the Scottish capital's single tram line is more than just a transport project, it is a shot at infrastructural redemption' (Mure Dickie, *Financial Times*, 16 April 2019). By way of justification, much was made of Edinburgh's population growth – up by 8 per cent in the ten years to 2026. The head of the council's transport committee commented: 'we would end up with gridlock . . . if we don't put in a mass transit option'. There was no suggestion that private cars be priced out of the city by a new congestion charge, and as we saw in the previous chapter, pricing in city centre parking spaces was part of the 'Edinburgh St James' deal.

Passenger revenues for 2016–17 showed an increase of 17 per cent over the twelve-month period (from £9.6m to £11.2m; DfT Light Rail and Tram Survey), and this was spun as 'tram profits arrive ahead of schedule'.[17] However, this is a long way short of paying off the debt, still less making a contribution to future trams extensions.

And the cost of that extension? When first mooted in July 2015, an extension to the Foot of the Walk was estimated at £78.7m; to Ocean Terminal, £126.6m; and to Newhaven, £144.7m (no mention however of an extension to Granton – clearly a line too far, at least at this stage of the tram game). By September 2017, the preferred option, to Newhaven, had been revised to £165m; and by February 2019, upped to £207m, an increase of 43 per cent on the 2015 estimate, a nice irony given that the Trams 1 budget was over by a similar percentage. There was even a price of £11m included to counter 'optimism bias', as if one could put a figure on a psychological weakness (q.v. Kahneman and Flyvbjerg). The trade magazine *New Civil Engineer* showed in May 2021 that it was not immune to optimism by stating: 'Lessons from over-budget Edinburgh tramway inform completion of the line' (lessons-from-over-budget-edinburgh-tramway-inform-completion-of-line-24-05-2021.pdf). And lessons from the Hardie Inquiry? 'As soon as practicable', said an inquiry spokesperson; which tells us nothing much.

How successful has Trams 1 (airport to city centre) been? Much is made of figures showing that this existing route carried 7.3m passengers in 2018, up 10 per cent on the previous year, but far less than the 11m the originally planned route was supposed to be carrying by 2011. The scheme supposedly achieved pre-tax profitability, but was running at an operating loss in 2018, especially when maintenance and infrastructure costs were included. Passenger numbers had increased from 6.67m in 2017, to 7.45m in 2019, and thereafter Covid-19 put paid to any comparative calculations. By October 2020 Scottish government were providing £4m emergency funding to Glasgow subway and Edinburgh trams via Transport Scotland, but without specifying what each was getting.[18]

The main contractor on Trams 2 is a consortium, Farrans Sacyr Neopul JV (https://www.farrans.com/project/edinburgh-tram-york-place-to-newhaven/), with Siemens making a comeback as a sub-contractor providing 'a broad range of intelligent infrastructure solutions' for trams to Newhaven under SCADA (Supervisory Control and Data Acquisition); but as a sub-contractor, unable to disclose the value of the sub-contract (https://www.transport-network.co.uk/Siemens-wins-Edinburgh-tram-extension-contract/16712). Siemens's surplus equipment was bought by the council, and stored in a shed somewhere in West Lothian at the end of Trams 1. The £165m is on top of the money it has to find for its share of the current scheme (£45m plus £231m for the 'overdraft', possibly as much as £291m index-linked). Taking those sums together, Edinburgh will have spent around £500m on trams, and 'remains saddled with £250m debt from this original line which was not completed' (https://www.newcivilengineer.com/latest/lessons-from-over-budget-edinburgh-tramway-inform-completion-of-line-24-05-2021/).

CONCLUSION: TICKET TO RIDE

What does the trams project tell us about who runs Edinburgh? It is easy to say who does not. Thus, elected councillors were kept at arm's length by arm's length companies. If any were co-opted on to such companies, they were shackled by commercial confidentiality clauses, and information is kept off formal board meetings. Council officials were hamstrung too, but only if they allow themselves to be. It took a much more proactive CEO in Edinburgh council, Sue Bruce, to break the deadlock on trams, and she came with a reputation for sorting thing out previously at East Dunbartonshire and Aberdeen City councils. Local capital? It is difficult to see what direct role they had in the trams project other than one in which they complained that their businesses were being disrupted (the Princes Street debacle being a case in point). Tellingly, the post-2011 director of economic development, David Anderson (2008–2012), spoke of the complaints he got from Harvey Nichols department store – not exactly one of Edinburgh's major employers. Anderson was not a key player, and complained in his evidence to the inquiry that at the time of the Mar Hall mediation, 'It was evident that key decisions were being taken without reference to my views' (TRI00000108_C_0112, para. 148b).

In terms of what the trams project tell us about who runs Edinburgh, we would be hard pushed to claim that it was the city council. In a revealing comment, the former CEO of Lothian Buses, Neil Renilson, observed:

> Most of TIE senior people had no connection with Edinburgh. They had no history of the city, no real knowledge of it and no commitment to it. To them it was just another job to do, and then move on. (TRI00000176_0012)

As local boy made good, Renilson had axes to grind, but his point arguably stands. Localism has ceased to matter.

City boosterism, however, has not gone away. Since the trams debacle, Edinburgh (and city region) has been the recipient of £1.1bn from the City Deal scheme funded by Scottish and UK government which will have as its key commitments[19]:

- £300m for world leading data innovation centres
- £140m for crucially needed upgrade to the A720 city bypass at the Sheriffhall Roundabout and transport improvements across west Edinburgh
- £20m capital funding for new world class concert hall
- £25m regional skills programme to support improved career opportunities for disadvantaged groups
- £65m of new funding for housing to unlock strategic development sites.

Would people stand for it? Do people want it? Among Leithers, nine out of ten are content with current provision – that is, *sans* trams (BBC News 2018). But six out of ten thought trams would benefit Leith, and that it would be easier to get around by tram. Four out of ten even believed it would benefit local businesses. So, after all, there might just be *Sunshine on Leith*, which is where most of us came in during this particular movie. It has been, nevertheless, a very expensive ticket to ride.

NOTES

1. Where these data are used, reference has been made to the date at which evidence was given to the public inquiry, and/or to the statement made prior to that date (usually with a reference number prefixed by 'TRI'). All such data are in the public domain at <http://www.edinburghtraminquiry.org/evidence-and-hearings/public- evidence/>.

2. In cost/benefit analysis, the higher the ratio, the more profitable the project is likely to be. Anything close to 1:1, as this was, implies a weaker case.

3. The smart move would have been to introduce a temporary congestion charge and make it permanent when drivers had got used to it; as Stockholm did in 2007 after eighteen months.

4. <https://www.nytimes.com/2008/01/24/us/24dig.html>.

5. <https://www.scottishreviewofbooks.org/2010/11/the-route-to-nowhere-georgie-rosie/> (last accessed 29 November 2021).

6. Where available, text is referenced to its paragraph number as indicated here; where not, the date of evidence is given. The full account of the inquiry is at <https://www.edinburghtraminquiry.org>.

7. Mar Hall was a secluded hotel in west central Scotland, where the discussions took place.

8. *Clype* in Scots means to tell or inform on.

9. <https://canada.constructconnect.com/dcn/news/infrastructure/2008/06/ metro-vancouver-terminates-contract-with-bilfinger-berger-over-construction-delays- dcn028129w>.

10. Jim Inch, the director of corporate services, observed in his evidence that 'BB was in litigation everywhere they worked' (para. 134, p. 53), and furthermore, 'their business motto was to go in low and then work on developing their price through contract challenge' (para. 139, p. 55).

11. *Bourach* in Scots, possibly originating in Gaelic, means a mess, a heap of something nasty, but not quite a fiasco.

12. For an interesting collection of articles, see <http://econsoc.
mpifg.de/archive/ Newsletter_19.2_gesamt_Endfassung.pdf>, and
Marcus Wolf's in particular.

13. Two key characters in A. A. Milne's *Winnie-the-Pooh* (1926):
Tigger is an enthusiastic tiger, and Eeyore a pessimistic donkey.

14. Flyvbjerg did not explain how he reached the figure of 52 per cent,
given that the nominal cost overrun for Edinburgh trams is
42 per cent (£776m/£545m).

15. <https://www.scottishreviewofbooks.org/2010/11/the-route-to-
nowhere-georgie-rosie/>.

16. Cities were indeed 'corporations' from nineteenth-century urban
reform, able to operate as such, and have subsequently shrunk in
power and importance.

17. <https://edinburghtrams.com/news/tram-profits-arrive-ahead-of-
schedule>.

18. <https://www.transport.gov.scot/news/further-support-for-
glasgow-subway-and-edinburgh-trams/> (last accessed 29 November
2021).

19. <https://www.edinburgh.gov.uk/news/article/2329/city_region_
deal_secured>.

10

Does Anyone Really Run Edinburgh?

In Winter she really comes into her own,
the New Town grey under a watery sun,
its whinstone setts ghosting broughams and sedan chairs, silk
dresses swishing,
the Old Town, once haunt of cut-purses
and men of letters; today's imbalance
more east-windy
and west-endy than ever. Formerly prim spinster, then dowdy
dowager, now part princess,
part hen party hostess, at heart she possesses a sliver of ice . . .

('Ice Maiden', by Stewart Conn)

What kind of place is this Edinburgh? Why does it invite questions about who runs it? Consider that last question. On the
face of it, it would seem obvious – after all, it seems a city with
secrets; in Abercrombie's words, 'an ancient and venerated
shrine' – but who wants to live in a shrine? Behind the façade,
if that's what it is, there seems to be another story, or, rather,
stories. Indeed, perhaps it is best to think that there are multiple
Edinburghs behind Stewart Conn's sliver of ice.

ECOLOGY OF GAMES

Let us return to Norton Long's notion of a city as an ecology of
games. Perceptively, Long observed: 'It is psychologically tempting to envision the local territorial system as a group with a
governing "they"' (Long 1958: 252). In other words, we are
expecting to find, and none more so than in Edinburgh, a close
nexus of powerful people who make the key decisions. Why

Edinburgh? There would seem a prima facie case for there being a governing 'they'. After all, the city was run by a peculiar breed of parochial politics for a century, from the 1870s to the 1970s. Readers of this book will recall the hegemony of the so-called Progressive party until its collapse in the final quarter of the twentieth century. Furthermore, it drew disproportionately on the local business class, merchants in the main, who held the city's affairs firmly in its grip. They dominated its economy, its politics and its culture, its schools, even though it was left to James Bridie, a Glaswegian, to remark that 'Edinburgh prides itself in not being interested in anything at all' (quoted in Miller 1996: 3–4). One might argue that such insouciance was a front. Bridie's may seem a harsh judgement in a city of festivals as well as its accolade as a UNESCO World Heritage Site. Certainly, on the face of it, the city seemed self-contained, and arguably self-satisfied, at least for much of its recent history. There was considerable interlock between its economy, politics, culture, especially in terms of education and schooling. The merchant class even ran their own schools; and their university was the *Tounis* College. John Heiton's Edinburgh as a 'City of Castes' seems apposite more than century after he said it.

Presenting Edinburgh

So let us consider the question, who runs Edinburgh, in two parts. First, examine the plausible; in particular, how Edinburgh presents itself, and how it has been written about. Is it possibly a victim of its own mythology? Only then will we return to the facticity of the question. Let us start with a famous son of Edinburgh, Robert Louis Stevenson. It was he who came up with Dr Jekyll and Mr Hyde. True, his novella (1886) was based in London, but it was conceived and born in Edinburgh. Stevenson was interested in dualities, two sides of the coin. Of Edinburgh, he considered it 'half a capital and half a country town, the whole city leads a double existence; it has long trances [his word] of the one and flashes of the other' (Robert Louis Stevenson 1878: 2). Stevenson was aware that

> these sentences have, I fear, given offence in my native town, and a proportionable pleasure to our rivals of Glasgow. I confess the news caused me both pain and merriment . . . To the Glasgow people

I would say only one word, but that is of gold; I HAVE NOT YET WRITTEN A BOOK ABOUT GLASGOW. [the capital letters are Stevenson's]

So here we have interesting dualities: Edinburgh's 'double exis-tence' as capital and country town; and Edinburgh vis-à-vis Glasgow. That sounds like a modern take on the two cities (and see Robert Crawford's book on the pair (2013)); he describes them as alter egos, two sides of the coin, and by inference, of psychological conditions (split personality). This notion has literary form as the Caledonian *antisyzygy*, a term coined by Gregory Smith in 1919 to evoke the polar turns of realism and fantasy arguably characterising Scottish literature. This notion of duality was made famous by Hugh MacDiarmid in the 1930s, and used to explain cultural and political formations in Scotland. Jekyll and Hyde, then, have form (see McCrone 2017a: ch. 17).

Imaginary City

There is a long and illustrious pedigree for thinking of Edinburgh as 'in the mind', or more precisely, a place of the imagination. Writers and filmmakers have had fun with that. At the demotic level, Lanarkshire journalist Ian Black collected and pub-lished jokes about Glasgow and Edinburgh (*Merr Weegies vs Edinbuggers* [*sic*]), where each told jokes about the other. The (more printable) jokes about Edinburgh included the following:

> 'Three douce Morningsiders were in church one Sunday morning when the minister made a strong appeal for some very worthy cause, hoping that everyone in the congregation would give at least £10 or more. The three Edinbuggers became very nervous as the collection plate neared them, and then one of them fainted and the other two carried him out.' (p. 8)
> 'What's the difference between an Edinbugger and a coconut? You can get a drink out of a coconut.' (p. 10)
> 'You can always tell an Edinbugger, but you can't tell him much.' (p. 10)
> 'Said the Edinbugger to the boastful Weegie: "Take away your SNO, your BBC SSO, your Scottish Ballet, your Citizens Theatre, all that other national culture stuff, your Celtic, your Rangers, and what have you got?" "Edinburgh", replied the Weegie.' (p. 11)

'It is now generally accepted that golf did not originate in Edinburgh. No Edinbugger would invent a game in which it was possible to lose a ball.' (p. 26)

'A Weegie stopped before a grave in an Edinburgh cemetery, containing a tombstone declaring, "Here lies an Edinburgh lawyer and an honest man." "And who would ever think", he murmured, "there would be room enough for two men in that one wee grave."' (p. 45)

'To the Glaswegian, the glass is half full.
To the Aberdonian, the glass is half empty.
To the Edinbugger, the glass is twice as big as it needs to be.' (p. 57)

In his introduction, Black, who came from Motherwell, wrote: 'The people of the two cities have always traditionally regarded each other with the greatest possible loathing, mistrust and contempt. They are both absolutely right, which is one of the joys of living in Scotland' (Black 2005: 3).

We might dismiss this sort of thing as so much pub banter, but sociologically it is significant banter. Jokes have a side to them which draw upon cultural meanings and stereotypes in order to be considered funny; they help us, in the famous words of Robert Burns, to see ourselves as others see us (see, for example, Christie Davies's *The Mirth of Nations*, 2002). Edinburgh's jokes are about legendary meanness, pretensions and deviousness. They are not 'qualities' unique to the city and its citizens, but they confer meaning and understanding on which people trade socially and culturally.

Consider too the presentation of Edinburgh in the movies. There is, of course, Edinburgh as backdrop, its scenic qualities, such as the classic *39 Steps* (1935), and even as the locale for novel-into-film, such as Muriel Spark's *The Prime of Miss Jean Brodie* (1969), with the splendid Maggie Smith in the lead role. There are filmic curiosities such as Sylvain Chomet's *'L'Illusionniste'* (2010) described by Robert Crawford as 'an extended cinematic love letter to Edinburgh', set in the '1950s milieu of dark buildings whose grimy uncleaned sandstone seems to invite louring skies and rain' (Crawford 2013: 35). There is, infamously, *Trainspotting* (1996), the film of Irvine Welsh's novel (it is always open to Edinburghers to dismiss it as about Leith, Edinburgh's alter ego – Hyde to its Jekyll). There is *Shallow Grave* (1994); somewhat more cheerily, *Sunshine on*

Leith (2013) – Leith again, and *The Angels' Share* (2011), which though not 'about' Edinburgh, has one of the best 'takes' on Edinburgh at the movies:

> Albert: What is that? That there. What is that?
> Rhino: What, that big thing on top of the hill?
> Albert: You cannae miss looking at that. What is that?
> Rhino: It's Edinburgh Castle, Albert.
> Albert: Is it?
> Rhino: Aye.
> Albert: What did they put it up there for?

Truth to tell, Edinburgh Castle is a curious icon (and not simply to Albert). It is surely the key icon of the city, but to whom? In 2019 – pre-Covid – it had 2.2m visitors (you have to pay to get in; cue Black jokes). It is not cheap: £17.50 for an adult, and £10.50 for a child (5–15). In 2010, it had 1.2m visitors, and that's an increase over the decade of over 80 per cent. In essence, it is a tourist icon; you come to Edinburgh and you do the castle. There has been a rising proportion of overseas visitors to the castle in recent years. In 1984, 56 per cent of castle visitors came from overseas, and in 2007, the figure had risen to 66 per cent (Morris 2010: 22, table 2); those domiciled in Scotland fell proportionately from 19 per cent to 8 per cent. We have no way of knowing whether locals make much of it, unless they find it a useful place to take visitors on a day out.[1]

Edinburgh is, of course, its own tourist attraction, stone piled upon stone, and you would not mistake this or any other Scottish city for an English one. They, and especially Edinburgh, are different, thus adding to the visitor lustre. Before Covid-19, Edinburgh was preparing for a 'bed tax' (visitor levy, in the jargon[2]), passed by the council, frowned upon by Scottish government lest it damage a key economic engine, but stymied by the dramatic drop in visitor numbers during the pandemic. Recall the comment in Chapter 1 by journalist Peter Ross that 'lockdown Edinburgh is uncanny. Streets that should be busy with tourists, phones and voices raised, are deserted.' Still, you can always visit Greyfriars Bobby, an apocryphal tale of a dog guarding the grave of his master, Auld Jock (inevitably so named).

All of this suggests that there is more to Edinburgh than meets the eye. The city appears in many movies and television serials. All cities have identities; in the French sense of *personnage* (the

English term 'personage' is quite the wrong translation). Consider, for example, Hugh MacDiarmid's *Midnight*, where he described Edinburgh as 'a mad god's dream/fitful and dark/Unseizable in Leith/And wildered by the Forth . . .' (see Chapter 1 for the fuller version). The rest? All nothing to MacDiarmid: Glasgow is null, Dundee is dust and Aberdeen a shell. Lewis Grassic Gibbon saw Edinburgh as 'a disappointed spinster, with a harelip and inhibitions' (Gibbon 1969: 82). Recall that Stewart Conn, in his poem opening this chapter, also described Edinburgh as 'prim spinster'; and Robert Crawford alluded to the city 'of spinsterish, unmarried malt'. Something in Edinburgh draws out these sexed terms.

We can think of Scotland's four cities as 'toons with character' (McCrone 2005). As Grassic Gibbon's anthropomorphisms imply, they are female, urban wombs, and the High Street, in William McIlvanney's words, 'a second mother' (which he uses in his novel, *Docherty*, 1975). We tread on dangerous, and sexist, territory here (none of these writers imagines the town/city as male), but these stand as examples of the anthropomorphising of towns and cities as they appear in literature, and as iconicised by poets and writers. Such accounts are not drawn out of thin air, nor do they have little impact thereafter. They work best when they epitomise place and create its 'character'. None more so than Edinburgh. When we peer at Edinburgh, we do so with expectations and presumptions; these frame how we see the city.

Writers trade on this. Ian Rankin began his PhD on Muriel Spark but found a more lucrative line in crime novels centred on Edinburgh, around his kenspeckle character, John Rebus. Indeed, 'Rebus tours' come in various forms of walking tours, and Rankin has observed that tour guides know more about Rebus[3] than he does. Rankin's skill is to connect up 'respectable' Edinburgh with its seamier side.[4] For many, fictional reality becomes more meaningful than the real thing; a phenomenon observable in the likes of Dan Brown's *Da Vinci Code* which made fifteenth-century Rosslyn Chapel 'famous', or the entirely fictional TV series *Outlander* devised by Diana Gabaldon (https://en.wikipedia.org/wiki/Outlander_(TV_series). None of this 'living in fiction' is unique to Scotland, but it has a powerful resonance (McCrone 2017a: ch. 16), none more so than Edinburgh which doubles as liveable city and movie screen-set.

A GOVERNING THEY?

We come at Edinburgh, then, with a complex set of assumptions derived from many cultural sources. We look at the city in the expectation that there is, in Norbert Long's words, a 'governing they'. A ruling elite may be all too plausible. Let us review that case.

Making a Living

Recall the power and influence of the Merchant Company of Edinburgh (Chapter 3), and its 1914 claim to local patriotism:

> The Company is not merely a company of merchants. It is the Company of Merchants of the City of Edinburgh and nothing that concerns Edinburgh or the district included in the definition should be a matter of indifference to it.

Recall too John Heiton's Castes of Edinburgh, all too plausible long after he coined the description in mid-nineteenth century. The social differences in the city belonged more to gradations of social status rather than of social class as such. The point made in Chapter 3 is worth repeating: Edinburgh's bourgeoisie and proletariat did not stare fixedly across a uniform class divide; indeed, they had little opportunity and reason to do so, because the city's economies (plural) were diverse and variegated. That may make assumptions of a ruling elite somewhat dubious, but the Merchant Company was aware of the need to incorporate as many professionals as possible into its ranks. Furthermore, Edinburgh was, for much of the last century, a city of manufacture; as Bob Morris observed: 'Manufacturing has a reluctant place in the history of the city, but it dominated the life of much of the population' (Morris 2010: 15). His fellow social historian, Richard Rodger, agrees, and makes the key point that manufacturing was airbrushed out of the city's political economy despite its importance.

Even the Merchant Company connived at this, remarking in 1919, that, in the words of Madgin and Rodger (2013: 515): 'Edinburgh has no serious claim at present to be considered as an industrial or commercial centre . . . Its striking picturesqueness and historical associations attract visitors from all countries. Its qualifications used to be summarised as Beauty, Beer and Bibles.'

Edinburgh was not defined by a single industry, unlike Glasgow (shipbuilding), Manchester (cotton), Birmingham (engineering) or Sheffield (steel). A process of de-industrialisation, of reinvention, took place, with a complex service economy to fall back on, and a cultural history to exploit with the connivance of the likes of the Merchant Company. The lack of industrial dominance meant, paradoxically, that transition to a cultural economy was much smoother than it might have been, taking on a seamless quality, and with it, continuities of economic power.

Power and Politics

None of this would have been possible without parallel continuities in systems of political power. It was not until the late 1970s that 'rule by shopkeepers' (to borrow from George Bernard Shaw) came to an end in Edinburgh. The hegemony of the self-styled Progressive party in the city's local politics long outlasted such influence elsewhere. When, as in the years after the Great War, 'socialists' threatened to win council elections, the 'ratepayer' interest came to the fore and united opposition to Labour on the grounds of 'economy' and the defence of local property. The Merchant Company was happy to mobilise such interests, aided by the local newspaper *The Scotsman*, self-styled Scotland's national newspaper, and the Edinburgh Good Government League (EGGL). The defining enemy was 'municipal socialism', and the aim, oddly, was 'keeping politics out of council affairs'. This curious form of 'non-political politics' was not unique to Edinburgh (in other Scottish cities, self-styled 'Moderates' ruled) but in Edinburgh it lasted much longer, right down to the 1970s. Thereafter, the threat of Labour, which had never won power in the council despite coming close often enough, mobilised the Conservative party to push aside Progressives, and quite quickly 'parochial' politics came to an end. This 'war on the Right', as *The Scotsman* called it, threatened to let in Labour (those 'socialists'), but this did not happen until 1973 by which time the long hegemony of the Right had done its work. The comment by the master of the Merchant Company in 1873 that he was thankful that the town council had nothing to do with politics was a mantra which had lasted throughout the following century.

This was not simply a matter of 'politics' but of economy too. Not only had there been a close connection between politics and property (landlordism in particular), but land deals had a particular impact in Edinburgh. In the inter-war period in particular the corporation, as it then was, used low-interest loans and subsidies to encourage private builders to erect both private and public housing. The council released land on favourable terms to local builders and offered cheap loans for house-building. Running the council had a direct, material, pay-off. Parcelling up the city allowed 'land banking' by local developers (such as James Miller), and low-rise suburban developments and inner-city infill schemes such as those designed by city architect Ebenezer MacRae (1881–1951) could be accommodated within a conservative strategy of house-building. In any case, MacRae followed Adam Horsburgh Campbell who had been burgh engineer since 1910, and director of housing since 1919, and there was continuity over a long period. MacRae's slum clearance programmes largely avoided corralling the poor on peripheral housing estates, at least in contrast with the scale of other Scottish cities. What came after him, post-war, he could do nothing about.

By the 1960s, commentators were noticing patterns of social and spatial segregation in Edinburgh, at least in modern forms. The Third Statistical Account of Scotland published in 1966 noted that in Edinburgh social strata were spatially located, even separated by open space. By the 1970s, social geographers were remarking on 'extreme social segregation of social classes' in Edinburgh (Richardson et al. 1975), at least compared with studies of other cities. The politics and economics of land development in the city had largely brought this about. The nexus of politics, economy and land development made notions of a ruling elite all too credible.

Schooling and Status

And it is not simply a matter of politics and economics; hegemony is about culture. Thus, it is highly significant that the Merchant Company ran many of the city's senior schools. Even those schools like Heriot's, not, in fact, a Merchant Company school, fitted into the general model of fee-paying day schools. The point is not that such schools are unique to Edinburgh, but that they were a substantial sector (one-fifth) of senior schools in the city. While beginning as schools for boys, the schools saw that the future lay in co-educational establishments, educating males and females together. The effect was to finish off the lesser girls' schools, leaving St George's (independent) and Mary Erskine's (Merchant Company) standing alone. Schooling paid off. One respondent in the study by John Highet (1969) commented: 'I soon found out that if your parents did not meet certain people, doors did not open easily. Life seemed to revolve around what your father did and what school you attended' (see Chapter 6). By the 1960s, such schools had found niches, according to Highet: the Edinburgh Academy, and to an extent, George Watson's, were linked to the legal profession, Heriot's to medicine, and Melville's (later Stewart's-Melville) to accountancy. And while there was a notional hierarchy of schools in terms of social status and ability to pay fees, this ran into education authority schools too. Older senior secondary schools shared much of the high lifelong educational attainment with those in the 'private' sector. The dividing line lay between 'old' and 'new' schools rather than 'public' and 'private' (see Chapter 6).

Furthermore, as Lindsay Paterson observed, such schools 'were firmly rooted in local bourgeois culture, and tied to the local university' (Paterson 1993: 237). From a situation where in 1960 around three-quarters of university entrants in Lothians and the Borders went to the Tounis College, thirty years later it was just over one-quarter. And there was little difference between graduates of 'independent' and older 'educational authority' schools in the city; the majority of university entrants (and in those days, only one in ten went to university) ended up at Edinburgh University. There was a time, of course, when a substantial number of school pupils chose *not* to go on to university or into higher education. Here, in particular, wearing the 'old school tie' was almost a passport to a job, in, for example, banking, accountancy, chartered surveying. It may not have been sufficient, but it was usually necessary to wear the old school tie. Hence, 'what school did you go to?' became a question with serious social mobility implications in Edinburgh, and did much to define social status in the city.

Those who went on to university, usually Edinburgh, were entering a place they implicitly understood, and while its university was possibly the most cosmopolitan of Scottish universities in terms of intake, most male students had attended the city's fee-paying schools, and women students, the 'ladies colleges' in the city. The close ties between city and university were reflected in the Merchant Company's funding of university chairs in accounting, and in the organisation of business and commerce, thus pointing up the close nexus between the two.

Performing Edinburgh

More generally, there were close links with professions such as law, medicine and accountancy, reinforced by the national (Scottish) professional bodies being based in the city. Describing Edinburgh as a 'closed' society did not come as a surprise to many. More generally, there were social clubs and associations which conveyed the sense of exclusivity. Playing golf on the likes of Muirfield or Barnton was not simply (not even) a question of knocking balls around eighteen holes; it was about 'doing business' and meeting people. Doors might open, opportunities arise, friendships be made which one could bank as a pay-off for the future. If nothing else, it was a way of amassing social capital. The likes of the New Club may have been resolutely against the discussion of 'business' (except its own), but it was likely to happen all the same among like-minded members (Chapter 5). Being 'one of us', 'people like oneself', always stood one in reasonable if unknowing stead.

Bodies such as the High Constables of Edinburgh, and the Royal Company of Archers, may have lost their *raison d'être*, no longer required to keep the peace or defend the monarch, but to borrow the words of sociologist C. Wright Mills,

> to the outsider, the club to which the upper class man or woman belongs is a badge of certification of his status; to the insider the club proves a more intimate or clan-like set of exclusive groupings which places and characterises the man. (Quoted in Bond 2012)

Note the gendering; for this (still) is almost entirely a world of men. Women, as such, did not exist in this world of elites, unless they were defined as 'ladies'. They had walk-on parts as long as they deported themselves with due decorum and appropriate dress.

There were stages upon which to act out deportment; to dress and behave accordingly, just as there were in many British cities of the time. Consider the classic department store; not of course unique to Edinburgh, but with particular nuances and expectations. We recognise them most in their passing. Only in their demise are we able to judge their significance. The BBC's Scottish business and economy editor is currently Douglas Fraser, whose father, (Sir William) Kerr Fraser, was permanent secretary at the Scottish Office in Edinburgh before serving as principal (and chancellor) of Glasgow University. Brought up in Edinburgh, son Douglas wrote perceptively of the demise of the great Edinburgh department stores as follows[5]:

> For those of us who grew up in Edinburgh, Jenners was an institution like few others anywhere. Into its extravagant sandstone façade had seeped generations of middle-class tradition along with the city's culture and social hierarchy. Pushing through its heavy doors opened into a sense of couthy capital quality, and permanence. I recall RW Forsyth's – very stiff and stuffy, it smelled of polish, is now home to TopShop. Patrick Thomson's on North Bridge was too small to last. At the west end of Princes St, Binns' had the clock where teenagers met friends (and in my dreams) a date. More recently branded Fraser's, it is currently being distilled and blended into a vast whisky visitor experience. Goldberg's[6] was downmarket and breezily brash. All were Edinburgh institutions. (25 January 2021)

It goes without saying that such department stores (in John Heiton's terms, most definitely 'big windaes' and not 'little windaes') were frequented by women, or rather 'ladies', with morning coffee and afternoon tea a specialty; to such an extent that 'Jenners' ladies' became a sobriquet of the city.

And that is the case for considering Edinburgh's ruling elite. Perceptive readers will notice the frequent use of the past tense, for the argument here is that much of that has passed away, or at least transformed into something different. Now we will consider how valid that claim is.

ERODING POWER

Nothing says more about the loss of economic autonomy in Edinburgh than the effective demise of Scottish banking. In 2016, Alf Young, the former economics editor of *The Herald*, wrote:

> In terms of market capitalisation, the Royal Bank is the second largest company with its head office in Scotland. It is not putting it too strongly to say that if the Royal Bank goes, it will be the beginning

of the end of the indigenous private sector in Scotland, with all
which that implies for the regeneration of Scottish industry. (Young
2016: 72)

And it has come to pass. The Royal Bank of Scotland and its
partner/rival the Bank of Scotland had stood at the centre of
Scottish capitalism, the hubs around which so many businesses
turned (see the fine study by John Scott and Michael Hughes,
The Anatomy of Scottish Capital, 1980). After the financial
crisis of 2008, the wheels came off the wagon. At the turn of
the millennium, Edinburgh was second to London as a financial
centre, with two of the top ten European banks, large life assurance companies, a substantial fund management sector and a
legal apparatus supporting that (see Chapter 3).

The Decline of Money

Two decades later, vestiges remain, but much has gone, including the title 'the Royal Bank of Scotland' (RBS) in England,
reverting to NatWest, but not in Scotland. The Bank of Scotland
has crawled out from under the wreckage of HBoS, its tie-up
with Halifax building society, and is doing its best to pretend
that none of it really took place. There are exceptions to this,
notably finance house Baillie Gifford whose astute, long-term
investments have paid off handsomely.[7] Nevertheless, removing
the two banks from the centre of things, or at least drastically
reducing their clout, means that finance capitalism in Edinburgh
is nowhere as significant as it was, and with that, the economic
heart of power in the city has been seriously damaged.

Space and Place

As if to underscore the point, the flows of investment capital
into city building projects have been transformed (Chapter 8).
Consider the complex ownership of the new St James Centre,
self-styled Edinburgh St James. The real estate company Nuveen
is a subsidiary of an American college insurance and annuity fund; its parent TIAA is the third largest commercial real
estate manager in the world. In 2016, it sold a large stake to
the Dutch pension asset manager APG, which holds funds for
The Netherlands' biggest pension fund, ABP. Similarly, The

Waterfront in north Edinburgh has a complex ownership pattern, whereby Forth Ports Authority sold its share of the development to an Australian investment company, which sold it on a few years later to the Public Sector Pension Investment fund of Canada; so the Mounties have a stake in Edinburgh. There are minority stakes held by London and Australian investors. Caltongate/New Waverley in downtown Edinburgh has an even more convoluted history, with its original developer going bust (when HBoS, ironically, withdrew funding). The site was subsequently sold to a South African developer, and who now owns the complex is almost anyone's guess; but there is little local money in it. These cases are not exceptional, but they tell a similar story: capital invested is not local. Site ownership is increasingly global; overseas investors, pension funds and hedge funds predominate. We might take the view that this is the way of the world, but it has direct implications for claims that there is a local elite which dominates Edinburgh in financial terms.

The trams saga tells a similar tale. True, public investment, from Scottish government and Edinburgh council have bankrolled the projects, but almost by default, because, like The Waterfront, only public investment can make such projects happen. Furthermore, those who did the work were certainly not local. In Trams 1 (from airport to city centre) the main contractor was Bilfinger Berger, and Siemens (both German), with the Spanish company CAF supplying the trams. In Trams 2 (from city centre to Newhaven), the contractor is a complex mouthful, Farrans Sacyr Neopul JV, in which Farrans, a Northern Ireland construction company is the lead contractor, Sacyr is a Spanish infrastructure company, and Neopul (JV means 'joint venture', so there are wheels within wheels) is a specialist rail company headquartered in London.

The key point is not the minutiae of who owns what, but that there is very little involvement or investment locally, other than public capital from Edinburgh council and Scottish government. It makes the point that in economic terms, local elites are not the key players in these development games, other than providing mediating legal and architectural services. These are by no means unique to Edinburgh. Furth of the city, George Rosie has pointed out that the Queensferry Crossing over the Firth of Forth (opened in 2017) is significantly different from its rail and road predecessors which were British-designed and

British-built from mainly British materials. The British, never mind Scottish, share in the consortium who built the new bridge is paltry (Rosie 2018). The point is made: local finance does not fund local projects, and by implication, local elites thereby lose their power and influence.

Spreading Power

Neither can we make a strong case for the power of *political* elites. After a century of rule by the parochial Right, political power on the council has become unpredictable. Proportional representation would seem to explain the lack of dominance of any single political party, but that is an effect rather than a cause (see Chapter 2). At the turn of the millennium, Labour ran the council by dint of its thirty-one to fifty-eight seat majority, but only on a third of the popular vote. In 2007 when PR was introduced, there was a four-way split of electoral votes, almost equally between Labour, Conservative, Liberal Democrat and SNP (each got around one-fifth of the vote). Since then, the Scottish Greens have made proportional gains, which adds to the unpredictability of electoral outcomes in which no party has a clear majority, and horse-trading and coalition is the order of the day. To date, since PR was introduced, the City of Edinburgh Council has been governed by coalitions, in order of numerical preponderance, between the Liberal Democrats and SNP (2007), Labour and SNP (2012), and SNP and Labour (in 2017). Smart money might suggest that a forthcoming 2022 election might see a Conservative/LibDem coalition emerging if the numbers fall out that way. Whatever the outcome, it is clear that the long hegemony of parochial right-wing rule which did so much to shape modern Edinburgh is over; and in any case, central government funds 85 per cent of local government expenditure. He who owns the piper calls the tune. The political elite in the city has been transformed.

Reading the Papers

Likewise, the local press, notably *The Scotsman* and the *Edinburgh Evening News* are no longer cultural powers in the city. Recall how *The Scotsman* in particular bolstered the Right against the 'socialist menace' well into the second half of the

twentieth century before it read the writing on the wall. It is
not that *The Scotsman/EEN* became the voice of the Left; it
is that people do not read them much anymore. In the early
1970s, more than 80,000 subscribed to *The Scotsman*, and as
many as 148,000 took the *Edinburgh Evening News* (see Kellas
1975: 172). These were powerful mouthpieces in the city. Over
the next forty years, *The Scotsman* lost almost three-quarters of
its readers (McCrone 2017a: table 22:1), and according to definitive ABC circulation figures,[8] only 10,000 buy the paper nowadays. Its stablemate, the *Edinburgh Evening News* is even more
curious. Despite its title, it sells in the morning,[9] which might
seem to make it *The Scotsman*'s competitor, and once more, it
sells just over 10,000 copies daily. The difference between the
two newspapers in terms of sales is non-existent, but whereas
The Scotsman relies on a fifty/fifty split between single paid
copies and paid subscriptions, the *Edinburgh Evening News* is
almost wholly single paid copies (90 per cent). The assumption
is that those who like their news 'really local' rely on the *Evening
News* and *The Scotsman* tries to live up to its title as Scotland's
national newspaper. To stretch a point, Edinburghers will tell
you that they take *The Scotsman* largely for the obituaries, as
well as out of habit. Whatever the case, it is hard to see either
as powerful mouthpieces in the city; which may not prevent the
local political class running scared of being badmouthed in the
local press, however small their readership. Indeed, cranking up
the scandal may be a sign of desperation in a declining readership, which may come to rely in any case on the broadcast and
social media picking up their stories for wider amplification.

To reinforce the point of a declining print media (a process
not unique to Edinburgh), ownership and location have rapidly changed. In 1860 in its heyday, *The Scotsman* was based
in purpose-built premises in Cockburn Street and owned by
founder John Ritchie. In 1904, it moved to grand premises on
North Bridge running down to Market Street where the paper
was printed. In 1953, the paper was bought by Canadian Roy
Thomson, who brought it onside as a supporter of Scottish home
rule. In 1995, it was bought by the reclusive and right-wing
Barclay Brothers, who moved the offices to new buildings on
Holyrood Road near the Scottish parliament building. Ten years
later, *The Scotsman/EEN* was sold to Johnston Press who specialised in local newspapers, usually weeklies across Scotland.

In 2013, the purpose-built building was sold and became the premises of a video games company (Rockstar North of Grand Theft Auto, no less), and *The Scotsman* was downsized to the top of an anonymous office block in Queensferry Road/Orchard Brae a few miles from the city centre. By 2018, its owners, Johnston Press, went into administration, and the newspapers became the property of JPI Media, and media executive David Montgomery, for a sale price of £10.2m. DC Thomson, best known for publishing the *Dundee Courier*, *Aberdeen Press and Journal* and the *Sunday Post* (to say nothing of *The Beano*) pulled out of the bidding judging that the price was too high for the products. *The Scotsman/Evening News* are shadows of their former selves.

Education and Status

And what of schools? Surely they have survived and even prospered? And the Tounis College has swallowed up smaller colleges of art (Edinburgh College of Art) and education (Moray House), to become one of the largest employers in the city.[10] Is the city's elite not still structured around such educational institutions? Up to a point, but as we saw in Chapter 6, the key divide in terms of lifelong career attainment is being educated at *older* schools, public and private, and not simply attending fee-paying schools. Older senior-secondary schools and fee-paying schools have much in common as regards achievements of pupils than their younger counterparts. And arguably the 'old school tie' is no longer as significant as it once was. When only one in ten senior school pupils went on to university in the 1960s, the 'tie' mattered as far as local employers were concerned.

Fifty years later, when more than half of school-leavers go on to higher education, exam credentials matter far more than the school you had attended. Furthermore, whereas in the old days students simply went on to the local university taking their culture with them, nowadays the norm is to go to university elsewhere (but still within Scotland), while at the same time, university intakes are more diverse; students thereafter make cultures of their own. Diversifying the intake to university has not meant, *pace* George Davie, the Englishing of Edinburgh, so much as 'Scotticising' the intake insofar as many students hitherto domiciled in England stay on after graduation and make their careers, and contributions, north of the border. The result is the diversification of educational and cultural experiences. The 'private' schools still matter, but they no longer funnel their graduates simply into local positions of power and responsibility; and in any case, furth of Edinburgh has become their oyster.

To recap. There has been considerable loss of local economic clout in Edinburgh; its electoral politics are now multi-party with none having expectations of an easy ride to power; the local print media, who amplified the concerns of the local ruling elite and made sure as best they could that the balance of power would not be upset, is a shadow of its former self. Educational capital tied into fee-paying schools no longer ostensibly dominates ruling institutions in the city. We might still wish to claim that social organisations such as the New Club, the High Constables of Edinburgh, and even the Honourable Company of Edinburgh Golfers still pack a punch, but without the requisite political-economic nexus behind it, such a claim is harder than ever to make. To cap it all, the great Edinburgh department stores such as Jenners, and Forsyth's, have had their day, which may be neither here nor there in the schemes of things, but is surely symptomatic of changing cultural habits. And if Edinburgh has transformed itself into a city of festivals, then it is chasing a highly competitive, post-industrial, market for such business. There is a pattern here, which we will return to later in this chapter, that virtually all cities are chasing the same game. Consider this comment: 'the only way municipalities in an age of austerity can keep the flywheel of internal revenue acceleration going is through real estate development, dependent on private capital to drive up land values and real estate prices' (Engelen et al. 2017). This is the new urbanism: competitiveness focused on what is tradable. We will return to flesh out that argument in the context of our question: who runs Edinburgh?

EDINBURGH OTHERS

There is one prior task to carry out before we do that. What of others who do not figure prominently, if at all, in this Edinburgh story? What of those who seem to have walk-on parts in this saga: women, the working class, ethnic groups in particular, none of whom have played central roles?

Female Edinburgh

As far as women were concerned, one class of that gender did matter: ladies. They appear, historically, as adornments and accompaniments of more powerful males, whether in the Merchant Company or the New Club. True, there is no longer an embargo on women members of these institutions, or the High Constables of Edinburgh, but this is relatively recent. This is odd, because the city long had a preponderance of women residents. Historian Bob Morris (2010) has made the import-ant point that in the middle of the twentieth century, women outnumbered men in Edinburgh in the ratio of 118 to 100; in 1911, the ratio was 123 to 100, so the lack of men was not to be accounted for by the Great War. This was by no means simply a reflection of the importance of domestic service in the city, which was, in any case, of declining significance. There was a rising number of female clerical workers, teachers and print-workers. Morris observed: 'Edinburgh was a place which proved especially attractive to young adult women' (Morris 2010: 13), and they favoured areas like Morningside, Haymarket and Newington, and avoided poorer districts like Gorgie/Dalry, Canongate and Calton. Morningside, especially, was favoured – it had a female to male ratio of 165:100 in 1951 – and probably gave rise to those Morningside jokes always heard in a female voice, with its slightly strangulated vowel sounds.

As Bob Morris observes, Muriel Spark was especially good at the female voice, and its variations of status and culture. Consider Spark's descriptions of sorts of Edinburgh women in *The Prime of Miss Jean Brodie*:

> There were legions of her kind during the nineteen-thirties, women from the age of thirty and upward, who crowded into their war-bereaved spinsterhood with voyages of discovery into new ideas and energetic practices in art or social welfare, education or religion. (1965: 42)[11]

These

> progressive spinsters of Edinburgh could be seen leaning over the democratic counters of Edinburgh grocers' shops arguing with the manager at three in the afternoon on every subject from the authen-ticity of the Scriptures to the question what the word 'guaranteed' on a jam-jar really meant. (Spark 1965: 42)

On the other hand

> the committee spinsters were less enterprising and not at all rebel-
> lious, they were sober churchgoers and quiet workers. The school-
> mistresses were of a still more orderly type, earning their keep,
> living with aged parents and taking walks on the hills and holidays
> in North Berwick. (Spark 1965: 43)

Note spinsterhood, characterised by poets Stewart Conn and
Robert Crawford as somehow typifying Edinburgh. There were
good reasons: women were required to resign from their posts
on marriage (known as the 'marriage bar' which lasted well into
the second half of the twentieth century). Those who wished
to continue in their professions had to remain spinsters; a feature well captured by Spark in her novels. In terms of elite positions, however, there were few women in positions of power in
Edinburgh, except as amanuenses to their husbands. There is
considerable irony, however, that it was a female chief executive
of the City of Edinburgh Council, Sue Bruce, who broke through
the trams stand-off in 2011 and was made a Dame Commander
of the Order of the British Empire in 2015 for her efforts.

Working Class City

If women only had decorative walk-on parts in Edinburgh's
story, so also did its manual working class. It was proportionately small – around 10 per cent in 2020, compared with
16 per cent in Scotland as a whole.[12] We have seen in Chapter 3
that Edinburgh was far more important as a 'professional' city as
well as a national capital; in the words of Madgin and Rodger:
'These capital city functions, with their superior courts, national
assemblies and institutional headquarters became deeply embedded in the city and influenced fundamentally its economic structure and social ecology' (Madgin and Rodger 2013: 509–10).
Not only had Edinburgh a diversity of industries, it was easier to
re-imagine it as a non-industrial city, and industry, and the city's
working class, were airbrushed out of the picture. This was
reinforced by the relative weakness of the Labour party, which
never managed to win political power on the council until the
1970s. It took the reorganisation of local government into two
tiers in the mid-1970s to give Labour power, but largely because
the 'landward' areas in the Lothians were disproportionately

strong, conferring dominance on Lothian Regional Council. This level had greater powers than Edinburgh District Council where Labour was weaker while managing to form administrations from 1984 onwards.

Class politics in Edinburgh were usually complex and nuanced, despite *The Scotsman*'s fear of the 'Working Class Other'. Furthermore, the city's working class was highly variegated. Recall Robbie Gray's comment in Chapter 3 about nineteenth-century Edinburgh: 'A range of old-established crafts catered for the large middle-class consumer market, while newer, more capital-intensive enterprise were geared to national and world markets. One feature common to many local industries was their high proportion of skilled labour' (Gray 1976: 26). At the cultural level, working class life was rarely part of the city's image (recall Labour's George Kerevan (he was chair of the district council's culture committee) opposing 'ingrained elitism' and 'the arts establishment in Edinburgh' as regards the Edinburgh International Festival (in Chapter 4): 'we declare war on it; we will abolish it; we will democratise it' (Miller 1996: 116). Little of those threats came to pass. Working class Edinburgh had low visibility in the city's affairs; except that Leith was a useful antithesis to 'Edinburgh', especially as it had been forced into merger with the city up Leith Walk in 1920 despite voting six to one against in a plebiscite. Old grievances were always useful and could be cited in evidence as occasions arose.

Every now and again working class Edinburgh breaks through such as when the City Arts Centre mounted an exhibition of photographs by Robert Blomfield in November 2018, taken when he worked as a doctor in the city fifty years earlier. This was followed up by a book, *Robert Blomfield: Edinburgh 1957–1966* (Bluecoat Press, 2020), and a few of his photographs are reproduced here, with the kind permission of his family. Here is another Edinburgh, of 'ordinary people', a gritty city based mainly in Stockbridge, Leith and the Southside, just at the point at which old neighbourhoods were being swept away. This is not a city recognisable to visitors and the tourist industry, but one known to many locals, as *their* Edinburgh. Blomfield was an incomer, who came from Leeds as a medical student and fell in love with what he found in ordinary Edinburgh: 'I think', he said, 'it's a form of love. You should love the picture. I love the photographs. I love the people' (p. 1).

Blomfield's is a useful corrective to the usual side of this caste-like city; bourgeois, professional, grand and status-conscious. Working class life almost becomes exotic (see *Trainspotting*). Even sport can be read off as a class indicator. Rugby for the middle classes (fee-paying schools, and FP teams like Heriot's, Watsonians, Academicals); and football for the working class. Edinburgh's two professional teams, Heart of Midlothian and Hibernian, served each half of the city, west and east, and while some tried to breathe religious sectarianism into each, as mini-me Rangers and Celtic, it never quite stuck except on the mad fringes, and never for very long. This was because football in Edinburgh had much more to do with pub bragging rights than with the vitriol of religious sectarianism to be found in parts of west-central Scotland. Religion, in any case, no longer mattered very much in Edinburgh despite the city's historic association with John Knox, the Disruption in 1843, when the Free Kirk broke away from the Auld Kirk, and led to competitive church building. Not many cities have a Holy Corner with four churches at a crossroads (in Morningside/Bruntsfield), which only in the late twentieth century was resolved as architects found new and imaginative ways of using old church buildings. Sectarianism had its odd moments, as in the so-called Morningside 'riots' in 1935, and the curious and idiosyncratic survival of John Cormack as Protestant Action councillor in Leith from 1933 until 1961 (the definitive account is by Michael Rosie, in *The Sectarian Myth in Scotland*).[13] The steam, however, had gone out of religion in Edinburgh a long time ago.[14] It was the exception which proved the rule that, by and large, religion in Edinburgh was a private affair.

City of Incomers

In terms of its population, Edinburgh gives off the impression of being a stable, staid and white city in terms of ethnicity. It has become, however, a much more multi-national and multi-cultural city in recent years, with the biggest increases among those born outwith the UK. In 1931, for example, 90 per cent of its population was born in Scotland; by 2011,[15] this had fallen to 70 per cent. Since 1981, the number of Edinburgh residents born in England had increased by 67 per cent.[16] People born in England are the largest number, representing 12 per cent of

Edinburgh's population in 2011, double the proportion of 1931. There has been a significant rise in people born on the continent of Europe; less than 1 per cent in 1981, but 6.5 per cent in 2011. Net overseas migration into Edinburgh between 2009 and 2019 is by far the largest component of population change, numbering over 53,000, eighteen times that of net migration from within the UK (2,900), and five times the figure for net births and deaths (10,390) (https://www.edinburgh.gov.uk/downloads/file/29314/edinburgh-by-numbers-2020). Poles now number 2.4 per cent of Edinburgh's population, with net growth in the French, German, Spanish and Italian populations. The growth in the Chinese population between 1981 and 2011 was almost seventeen-fold, from 243 to 4,100. According to the 2011 Census, Edinburgh was the most diverse of Scotland's cities, with 18 per cent defining themselves as an ethnic minority, closely followed by Glasgow and Aberdeen (both on 17 per cent), with Dundee some way behind at 11 per cent. The point of these figures is a simple one, and crucial to our argument. Edinburgh has become a highly cosmopolitan city, a reflection in part of its improving economy, and with it, job opportunities. Its overall population increase between 2009 and 2019 (at 61,700 net) was higher in absolute terms than any other UK city apart from Manchester and Birmingham which are, in any case, larger.

The population growth of Edinburgh, and especially its growing 'ethnic' diversity, might suggest that previously it was mono-cultural and mono-ethnic, but that was matter of perception rather than reality. Edinburgh was never, objectively, a closed city. Consider this observation by Ebenezer MacRae made in his chapter in the 1949 Abercrombie Report: 'At the beginning of the 17th century, an envoy sent to *"the Low Countreys for the hame-bringing of Flemyngs and utheris for making of broad claithe . . . and uther stuffis sic as is maid in Flanderis of our Scottis woll"*.' To expedite this, the city even built a village for Flemish weavers at Picardy Place, hence the name. Close by is Leith Walk which became a settlement for a succession of migrant groups: Irish, Italians,[17] Indians and Pakistanis, Chinese, and latterly, Poles. Jews tended to cluster on the Southside (see David Daiches' autobiography, *Two Worlds: An Edinburgh Jewish Childhood*, 1956); while the Irish settled in the Cowgate and Old Town, after the Irish famine in the 1840s, making it the second largest concentration in Scotland after Glasgow;

one of its best-known sons being the Irish revolutionary James Connolly, executed in the aftermath of the Easter Rising in Dublin 1916. More recently, while almost half (42 per cent) of Scottish Muslims live in Glasgow, 16 per cent live in Edinburgh. Edinburgh's Muslim population is smaller (12,500), but more diverse. Wardak's study (2000) of Edinburgh Pakistanis in the 1990s, who accounted for about half of the city's Muslims, found that they inhabited inner city areas like Gorgie, Leith and Broughton, and that most were Sunni of the Barelvi tradition. Edinburgh had eleven known mosques, nine catering for Sunnis and two for Shi'as.

Edinburgh, then, has long been a city of in-migrants as befits one of expanding economic opportunities, and a vibrant higher education sector. Its largest 'ethnic' group is undoubtedly the English, that is, people born in England,[18] who would, in any case, not consider themselves to be an ethnic group at all, but 'minus-one ethnics', a norm of the implicit 'we' from which others are deemed to deviate. Around one person in eight in Edinburgh was born in England, giving rise to claims that it is an 'English' city, but there is little justification for that, because the English in Scotland have a habit of 'going native', at least in terms of their own personal claims (see McCrone and Bechhofer 2015). It is worth underlining the point that Edinburgh, in terms of where its residents were born, can be considered the most cosmopolitan of the Scottish cities, even though this does not figure prominently in its cultural and social accounts. It does make the point, however, that cultural and ethnic heterogeneity have helped to erode the sense of Edinburgh as a closed social and cultural system.

SO DOES *ANYONE* RUN EDINBURGH?

The simple answer to that is to say that Edinburgh has ceased to be a city of castes in the sense that Heiton used the term in the nineteenth century. We search in vain for a 'Ruling They', except in the sense that the City of Edinburgh Council rules, but that does not get us very far. In the last twenty years, Edinburgh has grown in status as a national capital, but that carries a sting in the tail. Scottish government, which in any case funds around 85 per cent of local government expenditure nationally, especially wants a say in how Edinburgh is run. Consider the

Growth Accelerator model (GAM) which played a key role in the development of 'Edinburgh St James', as well as its reluctance to permit an Edinburgh 'bed tax'. Furthermore, its mantra 'open for business' applies particularly to Edinburgh as one of its leading economic engines. We have seen, too, that Edinburgh planners have bought into the mantra (Inch 2017). In any case, national capitals, of independent or semi-independent states, are required to face two ways, to be national as well as local, and they are compensated for their efforts.

Open for Business

Being 'open for business' also carries wider implications. Irving Lapsley[19] and his colleagues observe that 'The world of cities has increasingly become one of calculating and quantifying, as they compete in an increasingly explicit way with each other for population, economic resources and influence' (Lapsley et al. 2010: 308). We think of cities as a collection of physical assets, buildings and infrastructure, but they are in essence financial numbers (Arnaboldi and Lapsley 2010: 403), the 'calculable city', in which assets are sliced and diced, and fitted with numerical values. 'Cities have come to mimic large corporations as they engage in various kinds of exercises aimed at projecting and visualizing the city as it should become, and how it should transform itself to get there' (2010: 307).

Behind this notion of the 'calculable city' lies new public management (NPM). Hyndman and Lapsley (2016: 12) observe:

> despite the NPM emerging in the UK in a Conservative government era (between 1979 and 1997), it did not die with the advent of a New Labour Government in the UK in 1997; rather, policy 'translators' represented NPM ideas under another banner – the modernisation agenda.

NPM employs a suite of management devices: '"value for money" scrutiny, efficiency audits, benchmarking, targets' setting, cost comparisons, and greater scrutiny of public service delivery' (Hyndman and Lapsley 2016: 20). The point about NPM is that it is not a simple set of reform ideas, but a loose umbrella term embracing a range of administrative and managerial ideas. Hyndman and Lapsley conclude that NPM has penetrated UK (including Scottish) pubic services 'virus-like' over a lengthy period, with little sign that policy-makers are immune to its attractions. 'Different ideas are added over time, as the NPM virus adapts and mutates' (27). The use of the 'virus' metaphor has a particular resonance since 2019 even though the authors were using it before Covid-19 came on the scene, transforming social and economic life. One might observe that so has NPM.

Embedded in NPM is the mantra of 'modernisation', which was the leitmotif of the New Labour era, with its obsession with 'audit' and 'NPM-style numbers games'. The problem is, however, that 'modernisation is a never-ending process where politicians and civil servants chase the perfect way to organise the public sector and its services. The perfect is illusive, alas, and so the Sisyphus work has to go on' (Bergstrom and Lapsley 2017: 19). NPM, they observe, continues unabated contrary to the proposition that we live in a post-NPM world (16). In Newman's words:

> Local governments have been constituted as self-governing economic actors, as responsible political and managerial subjects, as good partners, as reflexive and flexible business leaders, as competitive entities constituted through performance discourse and as 'delivery agents' within a centralised system of governing in which there is little room for discretion. (Newman 2014: 3294)

And Edinburgh? Consider, for example, Andy Inch's evidence that city planners have bought wholesale into the 'modernisation' mantra, in which those opposed to it are considered 'dinosaurs': hence, the drive for 'efficiency and effectiveness'. Recall the use of arm's length companies to develop The Waterfront, and the trams project. ALCos are a direct expression of 'modernisation': except that in each case, they manifestly did not work, and developments had to be taken back into direct council control. The trams project, furthermore, is a poor example of 'efficiency and effectiveness', being way over budget (by 43 per cent), and arm's length inefficient. One might have expected further such projects to be shelved, at least until we knew more about why such megaprojects were liable to fail, or at least run well over budget. To the contrary. The council ploughed on with trams extensions without knowing the outcome of the Hardie Inquiry, which, two years on, has still to report in any case. The way to comprehend the trams is not in terms of tight cost-efficiency, but as a public statement of 'modernisation' itself, regardless of cost, for 'modernisation' is not about precise measurement of change: it is a governing mantra.

Scottish government's Growth Accelerator model (GAM) belongs firmly to this family of 'modernisation' concepts, as does its modified versions of PFI/PPP, the Scottish Futures Trust and the Infrastructure Investment Board. Encouraging City Regions such as South-East Scotland with Edinburgh as its hub, makes the point that 'cities and their hinterland do not compete but are instead complementary to one another' (Engelen et al. 2017: 410). 'If the governor [central government, and global capital] is external the only way municipalities in an age of austerity can keep the flywheel of internal revenue acceleration going is through real estate development, dependent on private capital to drive up land values and real estate prices' (415).

Edinburgh's assets are calculable and tradable, and by and large on an upward trajectory in which slicing and dicing its assets, in terms of property values or cultural products such as festivals are attractive to outsiders and to central government as long as the merry-go-round revolves. It is, in Molotch's term, a growth machine, but only as long as the wheels go round and money is made. None of this is inevitable, nor that investments of external capital continue evermore. Nor is it simply a question of assuming that the 'money machine' is predominant and flattens everything in its path. As Newman points out, there are 'landscapes of antagonism' involved whereby 'different enactments of neo-liberalising projects take place in a contradictory field of political forces' (Newman 2014: 3291), and in any case, 'neo-liberalism' is a promiscuous term, 'widely over-used and notoriously difficult to pin down' (Newman 2014: 3291).

CONCLUSION: SMOKE AND MIRRORS

Which is where we began this book. How broader forces play out depends on local conditions, of histories and cultures tied to place. In asking who runs Edinburgh, we glimpse those landscapes of antagonism, and see how they play out in the making and remaking of a city. Edinburgh is, of course, not unique in that respect, but arguably it has/had a degree of economic, political and social containedness which makes asking who runs the place more plausible than most. There is nothing to stop anyone asking the question of other towns and cities.

The question, who runs Edinburgh, turns out to be a question of considerable heuristic value, because it makes us focus on where various forms of power lie, and how these have changed over a century or more. If, as this book argues, we cannot put our finger neatly on the complex of elites any more, that is because power in the city has been transformed. It is not the case, of course, that *no one* runs the city, but that systems of power, economic, political and cultural, are no longer manifestly local. The hands of central government and of global capital are all too obvious in how Edinburgh works. Furthermore, there are financial devices like NPM which are highly significant. It would be taking it too far to say that Edinburgh is a 'calculable city', hence run by algorithms, but it is a measure of how attenuated systems of power have become that asking who runs Edinburgh still makes heuristic sense.

And yet, and yet . . . there are two sides to this Edinburgh story. On the one hand, it is ostensibly clear that if the city is not quite run by algorithms, then a framework of external rules, certainly well beyond its confines, sets the parameters for decisions to be taken. Those who pay the piper certainly call the tunes. The other side, however, is that in a relatively small and self-contained city of half a million people, there are, as the saying goes, those and such as those. Scale is important because it is easier to get to know people 'like yourself'. Indeed, they probably already do, for they will have attended the same schools, joined the same clubs, and engaged in similar pursuits, whether golf, archery (purely symbolic, of course), and above all, dining. Although the Merchant Company is no longer keeping the company it once was, there will considerable overlap with other forums and activities, whether the New Club, the RSE Dining Club,[20] the Caledonian Club, the Law Society, and so on. Times, of course, change, and the University of Edinburgh, unlike the days of principals Appleton and Swan, no longer has formal dinners for senior professors at which plotting and persuasion could occur. If nothing else, universities are much larger, and have too many professors to make that feasible these days. Nevertheless, it is a key expectation of university principals that, where deemed appropriate, they are able to wield influence in matters of campus planning, always touchy as we have seen in Chapter 7, or where there is overlap between the academy and public practice such as medicine and hospitals. The shift of the

Royal Infirmary to Little France would certainly have been such a matter where informal discussions between university, health board, Scottish government and city council took place.

If eating dinner with people you know is by definition a private social activity, and not a public one, it is not about assuaging hunger: it is about having a quiet word about matters of common interest. Having X on your board may seem of little value – after all, they may say very little at meetings – but their interests and connections can be activated as and when. Fundraising for charities, good causes or schools is a matter of calling in favours and friendships, usually on a reciprocal basis. Public bodies such as university courts, council development forums, private school boards, cultural bodies like the Edinburgh Festival, Scottish Opera and Ballet, the Museum of Scotland and so forth, will invite similar people, often the same people to share knowledge and expertise, as well as money. They also have veto power, in that kite-flying may test out projects before they get off the drawing board, never mind off the ground, and they may never do.

In a small city like Edinburgh, such people may have undue influence insofar as they move from one body to another. The novels of Alexander (Sandy) McCall-Smith,[21] notably the genre of 'Isabel Dalhousie' stories, give a good sense of the charmed circle of Edinburgh. If you happen to live in parts of Edinburgh's New Town, for example, you cannot be unaware that social life operates almost unknowingly around you.[22] It is also the case that such networks are frequently overlapping, but also informally 'policed' so that those who might wish to break into the circle are managed out of it. One cannot, after all, police private dinners and who one associates with. All this might assume the operation of 'hidden hands', but that is to assume a degree of formality which is not how they operate, and certainly would be denied by those who participate. They might eschew influence and power; it is, after all, the *private* sphere. To borrow a phrase from a close colleague, this is an apocryphal miasma of a closed, exclusive elite. It can be denied (apocrypha) and it is atmospheric (all around).

Studying 'who runs Edinburgh?', then, runs between two faultlines; assuming too much, and assuming too little. On the one hand, we can point to the fact that much money and power comes from the outside these days; the tunes are called by others; and there are complex rules and routines to be followed. On the other hand, the myth – in the sense of a truth held to be self-evident – that Edinburgh is a city of castes dies hard. There are too many anecdotal examples to dismiss it out of hand. In social statistics, to draw an analogy, there are two forms of error which researchers have to steer a line between: type I and type II errors. Put simply, there are errors of commission (type I), what are called 'false positives', in our case, assuming that there *is* indubitably an elite which runs Edinburgh. And there are errors of omission – 'false negatives' or type II errors – where we assume that rule and regulations, even algorithms, run the city; so no ruling elite to speak of. The skill in social research is to run the fine line between the two, neither rejecting too much, nor accepting too little. Asking who runs Edinburgh turns out to be not such a bad question after all.

NOTES

1. You can, of course, visit the War Memorial inside the castle free of charge, but you will be escorted there and back by a warder in case you wander off on to the tourist trail and try to dodge the entry fee.
2. <https://www.bbc.co.uk/news/uk-scotland-47157011>.
3. A 'rebus' is a picture puzzle made up of objects or things (derived from 'res' in Latin, 'rebus', the ablative plural, means 'by things').
4. <https://www.bbc.co.uk/news/uk-scotland-42263780>.
5. <https://www.bbc.co.uk/news/uk-scotland-scotland-business-55805481>.
6. Goldberg's was actually a Glasgow institution (since 1908); it opened the store in Edinburgh's Tollcross in 1960.
7. Baillie Gifford's views ('Don't Give up on China' as a source of investment opportunities) would have drawn attention in late 2021 <https://www.ft.com/content/c7002c97-4d81-4e2d-a23e-0c26582fd072>.
8. ABC is Audit Bureau of Circulations, the definitive count of newspaper sales, designed to aid advertisers, but open to a wider pubic as information. See <https://www.abc.org.uk/reporting-standards/national-newspapers>.
9. Or rather all day; a bit like that other oxymoron, the 'all-day breakfast'.
10. NHS Lothian has around 20,000 employees, City of Edinburgh Council 18,600, and Edinburgh University, 13,300 (2013–14 figures).

11. I am grateful to Michael Anderson for pointing out that Spark over-simplifies because if there was a shortage of men it was because of pre-war emigration and not simply war deaths (see Anderson 2018).

12. We can, of course, construe the working class as much more than manual workers, but it serves the purpose here to depict it as such, reflecting its relative numerical weakness.

13. And see M. Rosie and T. Devine 'The rise and fall of anti-Catholicism in Scotland', in Claire Gheeraert-Graffeuille and Geraldine Vaughan (eds): *Anti-Catholicism in Britain and Ireland, 1600–2000: Practices, Representations and Ideas* (London: Palgrave, 2020).

14. For a splendid account of growing up a Catholic in Edinburgh, see Sean Damer's 'Memoirs of a Catholic boyhood: a map of Catholic Edinburgh', *History Workshop Journal*, no. 44, Autumn 1977, pp. 189–96.

15. The Census of 2011 is the latest we have data for. Scottish Government decreed that there would be no Census in 2021 because of Covid-19.

16. The figure for Northern Ireland is 118 per cent, the Republic of Ireland, 83 per cent, and Wales, 43 per cent, but in each case from much smaller bases than England.

17. The Edinburgh institution Valvona and Crolla is in Elm Row at the top of the Walk.

18. This is not to presume that people born in England and who settle in Scotland consider themselves to be 'English' in terms of their national identity. Our research (2015) showed that they were more likely to think of themselves as 'British'.

19. Irving Lapsley is Professor Emeritus of accounting at Edinburgh University, focusing particularly on public finance.

20. The RSE has a Dining Club strictly by invitation, such that even RSE Fellows like the author did not know of its existence; it had to be pointed out. How important, or self-important, it is one cannot tell.

21. Sandy, as he is known – itself a form of insider-knowledge – had another life as an eminent Professor of medical law at Edinburgh University.

22. In 2019, BBC ran a series called 'the secret history of our streets', which included the Moray Estate in Edinburgh's New Town <https://www.edinburghlive.co.uk/news/edinburgh-news/moray-estate-edinburgh-bbc-series-16172140>. I lived in a nearby street for ten years previously, and I was dimly aware of such social activities going on around me which I was not privy to.

Bibliography

Abercrombie, Patrick and Derek Plumstead (1949), *A Civic Survey and Plan for the City and Royal Burgh of Edinburgh*, Edinburgh: McLagan and Cumming.

Anderson, Michael (2018), *Scotland's Populations from the 1850s to Today*, Oxford: Oxford University Press.

Anderson, Robert (1983), *Education and Opportunity in Victorian Scotland*, Edinburgh: Edinburgh University Press.

Anderson, Robert, Michael Lynch and Nicholas Phillipson (2003), *University of Edinburgh: an illustrated history*, Edinburgh: Edinburgh University Press.

Arnaboldi, Michela and Irving Lapsley (2010), 'Asset management in cities: polyphony in action?', *Accounting, Auditing and Accountability Journal*, 23(3), 392–419.

ARUP (2004), *Review of Line 1: Review of Business Case* (CEC01799560_0002).

Audit Scotland (2007), Edinburgh transport projects review, <http://www.audit-scotland.gov.uk/docs/central/2007/nr_070620_edin_transport_project.pdf>.

Audit Scotland (2011), Edinburgh trams: interim report. <http://www.audit-scotland.gov. uk/report/edinburgh-trams-interim-report>.

Bachrach, Peter and Morton Baratz (1962), 'Two faces of power', *American Political Science Review*, 56(4), 947–52.

Bain, Wilson (1985), 'The historical perspective', in Gordon Kirk (ed.), *Moray House and Professional Education*, Edinburgh: Scottish Academic Press.

Bartie, Angela (2013), *The Edinburgh Festivals: Culture and Society in Post-war Britain*, Edinburgh: Edinburgh University Press.

BBC News (2018), Leith trams survey questions the need for extension, 7 March, <http://www.bbc.co.uk/news/uk-scotland-edinburgh-east-fife-43304747>.

Begg, Tom (1997), *The Excellent Women*, Edinburgh: John Donald.

Bell, Colin and Howard Newby (2022 [1970]), *Community Studies*, London: Routledge.

Bergstrom, Tomas and Irving Lapsley (2017), 'On the elusive nature of modernisation in government', *Statsvetenskaplig tidskrift*, 119(1), 7–22.

Binelli, Mark (2013), *The Last Days of Detroit: Motor Cars, Motown and the Collapse of an Industrial Giant*, London: Bodley Head.

Black, Ian (2005), *Merr Weegies vs Edinbuggers*, Edinburgh: Black and White Publishing.

Blair, Alastair (1988), *New Club Annals, 1937–1987*, Edinburgh: The New Club.

Blomfield, Robert (2020), *Edinburgh 1957–1966*, Liverpool: Bluecoat Press.

Bond, Matthew (2012), 'The basis of elite social behaviour', *Sociology*, 46(4): 613–32.

BOP Consulting (2011), *Edinburgh Festivals Impact Study, Final Report*, <http://bop.co.uk/projects/impact-study-2010-2011>.

BOP Consulting (2015), *Edinburgh Festivals 2015 Impact Study, Final Report Impact*, <https://www.edinburghfestivalcity.com/assets/000/001/964/Edinburgh_Festivals_-_2015_Impact_Study_Final_Report_original.pdf ?1469537463>.

BOP Consulting (2015), *Edinburgh Festivals: Thundering Hooves 2.0*: A Ten Year Strategy to Sustain the Success of Edinburgh's Festivals, <https://www. edinburghfestivalcity.com/assets/000/000/821/TH_2__0_-_24_page_summary_ original.pdf ?1432032670>.

BOP Consulting (2018), *Edinburgh Festivals: The Network Effect*. The role of the Edinburgh festivals in the national culture and events sectors, <https://www.edinburghfestivalcity.com/assets/000/003/791/The_Network_Effect__July_2018__original.pdf?1531301203>.

Bruce, G. (1975), *Festival in the North: The Story of the Edinburgh Festival*, London: Robert Hale and Co.

Buchan, James (2003), *Capital of the Mind: How Edinburgh Changed the World*, London: John Murray.

Campbell, N. and R. M. S. Smellie (1983), *The Royal Society of Edinburgh, 1783–1983*, Edinburgh: RSE.

Carlin, Norah (2009), *Holy Cross Academy Edinburgh: The Life and Times of a Catholic School, 1907–1969*, Edinburgh: New Cut Press.

Cockburn, Harry (1938), *A History of the New Club, Edinburgh, 1787–1937*, London: W. R. Chambers.

Crawford, Ian (1997), *Banquo on Thursdays: The Inside Story of 50 Years of the Edinburgh Festival*, Edinburgh: Goblinshead.

Crawford, Robert (2013), *On Glasgow and Edinburgh*, Cambridge, MA: Harvard University Press.

Crawford, Robert (2015), *Camera Obscura*, *London Review of Books*, 8 January, p. 15.

Crewe, Ivor and Anthony King (2013), *The Blunders of Our Governments*, London: Oneworld Publications.

Dahl, Robert (1961), *Who Governs? Democracy and Power in an American City*, New Haven: Yale University Press.

Daiches, David (1956), *Two Worlds: An Edinburgh Jewish Childhood*, Edinburgh: Canongate Books.

Dale, Michael (1988), *Sore Throats and Overdrafts: An Illustrated Story of the Edinburgh Festival Fringe*, Edinburgh: Precedent Publications.

Damer, Sean (1977), 'Memoirs of a Catholic boyhood: a map of Catholic Edinburgh', *History Workshop Journal*, no. 44, Autumn, 189–96.

Damer, Sean (2020), *Scheming: A Social History of Glasgow Council Housing, 1919–1956* Edinburgh: Edinburgh University Press.

Davie, George (1961), *The Democratic Intellect: Scotland and her Universities in the Nineteenth Century*, Edinburgh: Edinburgh University Press.

Davies, Christie (ed.) (2002), *The Mirth of Nations*, London: Routledge.

Delamont, Sara (1984a), 'The Old Girl network: recollections on the fieldwork at St Luke's', in R. Burgess (ed.), *The Research Process in Educational Settings*, Brighton: Falmer Press, pp. 15–38.

Delamont, Sara (1984b), 'Debs, dollies, swots and weeds: classroom styles at St Luke's', in G. Walford (ed.), *British Public Schools Policy and Practice*, Brighton: Falmer Press, pp. 65–86.

Delamont, Sara (2003), 'Planning enlightenment and dignity: the girls' schools 1918–58', in G. Walford (ed.), *British Private Schools*, London: Woburn Press, pp. 57–76.

Domhoff, William (2014), 'Who really ruled in Dahl's New Haven?', <https://whorulesamerica.ucsc.edu/local/new_haven.html>.

Edinburgh's Year Round Festivals 2004–2005: *Economic Impact Study. A Final Report*, <https://www.edinburghfestivalcity.com/assets/000/000/341/SQW_Economic_Impact_Report_-_01.09.05_original.pdf?1411036239>.

Elliott, Brian and David McCrone (1982), *The City: Patterns of Domination and Conflict*, London: Macmillan.

Engelen, Ewald, Julie Froud, Sukhdev Johal, Angelo Salento and Karel Williams (2017), 'The grounded city', *Cambridge Journal of Regions, Economy and Society*, 10, 407–23.

Flyvbjerg, Bent (2003), *Megaprojects and Risk: An Anatomy of Ambition*, Cambridge: Cambridge University Press.

Flyvbjerg, Bent (2009), 'Survival of the unfittest: why the worst infrastructure gets built – and what we can do about it', *Oxford Review of Economic Policy*, 25(3), September, 344–67.

Fraser, Ian (2014), *Shredded: Inside RBS: The Bank That Broke Britain*, Edinburgh: Birlinn.

Froud, Julie, Sukhdev Johal, Michael Moran and Karel Williams (2017), Outsourcing the state: new sources of elite power, *Theory, Culture and Society*, 34(5–6), 77–101.

Fry, Michael (2009), *Edinburgh: A History of the City*, London: Macmillan.

Gibbon, Lewis Grassic (1969), *A Scots Hairst: Essays and Short Stories*, London: Hutchinson.

Glendinning, Miles (2005), 'Housing and suburbanisation in the early and mid-twentieth century', in Brian Edwards and Paul Jenkins (eds), *Edinburgh: The Making of a Capital City*, Edinburgh: Edinburgh University Press.

Gray, Robert (1976), *The Labour Aristocracy in Victorian Edinburgh*, Oxford: Clarendon Press.

Harvie, Jen (2003), 'The cultural effects of the Edinburgh International Festival: elitism, identities, industries', *Contemporary Theatre Review*, 13(4), 12–26.

Hearn, Jonathan (2017), *Salvage Ethnography in the Financial Sector: The Path to Economic Crisis in Scotland*, Manchester: Manchester University Press.

Heiton, John (1859), *The Castes of Edinburgh*, Edinburgh: John Menzies.

Heiton, John (1860), *The Castes of Edinburgh*, 2nd enlarged edition, Edinburgh: John Menzies.

Heiton, John (1861), *The Castes of Edinburgh*, Edinburgh: W. P. Nimmo.

Henderson, John (1953), 'Seventy-year survey of Edinburgh voting', *Edinburgh Evening News*, 20 April.

Hennock, Peter (1973), *Fit and Proper Persons: Ideal and Reality in Nineteenth Century Urban Local Government*, London: Edward Arnold.

Heron, Alexander (1903), *The Rise and Progress of the Company of Merchants of the City of Edinburgh, 1681–1902*, Edinburgh: T. and T. Clark.

Highet, John (1969), *A School of One's Choice: A Sociological Study of the Fee-paying Schools in Scotland*, London and Glasgow: Blackie and Son.

Hunt, Norman and Harry Nicholls (1968), *Edinburgh's Economy: Present and Future Prospects*, Edinburgh: T. and T. Clark.

Hunter, Floyd (1969), *Community Power Structure: A Study of Decision-makers*, Chapel Hill: University of North Carolina Press.

Hyndman, Noel and Irving Lapsley (2016), 'New Public Management; the story continues', *Financial Accountability and Management*, 32(4), 385–408.

Hardie, Iain and Donald MacKenzie (2007), 'Assembling an economic actor: the *agencement* of a Hedge Fund', *Sociological Review*, February, 55(1).

Iannelli, Cristina (2013), 'The role of the school curriculum in social mobility', *British Journal of Sociology of Education*, 34(5–6), 907–28.

Inch, Andy (2013), *Changing the Culture of Scottish Planning: Interpreting New Regulations, Shaping New Practices, Relationships and Identities*, Edinburgh: Royal Institution of Chartered Surveyors (RICS).

Inch, Andy (2018), '"Opening for business"? Neoliberalism and the cultural politics of modernising planning in Scotland', *Urban Studies*, 55(5), 1076–92.

Johnson, James and Lou Rosenburg (2010), *Renewing Old Edinburgh: The Enduring Legacy of Patrick Geddes*, Glendaruel: Argyll Publishing.

Kallin, Hamish (2015), *Gentrification and the State of Uneven Development on Edinburgh's Periphery*, unpublished PhD dissertation, University of Edinburgh.

Kallin, Hamish and Tom Slater (2014), 'Activating territorial stigma: gentrifying marginality on Edinburgh's periphery', *Environment and Planning A*, 4(6), 1351–68.

Keir, David (1966), *City of Edinburgh: Third Statistical Account of Scotland*, Glasgow: William Collins.

Kellas, James (1975), *The Scottish Political System*, Cambridge: Cambridge University Press.

Kirk, Gordon (1995), 'The changing context of higher education in Scotland', *Moray House and Change in Higher Education*, Edinburgh: Scottish Academic Press.

Lapsley, Irving and Peter Miller (2019), 'Transforming the public sector: 1998–2018', *Accounting, Auditing and Accountability Journal*, <https://doi.org/10.1108/AAAJ-06-2018-3511>.

Lapsley, Irving, Peter Miller and Fabricio Panozzo (2010), 'Accounting for the city', *Accounting, Auditing and Accountability Journal*, 23(3), 305–24.

Lee, Clive (1983) 'Modern economic growth and structural change in Scotland: the service sector reconsidered', *Scottish Economic and Social History*, 1, 5–35.

Lockhart, Brian (2009), *Jinglin' Geordie's Legacy: A History of George Heriot's School*, East Linton: Tuckwell Press.

Long, Norton E. (1958), 'The local community as an ecology of games', *American Journal of Sociology*, 64(3), 251–61.

Lukes, Steven (1974), *Power: a Radical View*, London: Macmillan.

mac Neil, Neil (2000), 'August, Edinburgh', in Bashabi Fraser and Elaine Greig (eds), *Edinburgh: An Intimate City*, Edinburgh: City of Edinburgh Council.

McArthur, E. (2013), *Scotland, CEMA and the Arts Council, 1919–1967: Background, Politics and Visual Art Policy*, London: Routledge.

MacCaig, Ewen (ed.) (2005), *The Poems of Norman MacCaig*, Edinburgh: Polygon.

MacCrae, Maurice (ed.) (2004), *The New Club: A History*, Edinburgh: The New Club.

McCrone, David (1990), 'Anglicising Scotland: University Admissions', *Scottish Government Yearbook*, 1990, pp. 195–208.

McCrone, David (2004), 'Devolving Scotland', in Alan Balfour (ed.), *Creating a Scottish Parliament*, New York: StudioLR.

McCrone, David (2005), 'Bidin' in the Toon', in J. Beech, O. Hand, M. Mulhearn and J. Weston (eds), *Compendium of Scottish Ethnology*, John Donald/National Museums of Scotland, Edinburgh, pp. 358–71.

McCrone, David (2017a), *The New Sociology of Scotland*, Sage Publications: London.

McCrone, David (2017b), 'In defence of parochialism: municipal politics in 20th century Edinburgh', *Book of the Old Edinburgh Club*, 13, 79-90.

McCrone, David (2018), 'Lost in Leith: accounting for Edinburgh's trams', *Scottish Affairs*, 27(3), 361–81.

McCrone, David (2019), 'Treading Angels: Edinburgh and its festivals', *Scottish Affairs*, 28(3), 290–317.

McCrone, David (2020a), 'What school did you go to? Education and status in Edinburgh', *Scottish Affairs*, 29(1), 24–49.

McCrone, David (2020b), 'The discreet charm of the Edinburgh bourgeoisie', *Scottish Affairs*, 29(2), 285–91.

McCrone, David (2021), 'Changing places: comparing 1986 and 2019 elites in Scotland', *Scottish Affairs*, 30(1), 1–30.

McCrone, David and Brian Elliott (1989), *Property and Power in a City: The Sociological Significance of Landlordism*, London: Palgrave Macmillan.

McCrone, David and Frank Bechhofer (2015), *Understanding National Identity*, Cambridge: Cambridge University Press.

MacDiarmid, Hugh (1978), 'Midnight', in *The Complete Poems*, London: Penguin Books.

MacDougall, Ian (1968), *The Minutes of Edinburgh Trades Council 1859–1873*, 4th series, vol. 5, Edinburgh: SHS.

McMillan, Joyce (1988), *The Traverse Theatre Story*, London: Methuen Drama.

McPherson, Andrew (1970), Review: Highet's *A School of One's Choice*, *Sociology*, 4(2), May, 263–4.

MacRae, Ebenezer (1949), 'Historical review', in Abercrombie and Plumstead, *A Civic Survey and Plan for the City and Royal Burgh of Edinburgh*, Edinburgh: McLagan and Cumming.

Madgin, Rebecca and Richard Rodger (2013), Inspiring capital? Deconstructing myths and reconstructing urban environments, Edinburgh, 1860–2010', *Urban History*, 40(3), 507–29.

Marshall, Rosalind (2015), *The Edinburgh Merchant Company, 1901–2014*, Edinburgh: John Donald Press.

Marwick, James D. (1865), *A Sketch of the History of the High Constables of Edinburgh, With Notes on the Early Watching, Cleaning, and Other Police Arrangements of the City*, Edinburgh: private circulation (reprinted by Kessinger Reprints, 2010).

Marwick, W. H. (1969), 'Municipal politics in Victorian Edinburgh', *Book of the Old Edinburgh Club*, xxxiii, 31–41.

Massey, Allan (1994), *Edinburgh*, London: Sinclair-Stevenson.

Miller, Eileen (1996), *Edinburgh International Festival, 1947–1996*, Aldershot: Scolar Press.

Miller, Mitch, Johnny Rodger and Owen Dudley Edwards (2010), *Tartan Pimps: Gordon Brown, Margaret Thatcher and the New Scotland*, Benderloch: Argyll Publishing.

Moffat, Alistair (1978), *The Edinburgh Fringe*, London: Johnston and Bacon.

Molotch, Harvey (1976), 'The city as a growth machine: toward a political economy of place', *American Journal of Sociology*, 82(2), 309–32.

Moore, Lindy (1984), 'Invisible scholars: girls learning Latin and mathematics in the elementary public schools of Scotland before 1872'. *History of Education* 13, 121–37.

Morris, Robert J. (2010), 'In search of twentieth-century Edinburgh', *Book of the Old Edinburgh Club*, New Series, vol. 8, 13–25.

Moss, Michael (2004), Review of R. D. Anderson et al. *The University of Edinburgh: An Illustrated History*, *The English Historical Review*, 119 (482), 810–11.

Newman, Janet (2014), 'Landscapes of antagonism: local governance, neo-liberalism and austerity', *Urban Studies*, 51(15), 3290–305.

Offer, Avner (1981), *Property and Politics, 1870–1914*, Cambridge: Cambridge University Press.

Paisey, Catriona and Nicholas J. Paisey (2000), *A Comparative Study of Undergraduate and Professional Education in the Professions of Accountancy, Medicine, Law and Architecture*, Edinburgh: Institute of Chartered Surveyors of Scotland (ICAS).

Paterson, Lindsay (1993), 'Regionalism among entrants to higher education from Scottish schools', *Oxford Review of Education*, 19(2), 231–55.

Paterson, Lindsay (1994), *The Autonomy of Modern Scotland*, Edinburgh University Press.

Paterson, Lindsay (2012), 'Review: Boys' and Girls' Schools of Edinburgh', *Scottish Affairs*, 80, 176–9.

Paterson, Lindsay, Alan Gow and Ian Deary (2014), 'School reform and opportunity throughout the lifecourse: the Lothian Birth Cohort 1936', *School Effectiveness and School Improvement: an international journal of research, policy and practice*, 25(1), 105–25.

Peacock, Helen (ed.) (1974), *Forgotten Southside*, Edinburgh: EUSPB.

Peacock, Helen (ed.) (n.d.), *The Unmaking of Edinburgh*, Edinburgh: EUSPB.

Perman, Ray (2012), *HUBRIS: How HBOS Wrecked the Best Bank in Britain*, Edinburgh: Birlinn.

Perman, Ray (2019), *The Rise and Fall of the City of Money: A Financial History of Edinburgh*, Edinburgh: Birlinn.

Polsby, Nelson (1963), *Community Power and Political Theory*, New Haven: Yale University Press.

Power, Michael (2004), 'The risk management of everything', *Journal of Risk Management*, 5(3), 58–65.

Richardson, Harry, Joan Vipond and Rob Furbey (1975), *Housing and Urban Spatial Structure: A Case Study*, Farnborough: Saxon House.

Robb, Steven (2017), 'Ebenezer MacRae and interwar housing in Edinburgh', *Book of the Old Edinburgh Club*, 13.

Roberts, Alasdair (2007), *Crème de la Crème: Girls' Schools of Edinburgh*, London: Steve Savage.

Roberts, Alasdair (2009), *The Ties That Bind: Boys' Schools of Edinburgh*, London: Steve Savage.

Roberts, Alasdair (2010), *Crème de la Crème: Girls' Schools of Edinburgh*, 2nd edn, London: Steve Savage.

Rodger, Richard (2001), *The Transformation of Edinburgh: Land, Property and Trust in the Nineteenth Century*, Cambridge: Cambridge University Press.

Rodger, Richard (2005), 'Industry and the built environment, 1750-1920', in Brian Edwards and Paul Jenkins (eds), *Edinburgh: The Making of a Capital City*, Edinburgh: Edinburgh University Press.

Rosie, George (2010). 'The route to nowhere', *Scottish Review of Books*, 11 November.

Rosie, George (2018), 'Double crossings: the tangled tale of the Forth road bridges', *Scottish Affairs*, 27(3), 342–60.

Rosie, Michael (2004), *The Sectarian Myth in Scotland: Of Bitter Memory and Bigotry*, London: Palgrave.

Rosie, Michael and Tom Devine (2020), 'The rise and fall of anti-Catholicism in Scotland', in Claire Gheeraert-Graffeuille and Geraldine Vaughan (eds), *Anti-Catholicism in Britain and Ireland, 1600–2000: Practices, Representations and Ideas*, London: Palgrave.

Scott, John and Michael Hughes (1980), *The Anatomy of Scottish Capital*, London: Croom Helm.

Shapin, Steve (1974), 'Property, patronage and the politics of science: the founding of the Royal Society of Edinburgh, *British Journal for the History of Science*, 7(1), March.

Shepley, Nigel (2008 [2007]), *Women of Independent Mind: St George's School Edinburgh and the Campaign for Women's Education*, 2nd edn, Edinburgh: St George's.

Smith, Adam (1904 [1776]), *An Inquiry into the Nature and Causes of The Wealth of Nations*, London: University Books.

Spark, Muriel (1965), *The Prime of Miss Jean Brodie*, London: Penguin Books.

Stacey, Margaret (1969), 'The myth of community studies', *British Journal of Sociology*, 20(2), 134–47.

Stevenson, Robert Louis (n.d. [1878]), *Edinburgh: Picturesque Notes*, Edinburgh: Valde Books.

Stevenson, Robert Louis (1886), *Strange Case of Dr Jekyll and Mr Hyde*, London: Penguin Books.

Sullivan, Alice and Anthony Heath (2003), 'Intakes and examination results at state and private schools', in G. Walford (ed.) *British Private Schools*, London: Woburn Press, pp. 77–104.

Taleb, Nassim N. (2007), *The Black Swan: The Impact of the Highly Improbable*, New York: Random House.

Walford G (ed.) (1984), *British Public Schools: Policy and Practice*, London: Routledge.

Walford, Geoffrey (1987), 'How important is the independent sector in Scotland?', *Scottish Educational Review*, 19, 108–21.

Walford, Geoffrey (1988), 'The Scottish Assisted Places Scheme: a comparative study of the origins, nature and practice of the APSs in Scotland, England and Wales', *Journal of Education Policy*, 3, 137–53.

Walford, Geoffrey (ed.) (2003), *British Private Schools: Research in Policy and Practice*, London: Woburn Press.

Wardak, Ali (2000), *Social Control and Deviance: A South Asian Community in Scotland*, Aldershot: Ashgate Publishing.

Weber, Max (1966 [1921]), *The City*, New York: Free Press.

Wynyard, Montague (1900), *The New Club from its Foundation in 1787*, Edinburgh: New Club.

Young, Alf (2016), 'Forty turbulent years: how the Fraser economic commentary recorded the evolution of the modern Scottish economy', *Fraser of Allander, Economic Commentary*, <https://strathprints.strath.ac.uk/54786/>.

Youngson, A. J. (1966), *The Making of Classical Edinburgh*, Edinburgh: Edinburgh University Press.

Index

Note: *italic* page number indicates illustrations; n indicates note

39 Steps (film), 251

Abercrombie, Patrick, 65–8
Abercrombie Plan (1949) *see Civic Survey and Plan for the City and Royal Burgh of Edinburgh, A* (Abercrombie and Plumstead)
Aberdeen, 26, 34, 142, 169, 184, 189
accountancy, 189–90
Aitchison, Tom, 231
Alexander, Wendy, 226
Alfred McAlpine Infrastructure Services, 227, 228
Allan Murray Architects (AMA), 203–4, 207, 208, 209, 211
Anderson, David, 245
Anderson, Donald, 197–8, 225, 228, 229, 231, 242
Anderson, James, 76
Anderson, Robert, 143, 145–6
  and University, 169, 172, 175–6, 177, 178–9, 181, 184
Andrew, Rebecca, 229–30
Ane Satyre of the Thrie Estaites (Lyndsay), 90–1, 94
Angels' Share, The (film), 252
Anne, HRH Princess, 114
antisyzygy, 250
Appleton, Edward, 179–80
Archer, Gilbert Baird, 138n13
architecture, 189–90

'arm's length companies' (ALCos), 236–7, 244–5
Artisan Real Estate Investors, 208
Arts Council (of Great Britain), 88, 91, 93, 94, 97
ARUP, 226–7, 228
Assembly Hall, 90, 94
Assembly Rooms, 89–90, 107, 123
'assisted places scheme' (APS), 152–3
Atholl, Duke of, 85
Atlanta (GA), 8–9, 11

Bachrach, Peter
  'Two faces of power', 7
Bagshaw, Nigel, 209
Baillie Gifford, 76, 260
Baker, Joanna, 105
Balfour of Burleigh, Lord, 73
Bank of England, 71, 75, 80n19
Bank of Ireland, 80n17
Bank of Scotland, 71–2, 73, 74, 75, 76, 260
banking, 9, 18, 55, 71–4, 75–6, 259–60
Banks, Sir John, Lord Provost, 97–8
Baratz, Morton
  'Two faces of power', 7
Barclays Bank, 74
Barrie, Gavin, 203
Bartie, Angela, 93, 94, 96
Bartlam, Ed, 107
Bechhofer, Frank, 2–3

Beecham, Thomas, 91–2
Bell, Colin, 11
belonging, 2–3, 12
Bertram of Sciennes, 61, *62*
'Beyond the Fringe', 99
Bilbao, 81
Bilfinger Berger (BB), 227, 228, 231–2, 239, 261
Billington, Michael, 107
Bing, Rudolf, 85–6, 88, 89, 92, 93, 95
BioQuarter, 199
Birmingham, 42, 77
Black, Ian
    Weegies and Edinbuggers, 250–1
Black Lives Matter, 180
Blair, Sir Alastair, 74
    and New Club, 124, 125, 127, 128–9, 130, 132, 134–5
Blomfield, Robert, 268–9
boarding schools, 142, 144
Bond, Matthew, 126, 127
BOP consulting company, 81–3
branding, 82–4
Brechin, Herbert, Lord Provost, 99–100
breweries, 17, 61, 212
Bridie, James, 86, 87, 92, 93, 95, 109, 249
    The Anatomist, 91
    'Knox', 89
    and Unity Theatre, 96
Brown, Dan
    The Da Vinci Code, 253
Brown, Gordon, 178, 180, 181
Brown, Keith, 203
Bruce, Sue, 230, 245, 267
Buccleuch, Duke of, 19, 84–5, 186
Buchanan, Tom, 208
building industry, 43, 45, 53
Burdett-Coutts, Bill, 107
Burns, Andrew, 231
Bush, George H. W., 10
Bush, George W., 10
Bush, Prescott, 10

CAF (Construcciones y Auxiliar de FerroCarriles), 227, 228, 261
Calton Road, 212
Caltongate, 207–13, 220, 261
Cameron, Gen Sir Archibald, 127

Cameron, Lord, 86, 87
Canongate Venture, 208–9
capitalism, 2, 4, 73–4, 239, 260
Carillion, 227, 228, 238
Carlin, Norah
    Holy Cross Academy Edinburgh: The Life and Times of a Catholic School 1907–1969, 158–9
Carstares, William, 171
castes, 12–13, 16, 17, 18–19, 52–3, 112–14
    and political economy, 40–1
    and schools, 143, 162–4
CEMA *see* Arts Council (of Great Britain)
China, 2
cholera, 29
Christie, Sir John, 93
Christine Orr Players, 91
Christmas *see* Edinburgh Winter festivals
cities, 2, 3–5, 8–11, 240, 241; *see also* Edinburgh
citizenship, 4
city bypass, 70, 197–200
City of Edinburgh Council (CEC), 39, 115, 123, 206, 214–15, 262
    and trams, 225, 226, 227, 228, 229–31, 244–5
City of Edinburgh Rapid Transit (CERT), 225–6, 227
Civic Survey and Plan for the City and Royal Burgh of Edinburgh, A (Abercrombie and Plumstead), 47, 48, 61, 65–8, 77–8, 195
    and St James Centre, 202
    and University, 176–7
Clancy Docwra, 228
class, 4, 44–5, 160–1; *see also* castes; merchant class; status; working classes
clubs *see* golf; social clubs
Clydesdale Bank, 76, 80n22
coal industry, 66, 78
Cockburn, Harry, 123–4
Cockburn, Henry, 146
Cockburn Association, 176, 205, 208–9
Cohen, Anthony, 131–2

Colinton, 32
Communist Party, 96
community, 5–6, 7–11, 131–2
Company of Archers *see* Royal
    Company of Archers
Company of Scotland *see* Darien
    Company
Comprehensive Development Area
    (CDA), 177, 179–81
comprehensive schools, 159
congestion charge, 226, 227
Conn, Stewart, 267
    'Ice Maiden,' 248, 253
Connolly, James, 27, 271
Conservative Party, 7, 24, 26, 27, 34–5,
    36, 255
    and councillors, 44
    and district councils, 37–8
    and education, 152–3
    and festival, 101, 102
    and municipal councils, 39
consumption, 63–4
contracts, 237–9
Cook, Robin, 181
Cormack, John, 34, 269
corporations, 241
Corstorphine, 32
Covid-19 pandemic, 12, 205, 211, 244,
    252, 273
Cowgate, 270
craftsmen, 52–3, 63, 118
Craiglockhart, 147
Cramond, 32, 192n7, 213, 215
Crawford, Iain, 84, 85, 87, 88–91, 103
    and funding, 97–8, 99
    and Glasgow, 104
Crawford, Robert, 253, 267
    Camera Obscura, 14–15
Crewe, Ivor
    The Blunders of Our Governments,
    236
Cubie, John, 27
culture, 17, 18, 63, 81; *see also* festivals

Dahl, Robert, 2
    *Who Governs? Democracy and
    Power in an American City*, 7,
    8–11
Dale, Michael, 162

Dalry, 32, 66, 67, 78, 266
Damer, Sean, 50n41, 278n14
Daniel Stewart's School, 145
Darien Company, 71–2
David Hume Tower (DHT), 177, 180
Davie, Cedric Thorpe, 91
Davie, George
    The Democratic Intellect, 183, 264
day schools *see* schools
de-industrialisation, 60–1, 62–3, 77–8
Deary, Ian, 159–61
Delamont, Sara, 149
Deloitte, 208
Demarco, Richard, 100
department stores, 258–9, 265
Detroit (USA), 2
Deutsche Oper am Rhein, 100–1
development, 20–1, 48, 195–200,
    216–19, 260–2
    and small-scale, 47
devolution, 183, 193n18, 201
Dewar, Donald, 201
Diamand, Peter, 99, 100, 101, 102
dinners, 31, 118, 122, 123–4, 156,
    275–6
Disruption of 1843, 269
district councils, 37–8, 49n2
    and festival, 101, 102, 103, 105
Domhoff, Bill, 9–11
Douglas, Bill, 79n13
Drummond, John, 102–3, 109
Dundee, 26, 34, 64, 142
Dunfermline College of Physical
    Education, 175, 192n7
Dunlop, Frank, 103, 104, 107

Easson, Jacqueline, 122
East India Company, 71
Easter (Strindberg), 91
ecology of games, 5–6, 11–12, 16,
    248–9
economics, 17–18, 26, 28, 255–6; *see
    also* capitalism; money; political
    economy
Edinburgh, 1–2, 13–22, 271–2, 274–7
    and banking, 259–60
    and Caltongate, 207–13
    and clubs, 114–15, 136–7
    and council, 24, 25–30

and department stores, 258–9
and development, 179–81, 195–200,
    216–19, 260–2
and elites, 116–17
and enlightenment, 185–7, 190–1
and festivals, 81–4
and games, 12–13, 248–9
and High Constables, 120–3
and immigration, 164–5, 166n19,
    269–71
and industry, 254–5
and money, 70–6
and municipal politics, 30–3
and professions, 187–90
and St James Centre, 201–7
and self-presentation, 249–53
and social worlds, 112–13
and Waterfront, 213–16
and women, 266–7
and working classes, 267–9
see also City of Edinburgh Council;
    Merchant Company of Edinburgh;
    New Club; politics; schools;
    trams; University of Edinburgh
Edinburgh Academy, 142, 146, 155–6,
    257
Edinburgh Airport, 197, 199, 206,
    230–1
Edinburgh Art Festival, 82
Edinburgh Book Festival, 82
Edinburgh Castle, 90, 252
Edinburgh College of Art Theatre
    Group, 91
Edinburgh Evening News (newspaper),
    43, 262–4
Edinburgh Festival Fringe, 82, 91–2,
    95–6, 105–7
Edinburgh Festival Society (EFS), 92,
    94–5, 97, 98–100, 101, 103
Edinburgh Film Festival, 82
Edinburgh Good Government League
    (EGGL), 26, 32–3, 255
Edinburgh High School, 146
Edinburgh Institution for Young
    Ladies, 145
Edinburgh International Conference
    Centre (EICC), 241
Edinburgh International Festival (EIF),
    68, 82, 95–6, 106

and beginnings, 84–91
and funding, 96–102, 109
and ownership, 92–5
and regime change, 102–5
Edinburgh Jazz and Blues Festival, 82
Edinburgh Labour Festival Committee
    (ELFC), 96
Edinburgh Mela, 82
Edinburgh Military Tattoo, 82, 84,
    91–2
Edinburgh Napier University, 170,
    199
Edinburgh Park, 197–9
Edinburgh Science Festival, 82
Edinburgh St James *see* St James Centre
Edinburgh Storytelling Festival, 82
Edinburgh Town Council, 36, 92–5,
    96–102, 103–4
Edinburgh University *see* University of
    Edinburgh
Edinburgh University Press (EUP),
    168–9
Edinburgh University Student
    Publications Board (EUSPB),
    180–1
Edinburgh Winter festivals, 82
Edinburgh Workers Municipal
    Committee, 31
Edinburgh World Heritage Trust, 208
Edinvar, 181
education, 28, 55, 60; *see also* schools;
    universities
education-authority schools, 142
Educational Institute of Scotland (EIS),
    182–3
Edwards, Owen Dudley, 107
electricity, 29, 32, 34
elites, 4, 5, 7, 9–11, 41, 126
    and Edinburgh, 18–19, 116–17
Elliott, Brian, 4
Elm Row Community Centre, 94
Emery, Vic, 230, 231, 232–3, 237
Empire Theatre, 105
employment, 54–60; *see also*
    professional employment;
    unemployment
England, 269–70, 271
Englishing, 181–5
enlightenment, 185–7, 188, 190–1

Enterprise Scotland exhibition (1947), 90
environmentalism, 83, 199, 217
Erskine Stewart's Melville Schools (ESMS), 142
ethnicity *see* immigration
Eveling, Stanley, 108
Everyman (morality play), 91

Falconer, John, Lord Provost, 86, 88–9, 92, 96, 109
Family Reunion, The (Eliot), 91
Farrans, 228, 244, 261
Farrell, Sir Terry, 241–2
fee-paying schools, 140–6, 148, 151–2, 154–7, 159–62, 164
Festival *see* Edinburgh International Festival (EIF)
Festival Theatre, 105
festivals, 17, 18, 81–2; *see also* Edinburgh Festival Fringe; Edinburgh International Festival
Fettes College, 95, 142, 144, 146
Fiery Angel, The (Prokoviev), 101
Fiery Cross, 90
Fife, 69–70
films, 251–2
Filsell, Catherine, 36
finance industry, 54, 55, 75, 76; *see also* banking
Fireworks (Handel), 91–2
First World War, 29, 30, 32, 147, 173, 255, 266
FirstBus, 227
fishing, 117
Fleming, Robert, 73
Flemish weavers, 270
Flying Dutchman, The (Wagner), 100
Flyvbjerg, Bent, 234–5, 236
football, 269
Forsyth's, 259, 265
Forth Ports, 214, 215, 261
Forth Road Bridge, 69
Foulkes, George, 157
Fraser, Douglas, 259
Fraser, Peter, Lord, 201
Freemasonry, 136–7
Fringe *see* Edinburgh Festival Fringe
Fringe Society, 106

Froud, Julie, 237
Fry, Michael, 180
Fyffe, Will, 2, 22n1

Gallagher, Willie, 229
games, 5–6, 11–13, 248–9
Gardiner, Neil, 203
Garioch, Robert
    'Embro to the ploy', 110n13
    A Wee Local Scandal, 180
gas, 29, 31, 34
Gateway Theatre, 94
Geddes, Patrick, 47, 177, 179, 192n11
gender, 116; *see also* women
General Strike (1926), 26, 32
George Heriot's School, 116, 142, 143, 144, 145, 157, 257
George Square, 176–7, 180
George Watson's College, 142, 144, 145, 149, 155–6, 257
Gibson, David, 48
Gilded Balloon, 107
Gillespie's *see* James Gillespie's School
Glasgow, 2, 3, 14, 15, 249–51
    and accountancy, 189
    and banking, 72–3
    and culture, 81, 104
    and Edinburgh Festival, 87
    and housing, 48
    and immigration, 270–1
    and industry, 42, 77, 78
    and politics, 26, 33, 34
    and schools, 142, 163
    and university, 169, 182, 184
Glasgow, Mary, 94
Glasgow Unity Theatre, 91, 95–6
Glenalmond School, 146
Glendinning, Miles, 45, 46
Glyndebourne Opera, 85–6, 88, 92, 93, 109
golf, 18, 114–15, 117, 258
Goodwin, Fred, 199, 202
Gorgie, 32, 66, 67–8, 78, 266, 271
Gow, Alan, 159–61
Grant-aided schools, 151
Granton, 213–16, 226
Grassic Gibbon, Lewis, 253
Gray, Robbie, 41, 52–3, 268
Great War *see* First World War

green belt, 197, 199
Greyfriars Bobby, 252
Growth Accelerator model (GAM), 203, 206, 217, 272, 274
Gumley, Louis, 43–4
Guthrie, Tyrone, 90, 98
Gyle, The, 197

Hardie, Ian, 233
Hardie, Lord, 224, 231, 243–4
Harewood, Earl of, 98, 99
Harvie, Jen, 106
Haymarket, 66, 226, 228, 230
health, 29, 67
Heart of Midlothian FC, 269
Heiton, John, 12–13, 40, 41, 112, 254
    Castes of Edinburgh, 52
Heriot Watt University, 170, 175
Heriot's *see* George Heriot's School
Hibernian FC, 269
High Constables of Edinburgh, 114, 115, 120–3, 136, 258, 265
    and women, 266
Highet, John, 257
    A School of One's Choice, 151–2, 154–5, 157, 162, 163–4
Historic Scotland, 208
Hogmanay, 82
Holyrood, 201
Home, Henry Douglas, 132
Honourable Company of Edinburgh Golfers, 114–15, 136, 265
Horsburgh Campbell, A., 46–7, 256
hospitals, 199
housing, 30, 31, 42–4, 181, 212–13, 256
    and factors, 50n37
    and living conditions, 67, 68
    and segregation, 45–8
Housing Act (1924), 45
Howell, Michael, 229
Hume, David, 180
Hunt, Norman, 69, 77
Hunter, Floyd, 2, 8–9, 11
Hunter, Ian, 95, 97

I belong to Glasgow (song), 2, 12, 22n1
Iannelli, Cristina, 161

identity, 2–3
'*L'Illusioniste*' (film), 251
immigration, 22, 269–71
Imrie, John, 87
Inch, Andy, 217–18, 219, 273
income levels, 60
Independent Labour Party (ILP), 27
industry, 3, 17, 18, 40–2, 53
    and Abercrombie, 66–8
    and decline, 69–70
    and diversity, 64–5
    see also de-industrialisation; manufacturing
information and communication industry, 55
Institute of Chartered Accountants of Scotland (ICAS), 189–90
insurance industry, 54, 55, 73, 74–5
investment trust industry, 73, 74, 75
Ireland, 28
Irish immigrants, 270–1
iron manufacturing, 61

James VI of Scotland, King, 118
James Gillespie's School, 142, 145, 153, 154, 165n5
Jefferson, Thomas, 185
Jeffrey, Francis, 146
Jeffrey, Richard, 229, 232
Jenners, 259, 265
Jestico + Whiles, 203, 204
Jews, 270
Johnson, Boris, 7
Johnson, Jim
    Renewing Old Edinburgh: The Enduring Legacy of Patrick Geddes, 179, 212
Johnson-Gilbert, Ian Anderson, Lord Provost, 98
Johnson-Marshall, Percy, 20, 177–8
Johnston, Tom, 93, 94
jokes, 250–1

Kahneman, Daniel, 234–5
Kallin, Hamish, 216
Kay, John, 225
Kelsall, Moultrie, 91
Kemp, Robert, 90, 91
Kerevan, George, 103, 197

Kerr Fraser, Sir William, 259
Keynes, John Maynard, 88, 93, 94
Kidd, John D., 99, 101, 108
'Kinetic Sculpture, The', 205
King, Anthony
    The Blunders of Our Governments,
    236
King's Theatre, 14, 91, 100, 102
Kirk, 90, 94, 114, 174, 269
Kirk, Gordon, 175
Kirking, 114
Knox, John, 16, 269
Knox, Moira, 99
Knox, Robert, 187
Koren, Karen, 107

labour aristocracy, 52–3, 63
Labour Party, 24, 26, 27, 31–6, 255
    and district councils, 37–8
    and Edinburgh Park, 197–8
    and education, 152
    and festival, 101–2, 103–4
    and municipal councils, 39–40
    and trams, 230
    and working classes, 267–8
ladies *see* women
Laird of Tortwatletie, The (McLellan),
    91
land *see* housing
landlordism, 42, 43
Lapsley, Irving, 21, 240, 241, 272–3
Laurie, Simon, 147
law firms, 9, 71, 72, 116
    and employment, 188, 189–90
leisure pursuits, 117; *see also* golf
Leith, 18, 32, 78, 118
    and films, 251–2
    and Protestant Action, 33, 34
    and trams, 227, 246
    and working classes, 268
Leith Docks, 215
Leith Walk, 202, 205, 226, 228, 243,
    270
Liberal Democrat Party, 24, 39–40
Liberal Party, 26, 27, 30, 34, 35, 37–8
Linehan, Fergus, 105
Livingston, 69–70
Local Government (Scotland) Act
    (1973), 36

localisation, 2–3
Lockhart, Brian
    Jinglin' Geordie's Legacy, 158
Long, Norton E., 5–7, 11–12, 16, 248
Loretto School, 142
Lothian Birth Cohort 1936, 159–61
Lothian Buses (LB), 227
Lothian Region, 37, 105
Lower Depths, The (McLellan), 91
Lukes, Steven, 7–8
Lynch, Michael, 168–9, 170

McArthur, Euan, 93–4
Macbeth (Shakespeare), 91, 110n3
MacCaig, Norman, 15–16
McCall-Smith, Alexander, 276
McCarthy, Shona, 107
McCrae, Maurice, 124, 125, 133–4
MacDiarmid, Hugh, 89, 92, 250
    Midnight, 14–15, 253
MacDougall, Ian, 53
McIlvanney, William
    Docherty, 253
Mackay, David, 229, 232
McKay, James, Lord Provost, 100–1
Mackenzie, Donald, 233
Mackintosh, John P., 19, 23n10
McLaren, Duncan, 26–7, 144
Maclaurin, Colin, 72
McMaster, Brian, 104–5
McMillan, Joyce, 107–8
McPherson, Andrew, 154, 157
Macrae, Duncan, 91
MacRae, Ebenezer, 47–8, 208, 212,
    256
McVitie's biscuits, 53, 54, 61
Madgin, Rebecca, 40, 61, 63, 70
Mainland, Keith, 107
male occupations, 61
Manchester, 3, 41, 62, 64, 67, 77
manufacturing, 18, 40–1, 54, 61–2,
    254
markets, 17, 68
'marriage bar', 267
Marshall, Rosalind K., 118, 120
Marwick, James D., 121–2
Marwick, W. H., 26, 27, 28–9
Mary Erskine School, 142, 143, 146,
    149, 257

Massie, Allan, 180
Mathewson, George, 202
Mavor, Ronald (Bingo), 98
May, Theresa, 238
media, 5–6, 262–4
medicine, 189–90
medieval city-states, 4
Meek, Brian, 36, 108
megaprojects, 234–6
Menzies, William, 73
merchant class, 41, 249
Merchant Company of Edinburgh, 18,
    31, 51–2, 114, 117–20, 136, 254
    and industry, 65
    and politics, 255
    and property, 42
    and schools, 142, 143, 145, 153,
    256–7
    and universities, 258
    and women, 266
Merchiston Castle School, 142
Midlothian, 200
Mildmay, Audrey, 85–6
Miller, Eileen, 84–6, 102–3
Miller, James, 45–6
Milligan, Martin, 96
Mills, C. Wright, 126, 131, 134–5, 258
Mills, Jonathan, 105
Miralles, Enric, 201
Mitchell, Robert, 96
Moderates *see* Progressive Association
modernisation, 218–19, 272, 273–4
Moffat, Alistair, 106
Molotch, Harvey, 196, 207
monarchy, 134
money, 70–1
Moray House College of Education,
    174
Morgan, Jon, 107
Morningside, 14, 250, 266, 269
Morris, Bob, 60, 61, 70–1, 77, 254,
    266
Moss, Michael, 169
Mountgrange, 207, 208, 212
Muggeridge, Malcolm, 178
Muirfield golf course, 18, 74, 114–15,
    258
municipalisation, 28–9, 30–3, 38–40
Murder in the Cathedral (Eliot), 91

Murdoch, Bryden, 91
Murray, Allan *see* Allan Murray
    Architects
Murray, Andrew, Lord Provost, 26,
    86–7, 92
Muslims, 271

Nationalists *see* Scottish National Party
networks, 276
New Club, 19, 73, 114, 123–7, 258
    and anecdotes, 132–3
    and membership, 127–31, 137n5
    and politics, 133–6
    and professional members, 190
    and status, 265
    and women, 115, 266
New Haven (CT), 8, 9–11
new public management (NPM), 21,
    238, 272–3
New Town, 68, 276
New Waverley *see* Caltongate
Newby, Howard, 11
Newcraighall, 226
Newhaven, 21, 226, 227, 228, 243–4
Nicholls, Harry, 69, 77
Nuveen Real Estate, 204, 205, 260

occupations, 55–9, 61, 78n8
Ocean Terminal, 243
Old Town, 47, 66, 179, 270; *see also*
    Caltongate
Oliver, Cordelia, 106
opera, 97, 100–1, 110n12; *see also*
    Glyndebourne Opera
Outlander (TV series), 253
outsourcing, 236–40

Parnell, Charles Stewart, 28
Parsons Brinckerhoff (SDS), 227, 228
Paterson, Lindsay, 159–61, 162–3, 183,
    257
Paterson, William, 71–2
People's Festival, 96
Perman, Ray
    The City of Money, 71, 73–4
Perth, 93
Philip, HRH Duke of Edinburgh, 128
Phillipson, Nick, 169, 170–1
Philosophical Society, 185

Picardy Place, 205–6, 270
Pilgrim Players (London), 91
Pilton, 227
Plan for Edinburgh see *Civic Survey and Plan for the City and Royal Burgh of Edinburgh, A*
planning, 65–8
Pleasance, The, 107
Plumstead, Derek, 61, 65–8
poetry, 14–16
police *see* High Constables of Edinburgh
political economy, 40–8, 51–2, 69–70, 77–8
  and Abercrombie Plan, 65–8
  and modern day, 53–60
  and transformation, 60–5
  see also castes
politics, 4, 5–6, 16–17, 37–40, 255–6
  and clubs, 114
  and development, 196–7, 217–19
  and elites, 116
  and festivals, 92, 95–6
  and media, 262–3
  and municipal, 30–3
  and New Club, 133–6
  and parochialism, 25–30
  and post-war, 33–7
  see also political economy; Scottish parliament
Polsby, Nelson, 2, 8, 11
  Community Power and Political Theory, 7, 9, 10
Ponsonby, Robert, 97, 98
Portobello, 30
ports, 214
power, 2–3, 7–11, 255–6, 259–62
  and gender, 19
  and media, 262–3
  and property, 43
  see also elites
Power, Michael, 242
Prime of Miss Jean Brodie, The (film), 251
Princes Street, 66, 68, 205, 228, 232; *see also* New Club
printing industry, 61–2
Prism Developments, 208
production, 2, 63–4

professional employment, 55, 56–7, 59, 61, 63, 187–90
Progressive Association, 26, 33–5, 36, 44, 255
  and housing, 46
  and municipal politics, 38–9, 40
property, 42–4; *see also* housing
Protestant Action (PA), 33, 34
public bodies, 276
publishing industry, 61–2

Quartermile, 213
Queen Margaret University, 170
Queensferry Crossing, 233, 240, 261–2

racism, 10
radicalism, 26
Rankenian Club, 185
Rankin, Ian, 253
Red Paper on Scotland, 180–1
regional councils, 37, 49n2
religion, 16, 28, 72, 147, 269; *see also* Jews; Kirk; Muslims; sectarianism
Renilson, Neil, 227, 245
Richardson, Chris, 107
Risk, Tom, 74
road networks, 65–6, 68; *see also* city bypass
Robb, Stephen, 47
Roberts, Alasdair, 147, 148, 149, 150, 157–8
Robertson, William, 171, 173, 185
Robison, John, 186
Rodger, Richard, 40, 60–1, 70, 77, 254
  The Transformation of Edinburgh: Land, Property and Trust in the Nineteenth Century, 63
Rogan, Pat, 46
Rosebery, Earl of, 88
Rosebery, Lady, 86, 89
Rosenburg, Lou
  Renewing Old Edinburgh: The Enduring Legacy of Patrick Geddes, 179, 212
Rosie, George, 202, 204, 228, 239, 261–2
Ross, Peter, 12
Rosslyn Chapel, 253

Royal Bank of Scotland (RBS), 71, 72, 74, 75, 76, 259–60
and Gogarburn, 197, 199, 202
Royal Company of Archers, 19, 258
Royal High School, 151, 153, 154, 158
Royal Infirmary of Edinburgh (RIE), 199, 226, 227, 275–6
Royal Scottish Museum, 90, 103
Royal Society of Edinburgh (RSE), 185–7, 190
rubber industry, 61
rugby, 269
Russel, Alexander, 26–7

Sailor's Ark, 208–9, 210
St George's School, 142, 147–9, 150, 153, 158, 165n5, 257
St James Centre, 201–7, 220, 260, 272
Salmond, Alex, 231
schools, 16, 19, 112, 157–9
and careers, 173
and caste, 162–4
and definition, 140–2
and elites, 116–17
and fee-paying, 140–6, 159–62
and gender, 115
and girls, 146–50
and grant-aid, 150–3
and independent, 154–7
and Merchant Company, 114, 118, 137
and status, 256–8, 264–5
scientific employment, 55
Scotsman, The (newspaper), 26–7, 28, 30–1, 32, 33–4, 255, 262–4
and Festival, 86
Scott, Walter, 146
Scottish Arts Council, 103, 105, 109
Scottish Community Drama Association, 91
Scottish Equitable, 74
Scottish Executive, 226
Scottish Labour Party, 27
Scottish Mortgage Investment Fund, 76
Scottish National Opera (SNO), 100
Scottish National Party (SNP), 24, 25, 35, 37–8, 39
and trams, 227–8, 230

Scottish parliament, 24–5, 40, 49n3, 200–1, 227–8
Scottish Television (STV), 182
Scottish Widows, 72, 73, 74
sectarianism, 33, 269
segregation, 18, 20–1, 44–8, 66, 115
selective employment tax (SET), 69
Shallow Grave (film), 251
Shaw, George Bernard, 25, 29, 255
Shawfair, 200, 216
Sheffield, 11, 41, 64, 77, 255
Shepley, Nigel, 148–9, 158
shooting (sport), 117
shopkeepers, 25, 29, 41, 52, 255
Sibbald, Robert, 210
Siemens, 227, 228, 244, 261
significant areas of social deprivation (SIMDs), 20–1
single transferable vote (STV) system, 24, 37–8, 39–40
Slevin, Gerry, 106–7
slum clearances, 20–1, 48, 256
Smith, Adam
Wealth of Nations, 6
Smith, Colin, 230
Smith, Gregory, 250
Smith, Robert C., 74
Smith, William, 31
SNP *see* Scottish National Party
social clubs, 9, 18–19, 114–15, 131–2, 136–7; *see also* New Club
social welfare, 43
Socialists *see* Labour Party
Society for the Improvement of Medical Knowledge, 185
Society of Antiquaries, 185, 187
Southside, 20, 179, 181, 268, 270
Soviet Union, 100
Spark, Muriel, 253
The Prime of Miss Jean Brodie, 165n5–6, 266–7
special purpose vehicles (SPVs), 214, 226
Stacey, Meg, 11
Stair, Earl of, 73
Standard Life, 74–5
status, 18–19, 155–7, 256–8, 264–5; *see also* castes
Steel, Sir James, Lord Provost, 31, 119

Stevenson, Bailie, 86, 92
Stevenson, Robert Louis, 77, 249–50
Stewart, Charles, 178
Stewart's-Melville School, 142, 149, 257
Stockbridge, 268
Student, The (newspaper), 177–8, 180
students *see* universities
Summerhall Arts Hub, 107
Sunday activities, 31
Sunshine on Leith (film), 251–2
surveyors, 194n28
Swann, Michael, 178
Swinney, John, 228, 233

Tattoo *see* Edinburgh Military Tattoo
taxation, 42, 69
Teachers Insurance and Annuity
    Association of America-College
    Retirement Equities Fund (TIAA),
    204, 260
technical employment, 55
Telfer, Andrew, 27
temperance, 31
Tesla, 76
TH Real Estate, 204
Thatcher, Margaret, 182, 184
theatre *see* Edinburgh Festival Fringe;
    Edinburgh International Festival;
    Traverse Theatre
Theurer, George, 46, 100
Thomson, Godfrey, 147, 174–5
tobacco trade, 72
Tories *see* Conservative Party
Tounis College *see* University of
    Edinburgh
tourism, 3, 12, 63, 190–1, 205, 252
Town and Country Planning Act
    (1947), 65
trade, 118
Trades Council, 27, 53
Trainspotting (film), 251, 269
trams, 21, 214, 224–5, 239–42, 244–6, 261
    and 1870 Act, 29
    and *agencement*, 233–4
    and bias, 237
    and blame game, 231–3
    and council, 229–31

and governing, 227–9
and megaproject, 234–6
and modernisation, 273–4
and Newhaven, 243–4
and re-invention, 82, 225–7
and Socialism, 32
Tramways Act (1870), 29
Transport initiatives Edinburgh (TiE),
    214, 226–33, 237, 242
Traverse Theatre, 82, 105, 107–9, 195
Trump, Donald, 7
Tweedbank, 217
typhus, 29

Underbelly, 107
unemployment, 69
UNESCO, 208, 249
United States of America (USA), 2,
    8–11, 73, 196
universities, 20, 117, 163–4, 275; *see
    also* University of Edinburgh
Universities Act (1858), 172
University of Aberdeen, 169, 184
University of Edinburgh, 20, 168–76,
    257–8, 264
    and city, 176–81
    and Englishing, 181–5
University of Glasgow, 169, 182, 184
University of St Andrews, 181–2, 184
University of Strathclyde, 169, 182

Walford, Geoffrey, 143, 151, 152,
    153
Walker, David, 188
Warren, Sir Victor, 87
water supplies, 29, 31
Waterfront, The, 213–16, 217, 220,
    260–1
Watson, James Murray, 86
Watson's *see* George Watson's College
Waverley station, 66, 207, 210, 212
Weber, Max
    The City, 4
Webster, Alexander, 72
West Lothian, 69–70
Wester Hailes, 46
Western Harbour, 215
Westminster parliament, 25
Wheatley Commission, 36, 37

Who's Who in Scotland, 116, 117–18, 137n7
Wilding, Clive, 211
Williams, Marion, 208–9
Williamson, Magnus, 98–9
Wills, Jonathan, 177–8
Wilson, Peter, 101
Wodehouse, P. G., 132
women, 18, 19, 115, 122, 258, 266–7
   and education, 146–50, 157, 158, 257
   and employment, 64
   and Jenners, 259
   and Merchant Company, 118
and New Club, 126, 127, 130–1, 137n6
   and university, 172, 173
   and voting rights, 28, 31
Wood, Charlie, 107
Wood, Harry Henry, 86–7, 88
working classes, 27, 52–3, 267–9
Wright, Allen, 107
Wyllie, Cameron, 157
Wynyard, Lt Col Montagu, 124, 130

Yale University (USA), 8, 9–11
Young, Alf, 259–60
Youngson, A. J. (Sandy), 171